D1616449

The New True Crime

THE NEW TRUE CRIME

**HOW THE RISE OF
SERIALIZED STORYTELLING
IS TRANSFORMING INNOCENCE**

Diana Rickard

NEW YORK UNIVERSITY PRESS

New York

NEW YORK UNIVERSITY PRESS
New York
www.nyupress.org

Please contact the Library of Congress for Cataloging-in-Publication data.
ISBN: 9781479816040 (hardback)
ISBN: 9781479816071 (library ebook)
ISBN: 9781479816064 (consumer ebook)

New York University Press books are printed on acid-free paper, and their binding materials are chosen for strength and durability. We strive to use environmentally responsible suppliers and materials to the greatest extent possible in publishing our books.

Manufactured in the United States of America

10 9 8 7 6 5 4 3 2 1

Also available as an ebook

Contents

Introduction: True Crime Meets Wrongful Conviction and
Lives to Stream about It   1

1 True Crime   15

2 The New True   38

3 Exhibit A   73

4 Where the Devil Truly Resides   103

5 Conviction and Wrongful Conviction   129

6 Judging the Jury   155

7 Where Truth Lies   181

8 The Will to Punish   208

9 Wrongful Conviction and Society   224

Conclusion: Truth and Consequences   237

Acknowledgments   243

Notes   245

References   263

Index   275

About the Author   291

Introduction

True Crime Meets Wrongful Conviction and
Lives to Stream about It

O N October 3, 2014, Sarah Koenig of NPR's *This American Life* spoke to her new podcast listeners in a direct, frank, almost confessional voice: "For the last year, I've spent every working day trying to figure out where a high school kid was for an hour after school one day in 1999—or if you want to get technical about it, and apparently I do—where a high school kid was for *twenty-one minutes* after school one day in 1999."[1] So began the first episode of *Serial*, a twelve-episode podcast that has since become the most downloaded podcast of all time.[2] In Koenig's first words, she invites us to follow her down the rabbit holes of her new obsession as she tries to figure out whether the teenaged Adnan Syed actually killed his ex-girlfriend. Her attempts to solve this mystery—or what she poses as a mystery (Syed had been convicted fifteen years before)—transfixed her audience and became a national sensation. Millions of Americans became familiar with the intricate lives of a group of teenagers at Woodlawn High School in the suburbs of Baltimore.

At the time *Serial* was first airing, I began to hear more and more about it from friends and colleagues who urged me to listen. People thought it was perfect for me for a number of reasons: I am a professor of criminal justice; I was studying wrongful conviction; and I enjoy crime entertainment, investigative journalism, and documentaries. I was also coming across articles on *Serial* in general publications I read regularly, such as the *New York Times* and the *New Yorker*. It seemed that everyone was talking about it. But because I did not consider myself "a podcast person," I did not get around to it. Then, in the last month of 2015, one person after another told me I had to watch *Making a Murderer* on Netflix. Somehow it caught on instantly upon its release and generated even wider media coverage than *Serial*. It inspired over twelve books, including a coloring book. This ten-part, twenty-hour documentary is about a Wisconsin man who had served eighteen years in prison for rape before being exonerated with DNA evidence, only to be accused of a murder two years after his release. This one I watched. And I finished it in four days.

Serial and *Making a Murderer* are the most prominent examples of a new true-crime phenomenon.[3] Fictional and journalistic true-crime stories have been a staple of American entertainment since at least the turn of the century, and television gave rise to an ever-evolving and continuous glut of crime shows, from *Perry Mason* to *Judge Judy*, *Hill Street Blues* and *Law & Order* to *Cops* and *Dateline*. Intentionally or not, they have become a source of information about the criminal justice system, disseminating an array of narratives, images, terms, and values about crime-related issues, while providing the public a sense of having insider knowledge.[4] Along with television fare, in the late twentieth century, two notable feature-length documentaries were released in theaters (*The Thin Blue Line* and *Capturing the Friedmans*) that questioned the innocence of their convicted subjects and were met with critical acclaim and box-office success, bringing wrongful-conviction issues into the mainstream.

Serial and *Making a Murderer* represent a new iteration of the long-standing true-crime craze. They differ in that they are told over multiple episodes and demand a significant amount of viewers' or listeners' time and attention. These detailed, nuanced docuseries are representative of the current binge era that we find ourselves in, in which viewers can and often do watch, in about two weeks, twenty-three-episodes-per-season network series that originally aired over the course of several years. This is made possible by new forms of communications technology enabling at-home entertainment that have transformed the way we consume crime stories.

Included in the new true-crime genre are popular series that specifically look at innocence issues in the criminal justice system. In addition to *Making a Murderer* (Netflix, 2015, 2018), these include the video documentaries *The Staircase* (Sundance Channel and Netflix, 2004, 2013, 2018), *The Innocent Man* (Netflix, 2018), and podcasts such as *Atlanta Monster* (2018). Most recently, *Mind Over Murder*, released by HBO in 2022, looks at the wide-ranging impact that a wrongful conviction in the 1980s had on an entire small town. In addition to these, which focus on (possible) wrongful conviction, there are a slew of other highly popular long-form, streamable true-crime documentaries such as *The Jinx* (HBO, 2015), *Evil Genius: The True Story of America's Most Diabolical Bank Heist* (Netflix, 2019), and *Love Fraud* (Showtime, 2020), among many, many others.

Audiences of the new true-crime series are not passive consumers. They bring their interest in the cases into the "real world," where they become investigators and advocates, following up on clues and weighing the import of evidence in obsessive detail. Online discussion forums such as Reddit include tens of thousands of threads and comments on the cases. Questions about the legal process of determining guilt are heatedly discussed, and this intense viewer/listener engagement is itself a noteworthy phenomenon.

These audiences are a particularly active part of the social media landscape. Research shows that over 60 percent of Reddit users often or sometimes discuss true-crime series on social media, and almost as many participate in true-crime-case-specific online communities.[5] As an example, a subReddit devoted to *Making a Murderer* generated four million views within the series's first month. Outcomes in the actual cases, such as appeals and motions, as well as public statements by court actors and politicians (including Barack Obama), have been influenced by the actions of audiences. And the attorney who took on Syed's case following *Serial*'s release claimed that it was the first ever "open-source investigation" and said that he benefited from "essentially thousands of investigators."[6]

As a scholar of criminal justice issues, I am drawn to the series that specifically focus on possible wrongful convictions because the issue of innocence highlights disturbing and crucial flaws in the system and makes visible the processes whereby the state can legally take the liberty of a citizen and inflict justified harm. These series contribute to discourses that are ongoing throughout the culture about punishment and how we calculate justice. In this book, I examine the relationship between our punishment practices and the new true-crime series, what I am calling the "New True." These series deserve our attention for what they reveal about our societal understanding of crime and punishment. Through them, audiences are receiving ideological messages about punishment. They are also sites where inequality, power, and racism are openly examined, playing a role in our public conversations about who is and is not deserving of punishment and who is and is not protected by law. In addition, by using the term "New True," I am also suggesting these series indicate a new way of constructing truth itself. Questioning the finality of verdicts, framing facts as in the eye of the beholder, the new series unmoor our faith in what is knowable.

Media and Crime Stories

The relationship between media and crime is dynamic: social issues are packaged and debated through representation, and those representations themselves become part of the social landscape. As Michelle Brown writes in *The Culture of Punishment: Prison, Society, and Spectacle*, "Representation is not separate from reality, it is part of reality."[7] As much as 90 percent of the American public cite the media as their most important source of crime news.[8] Like language, cultural products are both shaped by and reflective of the social world, and this holds also for the New True. As documentaries, they purport to document and present objective reality from a relatively neutral perspective, following most of the traditions of investigative journalism. At the same time, as media products, the New True become part of the world as they are consumed, shaping public sentiments about criminal justice.

The relationship between reality and entertainment is fluid, with each entering and altering the other. In a study of how our actual lives have merged with media, the cultural critic Neal Gabler describes the history of the "graphic revolution," arguing that journalism was "the first portal through which entertainment slithered into life and then conquered it."[9] Ever since, entertainment values have been entwined with news reporting. Print and film journalists must frame their accounts using established conventions of narrative storytelling, often with clearly defined good guys and bad guys. For a story to be deemed newsworthy, it must meet some of several criteria among an array of established news values, such as an ability to be simplified; the presence of violence, sex, or a high-status person; and events that can be framed in terms of individualism and conservative ideologies about crime.[10] Representations of crime in the news influence our beliefs about crime problems and our opinions about what policies best address them.

In an analysis of the coverage of high-profile crimes, Lynn Chancer observes that journalists tend to frame stories using "oppositional categories" and "dualistic frameworks."[11] Existing cultural frameworks that emphasize individualism tend to support conservative agendas that construct criminal behavior in terms of self-serving bad behavior and to favor harsh punishment. Newsmakers present crime through a set of familiar packages that condense meanings around easily transmittable phrases and symbols, such as "zero tolerance," "respect for authority," and "the rule of law."[12] Stories that feature violence are rousing and attention grabbing. Big, national news stories and small, local sensations alike can be seen as examples of "crime as public spectacle," where "experiences of victimization, justifications for punitiveness, and modes of policing all circulate widely and ambiguously, available for mediated consumption or political contestation."[13]

News stories are not known for providing sociological context or analysis and do not rely on data provided by experts so much as they are sourced from various government officials and other claims-makers.[14] They do not necessarily reflect the "reality" of crime. Instead, they focus on rare forms of extreme violence, such as murder, typically portraying predators as strangers rather than friends or family, who are the more common perpetrators. Crime victims deemed most newsworthy are usually white, female, and middle class, even though the group most likely to experience victimization is lower-income young men of color.[15]

The New True narratives are framed around sympathetic, innocent, and blameless victims and bad guys from groups that are already socially demonized. With one notable exception, they concern cases in which the victim is a young, middle-class female, but by presenting evidence of the convicted person's innocence, directors attempt to challenge stereotypical images of badness. The New True, like other high-profile cases, "provide an everyday conversational vehicle for debating social issues in a way that marries emotion and logic in lively argumentation."[16]

The public also receives information about crime issues from fictional depictions in popular movies and television dramas. In an analytic study of crime films, *Shots in the Mirror: Crime Films and Society*, Nicole Rafter observes that crime movies provide the general public with much of its knowledge about criminal justice and that these movies provide themes and viewpoints for understanding it. Like high-profile crime, "crime films are one of the world's most effective means of debating issues of crime and justice."[17] Rafter shows that crime films frame events in ways that support existing criminological theories, such as explanations for behavior that point to either inequality or social conditions, individual aspiration and thrills, or mental illness or the "bad seed."[18] She makes the important observation that "one of crime films' most potent ideological messages is, simply, that crime can be explained."[19] At the center of the New True is the enigma of the defendant's true nature and the audience's capacity for reconciling competing accounts of their motivations.

Given news' reliance on entertainment values and narrative conventions, distinguishing it from fictional forms of crime entertainment is not necessarily useful. In today's media vernacular, programming is categorized as either scripted or unscripted and sets aside the more thorny issue of "reality." Fact and fiction endlessly borrow from each other. Certainly, the New True are consumed as both. They are gobbled up like entertainment but inform the public of real issues and have led to public engagement with the cases that has in turn influenced outcomes. These activities are then documented in subsequent follow-up installments and become part of the story. This is an example of what cultural criminologists have called a "spiral": "the collective meaning of crime and deviance is made not once but time and again, as part of an amplifying spiral that wends its way back and forth through media accounts, situated action, and public perception."[20]

In fact, news media are characters in the New True in several ways. In most instances, the cases originally attracted documentarians' interest as prominent news stories they wanted to explore further. Thus, the cases were already mediated. Attorneys and prosecutors often make public media appearances that are also documented in the series. Here we see an example of the way Gabler describes real life becoming entertainment: "If the primary effect of the media in the late twentieth century was to turn nearly everything that passed across their screens into entertainment, the secondary and ultimately more significant effect was to force nearly everything to turn itself into entertainment in order to attract media attention."[21] Crime stories enter the realm of "cultural fluidity," where criminal justice and its representations become confounded and the distinction between "a mediated image and its effects" becomes fuzzier and fuzzier.[22] Innocence issues in particular have been shaped by the media, as in-depth journalistic accounts of cases have played a role in exonerations and lawyers have taken on defendants after reading some of these stories.[23]

Violence is at the heart of crime entertainment, and a discussion of the relationship between media and crime would not be complete without at least a brief look at the way violence is consumed. Rafter states that "crime films offer the ancillary joy of watching others suffer," and Brown similarly observes of some prison films that they are "iconic images of modern suffering."[24] The public's appetite for violence can be seen in the long-standing popularity of stories about serial killers, which include over one thousand films.[25] The New True are all about murders (only one concerns serial crimes) and can be counted as one of the "various contemporary forms of violence as entertainment."[26] The New True rely on the same visual tropes common in all true crime, such as graphic crime-scene photos of the victim, which are repeatedly presented to underscore the seriousness of the crime and remind audiences of the victims' reality. In *True Crime: Observations on Violence and Modernity*, Mark Seltzer argues that true crime is an exemplar of the pervasive commodification of violence in contemporary society: "The convening of the public around scenes of mass-mediated violence has come to make up a wound culture: the public fascination with torn and open bodies and torn and opened psyches, a public gathering around shock, trauma, and the wound. One of the preconditions of our contemporary wound culture is the emergence of popular genres of collective intimacy, such as, for example, the popularity of true crime."[27]

The spiraling effect of contemporary true crime is also evident in parodies of the New True narrative style. The two-season *American Vandal* series on Netflix (2017 and 2018) mocks the attention to minutiae and the earnest tone that characterizes the New True while chronicling a high school student's investigation into who defaced a teacher's car. In the final season of *Portlandia* (2017), the show did a send-up of NPR-style true-crime podcasts, with their characters quietly and self-seriously intruding on routine police work and commenting with condescension on stray details, as one form of entertainment ridicules another.

Wrongful Conviction and the Innocence Movement

Public awareness of wrongful convictions has greatly increased in the past twenty-five years due to the increase in high-profile exonerations since the availability of DNA evidence in 1989. Although journalists had sporadically covered cases of wrongful conviction since the nineteenth century, with increased attention since the influential 1932 publication of Edwin Borchard's *Convicting the Innocent*, it was not until DNA helped exonerate innocent people that what is known as the "innocence movement" began to take shape.[28] This movement has been defined as "loosely signifying the growing awareness that factually innocent people have been and continue to be wrongfully convicted of crimes coupled with a concerted effort to take preventive and corrective actions."[29] In a history of the movement, *Exonerated*, Robert J. Norris chronicles the rise of wrongful conviction as a social issue that began with the work of disconnected individuals, from chaplains to law students. It began to take its current shape in 1992, when the attorneys Barry Scheck and Peter Neufeld founded the Innocence Project, a nonprofit organization that has helped exonerate over three hundred innocent people using DNA evidence. The innocence movement now comprises a diverse group of organizations and activists, "be they journalist, lawyers, students, activists, formerly incarcerated people, or anybody, family members, who are trying to make sure that innocence is a force in criminal justice that people care about."[30] The official Innocence Network is made up of over seventy organizations.[31] Actions of these groups have led to important legislation, such as the 2004 federal Innocence Protection Act, providing for, among other things, postconviction DNA testing, and the 2015 Wrongful Convictions Tax Relief Act, which exempts compensation awards from taxes.[32] The National Registry of Exonerations was founded in 2012. This organization compiles and makes available yearly data on wrongful convictions. The issue now has a place in mainstream consciousness, as reflected in feature-length movies such as *Conviction*, a number of PBS *Frontline* episodes, and the popular documentary series explored in this book.

Precise estimates on the number of people wrongfully convicted are impossible to ascertain.[33] It is generally agreed among scholars that the number of innocent people convicted of felonies each year is in the thousands.[34] Some research has shown the exoneration rates of death-penalty convictions at 2.3 percent, and for sexual assault, it is as high as 7.8 percent.[35] To date, the National Registry of Exonerations, the most comprehensive source of data on the subject (reflecting all exonerations, not just those related to DNA), currently lists 3,172 exonerations since 1989. But exonerations reflect just the tip of the iceberg, not the total numbers of innocents in prison. While this number, sometimes referred to as "the dark number," is unknowable, given our high incarceration rate, a conservative estimate of 1 percent of the prison population would mean that there are thousands.[36] The majority (though not all) of exonerations are for cases that went to trial, and of DNA exonerations, the vast majority are for sexual assault and homicide.[37] In contrast to these, most cases are plea bargained, and rape and homicide are a small minority. As William S. Lofquist argues, this dark figure of wrongful convictions is largely "generated by procedures that render them virtually invisible and unknowable: ubiquitous use of plea bargains, significant trial penalties, perfunctory access to defense counsel, and waiver to rights to trial and appeals and the written public records that they create."[38]

The United States was founded in reaction to absolute monarchical rule, and the Constitution guards against excesses of the state. Criminal justice procedures are intended to protect the individual from abuses of government power and to ensure that liberty is only revoked in ways that follow due process.[39] A functioning democracy depends on a criminal justice system that upholds the presumption of innocence and ensures constitutional protections. Democracies depend on a general belief in the fairness of the law "that is fundamental to the legitimacy of state power."[40] Although many Americans may never come into contact with this system, its actual existence and belief in its substantive justness are integral to the lives of all. This is one reason "private calamities" are social matters.[41] In practice, prosecutors hold immense power in every stage of the criminal justice process. Their power is part of the structural dynamics that can make the presumption of innocence seem like merely theory or myth in actual practice.[42]

It is tempting to see wrongful convictions as tragic yet anomalous instances of mistakes in the system, but they are rooted in embedded structural processes that favor convictions over the pursuit of truth.[43] The growing body of empirical research conducted by a number of wrongful-conviction scholars identifies six independent but related factors that contribute to this situation. These significant factors can be seen as isolated and fixable problems.[44] But taken as a whole, they expose core and systemic institutional failures. Wrongful-conviction scholars have begun to understand that preventive reform "implies major changes in the entire criminal justice process concerned with the identification and prosecution of offenders."[45]

Most research on wrongful convictions has focused on "the prevalence and causes of errors," and much of this knowledge has been made available to the general public beyond academia through the innocence movement.[46] The six factors that constitute "the catalogue of errors" that contribute to wrongful conviction are (1) eyewitness misidentification, (2) misapplication of forensic science, (3) false confessions, (4) incentivized witnesses, (5) government misconduct, and (6) inadequate defense.[47] I will here briefly discuss the five that are raised as significant issues in the docuseries (leaving aside eyewitness misidentification for now).

False confessions occur when a suspect confesses to a crime they did not commit. The public has difficulty believing that someone would do this, and because of this, false confessions are highly persuasive to jurors and make for very strong leverage in plea bargaining. Factors that increase the likelihood of a false confession occurring during police interrogation include duress, coercion, intoxication, diminished capacity, mental impairment, ignorance of the law, fear of violence, the actual infliction of harm, and the threat of a harsh sentence. False confessions play a critical role in three of the series I focus on, *The Innocent Man*, *Paradise Lost*, and *Making a Murderer*. The video of the teen confessing in *Making a Murderer* is even taught in law school as a perfect example of a coerced confession.

Forensic evidence is also extremely persuasive. Many people have faith in science and are confident that it produces true facts. However, the misapplication of science is the second most common contributing factor to wrongful convictions. This is more likely to happen when a specific field itself, like bite-mark comparisons, is unreliable or invalid; when not enough research has been done on the method to validate it; or when forensic experts' testimony overstates the significance of a result or downplays or omits analysis that would exclude the suspect or does not explain the limitations of the result. Sometimes practitioners simply make mistakes (with samples, for example), and sometimes analysts have engaged in misconduct by hiding exculpatory results or stating that tests were done that were not. Forensics play an important role in the trials documented in the New True.

Misconduct by government actors refers to improper behavior or intentional wrongdoing by law enforcement officials and prosecutors who are motivated to secure convictions, which are important markers of professional success. Their importance is amplified by community demands for public safety.[48] The Innocence Project and the National Registry of Exonerations, as well as other researchers, report that DNA exonerations have exposed official misconduct at every level and stage of a criminal investigation. The National Registry of Exonerations found that 77 percent of homicide exonerations in 2021 involved some form of official misconduct.[49] Some forms of law misconduct include being suggestive during identification procedures, coercing false confessions, lying or intentionally misleading jurors about their observations, failing to turn over exculpatory evidence to prosecutors, and providing incentives to secure unreliable evidence from informants. For prosecutors, misconduct includes withholding exculpatory evidence from the defense (*Brady* violations); mishandling, mistreating, or destroying evidence; allowing witnesses whom they know are not truthful to testify; and knowingly relying on fraudulent forensic experts. State misconduct is at issue, to varying degrees, in all of the New True except *Serial*. It is most prominently of concern in *The Innocent Man* and *Making a Murderer*.

The New True and Contemporary American Culture

In my analysis of the New True series, I introduce readers to developments in entertainment technology and the new crime-related documentaries that have been called "the glam genre of the moment."[50] Readers need not be concerned if they have not seen all—or any—of the series, as I provide detailed summaries of the eight that are the focus of this book. However, please note, there will be many "spoilers."

The series chronicle a number of stages in the criminal cases, from trials to convictions and appeals and their aftermath. I have chosen throughout to refer to the subjects of the series as "the defendants" because I believe this best expresses their position, even though the trials are just one part of their story. The subjects of the series do not only start off as defendants, but after conviction and in the course of podcasts and films, their status as guilty (or innocent) is continually questioned and explored. I will not be putting forth my own opinion on these cases or speculating about who I think really did it. Nor do I present an aesthetic assessment of these series as "good" or "bad." Rather, this is a study of the way the issues the series raise about wrongful conviction intersect with larger issues in American culture and entertainment.

As sites of public discourse, the New True reach broadly into American homes at a time when criminal justice reform is a national issue. It was a consistent feature of debate in the 2020 election season, and since George Floyd's murder, many Americans feel an urgency to address systemic injustice and racism. The Black Lives Matter movement and police reform are now part of a steadily growing sense of urgency about the need to end harsh punishments that disproportionately impact young men of color. Calls to change policing practices, to reform bail, to end mandatory minimum sentences, to improve the abysmal conditions of prisons, to enhance inmates' rights, and to drastically reduce or end solitary confinement are all efforts to humanize criminal justice and achieve a more truly functional democracy.

I am interested in the ways the New True rely on existing narrative strategies (and clichés) while innovating and bringing the critique of criminal justice into a genre that many viewers perceive as a trashy "guilty pleasure." I am equally concerned with the ways new stories of wrongful conviction contribute to our ongoing and evolving discourses on punishment. Throughout this book, I look at the ambiguity and uncertainty that run through the New True. The lack of resolution in the series resonates in a particularly disconcerting way at the moment of this writing. I see the New True as coexisting symptomatically in the era of "post-truth politics." Entertainment platforms are creating fragmented, niche audiences who exist in curated content bubbles at a time when news is consumed in a similar way. We can no longer agree on facts any more than we can agree on whether Adnan Syed killed Hae Min Lee.

True Crime

I found myself, not for the first time, compulsively refresh-
ing a newspaper's story on the shooting, not knowing what
information I was looking for. I guess I was trying to divine
something about proximity, tragedy, and how random these
random shootings really were, since they seem to happen in-
credibly regularly in the twenty-first century United States.
—Alice Bolin, *Dead Girls: Essays on Surviving an American
Obsession* (2018)

N Alice Bolin's collection of personal essays *Dead Girls: Essays on
Surviving an American Obsession,* she intertwines insights about
representations of women in in popular culture and true crime with
her own biography. Her life is not explicable separate from the crime
stories and images that we are surrounded with. In Karen Kilgariff and
Georgia Hardstark's true-crime comedy podcast *My Favorite Murder,*
they share personal experiences and reflections as they recount the
details of various murders that hit a chord with them. Their fan base
of "murderinos" fill sold-out live shows across the country. True crime
is more than just a popular entertainment genre: its clichés, repetitions,
horrors, and images are an important part of how we understand risk
and violence, as well as ourselves and our social world.

American audiences devote uncountable hours of leisure time to de-
vouring stories about criminals and the workings of the criminal justice
system.[1] Contemporary true-crime documentary exists within a universe of crime storytelling that includes crime news reporting in print
and television, traditional true-crime literature, and fictional crime entertainment in film and television. Although there are important differ-

ences among these, they all share some features in common with the new series I am analyzing, which conform to some true-crime conventions while taking the genre into new, more critical terrain. These series concern cases that started as high-profile news stories that garnered a lot of media coverage, at least locally. Much like investigative journalists, documentarians have gained access to players and conducted their own research.

True crime has functioned to educate mass-media consumers about criminal justice as they become "increasingly savvy and sophisticated about murder and how various institutions deal with it."[2] The informative aspects of true crime are consumed by the American public as entertainment, and a number of scholars have noted the degree to which they are specifically pleasurable. Yvonne Jewkes observes that the stories focus heavily on violence, which is "commodified and desired to the extent where they are widely distributed through all forms of media to be pleasurably consumed."[3] In Nicole Rafter's study of crime films, she argues that these stories confer pleasure by offering "the attractions of transgression" and what the historian Karen Halttunen refers to as the "'dreadful pleasure' of imaginatively viewing terrible scenes of violent death."[4] But for those who do not love true crime, it can seem like "nothing more than a form of pornography."[5] At the same time that crime stories confer pleasure in these ways, they convey ideological messages that "shape social thought about crime."[6]

In Jean Murley's study of true crime, she shows how it "presents mystery in order to solve it, while perpetuating and assuaging anxiety and fears about crime, presenting multitudes of murder scenarios, almost superhuman killers, and an insider's view of the pain that people inflict on each other."[7] There seems to be no saturation point in sight for this ever-popular and evolving genre that continues to offer "the dizzying pull of a real-life mystery."[8] This chapter looks at how crime news is constructed and packaged for audiences, the conventions of fictional crime entertainment, and true-crime storytelling in literature and documentary. The themes, issues, and values continuously overlap among the three, creating an ecosystem of crime entertainment that lays the groundwork for the subgenre that is the focus of this study.

Crime News

Crime news consumed as entertainment has long been a staple of American culture.[9] Print crime stories have historically and continuously been widely read. Looking at how entertainment became intertwined with all aspects of American culture, Neal Gabler discusses the widely circulated penny papers that captured nineteenth-century Americans' attention with the advent of the mass-distributed "human interest story," which from the beginning "emphasized crime and murder."[10] These stories were told in the overwrought style of "sentimental novels" to enhance their value as entertainment and "made crime reporting a staple of working-class news, the more sensational the better."[11]

To this day, the line between crime news and crime entertainment "has been increasingly blurred."[12] In traditional newspapers, the percentage of column space devoted to crime rose 58 percent in the first two decades of the twentieth century.[13] With the new energy of the type of investigative journalism promoted by William Randolph Hearst, news stories were told with more depth, detail, and nuance, making newspapers (and their crime stories) possibly "the single most popular form of entertainment prior to the movies. . . . They were fun to read."[14] Just as the public closely followed the O. J. Simpson trial at the end of the century, the entire nation then fixated on certain high-profile crimes and daily read detailed reports of the trials.[15]

Crime news stories must conform to the conventions and demands of the news business, which depends on advertising revenue and must fulfill perceived audience demand. Thus, ratings-driven news production is shaped by media professionals' assumptions about audiences and a need to entertain.[16] In addition, in producing crime stories, reporters rely on official sources such as government and nongovernment agency officials, law enforcement, and politicians, offering their versions of events that reflect their messaging priorities.[17] Structured by organizational needs, motivated to entertain, and conforming to established news values, stories inevitably focus on the rarest, most sensationalist of crimes, most notably murder. In this way, crime news has produced "a distorted picture of the world of crime and criminality" that "contributes to the public's unending thirst for information on bizarre and violent crime."[18]

Newsmakers routinely assess the potential public appeal of their stories.[19] Across various forms of media, news organizations choose which stories to tell and how to tell them, relying on a standard set of priorities and judgments. In Jewkes's study of media and crime, she enumerates several news values that shape journalism's storytelling, most of which are relevant to true-crime entertainment. These include *threshold*, referring to overall level of importance of the events; *simplification*, which refers to the ability of newsmakers to reduce stories to easily recognizable categories such as good guys and bad guys within a short enough space not to strain viewers' attention span; *individualism*, which pertains to the ability to organize stories around individual actors and frame conflict as between people as opposed to complex sociocultural and political forces; *proximity*, referring to geographical and cultural nearness to the lives of audiences; *violence or conflict*, when the events also meet news thresholds' overall levels of importance; *visual spectacle or graphic imagery*; and *conservative ideology and political diversion*.[20] Lynn Chancer argues in her study of high-profile crimes that ideology is often communicated by presenting events using "dualistic frameworks" based in "long-standing American beliefs in individualism and in using the legal system to resolve myriad social problems."[21] Taken together, these news values present ideological messages and often one-sided worldviews while depicting crime issues in as frightening and salacious a form of entertainment as possible.

To meet some of these criteria, newsmakers frame events and social actors within conventional narrative tropes; it is a form of storytelling. Subjects emerge as characters as newsmakers selectively choose how they will be portrayed. This is particularly true of suspects/perpetrators and victims. For example, while most sexual crimes are perpetrated by someone known to the victim, media consistently focus on stranger danger, portraying offenders as outsiders to the community, not friends and families. Perpetrators are framed as deviant fiends or maniacs as opposed to regular people. In so doing, newsmakers avoid uncomfortable truths about sexual violence and are not able to provide an analysis that includes social structures, institutions, and everyday modes of oppression. Similarly, murderers are more likely to be deemed newsworthy when they are strangers to the victims, who too must be drawn in a certain set of ways. The news business prefers victims who are "innocent, virtuous, and honorable," and they are usually white, middle class, female, and conventionally attractive.[22] They must possess the credibility conferred on people with higher social status.

In spite of the fact that young men of color experience the highest rates of victimization, news stories continue to focus on dead white girls.[23] Catering to perceived viewer demand, depictions of crime in the news are at best distortions of reality rather than reflections of it. They are mediated through processes designed to make them easy to consume, conforming to news values that often reinforce rather than challenge or disrupt the status quo. Gaye Tuchman explains, "Journalists are often attracted to stories that are variations on standard news formulas. They seek novelty—stories unexpected in their content, proffering 'sexy' pegs and angles—but only so long as such variations take place within formats already structurally familiar and 'routine.'"[24]

The news values of individualism and conservative ideology tend to serve the needs of the criminal justice system by communicating the same explanations that are foundational to the expansion of punitive social control that has led to mass incarceration. Individualism lends itself to definitions of offenders as deviants "who should be isolated via policies of containment, incapacitation and surveillance."[25] In an article on "gonzo rhetoric" in the news, R. J. Maratea and Brian A. Monahan discuss how the consistent emphasis on murder contributes to a culture of fear, exaggerating "the nature and extent of crime, while promoting quick fixes via get-tough policies to solve the violent crime problem."[26] Some journalistic strategies around crime have been referred to as "gonzo rhetoric," which employs "the discourse and symbolism used to promote and justify exaggerated acts of punishment" while making claims about the weakness and leniency of existing crime policy.[27] Using gonzo rhetoric to portray crime as the "imminent threat" of uncontained villains, newsmakers contribute to the expansion of ever-harsher systems of social control.[28]

Conservative ideology, gonzo rhetoric, and sensationalism in the news, taken as whole, have in some instances contributed to the subject matter of the new documentary series: wrongful convictions. Historically there was no general or substantive belief that criminal justice could go wrong, and often when the media presented crime stories, "they tended to butcher the concept or the presumption of innocence and assume the guilt of the defendant."[29] Lurid, breathless, seemingly nonstop coverage of the alleged satanic ritual abuses of small children at the McMartin preschool in the 1980s led to many arrests, devastating the lives of the accused. But those journalists who questioned some of the assertions were given little media time.[30] Also in the 1980s, dozens of people were arrested as part of a high-profile child sex ring in Kern County, California. Stories of the alleged abuse dominated news cycles and gave no presumption of innocence for the accused. Of thirty-seven convictions, thirty-five were overturned after the convicted people had spent years in prison, with one man serving nineteen years. When five Black and brown teenagers were arrested in New York City for the rape of a woman in Central Park, media coverage escalated existing tensions and helped fuel a fury of vitriol directed against the teenagers (known previously as "The Central Park Five," now "The Exonerated Five"). At the time, their guilt was considered patently established and went unquestioned by journalists. The most critical of perspectives only speculated on why so many urban young people turn to violence in the modern era, but no news outlet voiced the possibility that they were innocent.[31]

At the same time, however, a few investigative journalists were gaining fame for stories that actually led to exonerations, such as Morley Safer, whose CBS *60 Minutes* story helped free an innocent man in Texas in 1983.[32] Around the same time that the McMartin preschool scandal burned through the media, DNA testing was becoming more available as forensic evidence. In 1989, Gary Dotson in Illinois became the first person to be exonerated with DNA evidence, and some parts of the media went "from reactionary to revolutionary."[33] Cornelia Grumman won the Pulitzer Prize in 2002 for a story in the *Chicago Tribune* about wrongful convictions and the death penalty. Her story advocated for specific reforms that are cornerstones of the innocence movement today, such as "reducing coerced confessions, modifying police lineup to reduce eyewitness error, etc. This work contributed to Governor [George] Ryan of Illinois emptying the state of death row inmates before he left office."[34]

CBS's *60 Minutes* is one of many prime-time news-magazine shows that regularly feature true-crime reporting. These include *Unsolved Mysteries* (1987–2002), *48 Hours* and *48 Hours Mystery* (1988–present), *America's Most Wanted* (1988–present), *Cold Case Files* (1999–2017), *Forensic Files* (1996–2011, 2020–present), and *The First 48* (2004–present).[35] These in-depth journalistic treatments of crime stories blend news values, documentary techniques, and the narrative strategies used in true-crime literature. More so than segments in regular news programming, news magazines often offer satisfying endings. They "both present and then solve mystery, offering that deeply satisfying diversion as entertainment; and the TV shows both perpetuate and assuage anxiety and fears about crime, presenting multitudes of murder scenarios, almost superhuman killers, and an insider's view of the pain that people inflict on each other."[36] Yet others do not solve the mystery for the viewer so much as they ask the viewer to solve it themselves. *America's Most Wanted*, hosted by John Walsh, the influential victims' rights advocate who cofounded the National Center for Missing and Exploited Children, asks its audience to take an active role in crime solving, creating a prototype of what are today known as web- or internet-sleuths. A father of a murdered child, Walsh claims that the aim of the show is to put "the creeps behind bars where they belong." Unsurprisingly, this show has been criticized for disregarding the presumption of innocence by profiling suspects as de facto guilty.[37] It has also been critiqued for inspiring and encouraging vigilantism, because audiences track down suspects and assume roles of investigators, but the interactive quality, the bringing the audience into the process of solving the crime, remains a feature of some crime storytelling.[38]

Although news-magazine shows generally focus on the deviant killer, they have begun to look more critically at our legal system. In 2021, *Dateline NBC* aired a special report on the wrongful conviction of a man in 1988 who was exonerated and released in 2020. This episode explored the official misconduct of a number of Philadelphia police officers and was part of a weeklong investigation into criminal justice and wrongful conviction.

Fictional Crime Drama

Audiences of contemporary documentary series have been primed in murder stories and courtroom procedures through decades of fictional programming that includes police procedurals, forensic-driven detective series, and legal dramas. The fictional crime drama is deserving of mention in discussions of contemporary crime documentaries, as the two share important characteristics and rely on much the same values informing crime news reporting. Fictional crime entertainment includes movies and television shows that center on police work and investigations (police procedural dramas), the inner workings and motivations of criminals (such as the shows *Dexter* and *Criminal Minds*), or the trial process and court actors (legal dramas). These shows consistently show high Neilson ratings.[39]

Each form of true-crime entertainment packages conventions about victims and offenders and law enforcement that include a set of scenarios and legal concepts that inform the experience of other forms of true-crime entertainment. The fictional crime drama has cemented these in the American imagination and constrained our understanding of crime issues, particularly in ways that justify specific policies. Crime stories articulate three general causal explanations of crime, including "environment or subculture; psychopathy or mental illness; or higher material aspirations/excitement or a better life," the last two of which lend support to law-and-order policies.[40] Popular series such as *Law & Order* present stereotypical representations of criminals within racial and moral frames, where an "ontological criminality" is attributed to people of color, and white women, when engaged in criminal enterprise, are presumed to be the innocent and passive victims of the real bad guys.[41] Some evidence suggests that crime dramas "increase support for retribution as the most important goal of punishment."[42]

Katherine Beckett and Theodore Sasson provide an overview of evolving themes in fictional crime entertainment in the late twentieth century, from the relatively simplistic formulas of police dramas in the 1950s and 1960s, which presented "a two-dimensional moral order" with unambiguous good guys and bad guys, including such vintage favorites as *Hawaii Five-O* and *Columbo*.[43] This formula also operates in police films in which criminals are easily recognizable and categorized and police are righteous and justice driven.[44] The "vigilante cop" emerged as a prominent hero in the 1970s, both on television and in film. Civil liberties, which had recently been strengthened by landmark Warren Court rulings, were "depicted as impediments to police investigations," letting criminals off easy through "technicalities."[45] For justice to be served and wrongs to be righted, cops had to take the law into their own hands and defy legal constraints. Because in these shows it is taken for granted that police know who the perpetrator is and that their theories are correct, the crucial fact that they often do not know is not even considered a possibility. Examples include the "gritty" 1970s hit *The Streets of San Francisco* and today's *Law and Order: SVU*. The traditional narratives produced up until and through this era present right and wrong as unquestioned categories and assume a consensus on these values throughout society.[46] Rafter explains that movies in this tradition have a clear logic in the sequencing of events from "violation [and] discovery" through "punishment [and] resolution."[47]

Standard fictional crime entertainment solves the murder and re-stores order, but in the latter part of the twentieth century, a more critical and less romanticized view of crime and justice emerged in television and film, showing crime events in a social context, turning away from neat resolutions, and, in some instances, depicting crime as a feature or symptom of a bleak and alienated society—what Rafter refers to as "alternative tradition" films that present crime "in terms of a fallen world."[48] Eschewing criminological theories, films such as *Badlands*, *The River's Edge*, and *Natural Born Killers* present violence as senseless. American society is seen as riddled with malignant forms of oppressions built on and organized through racism, inequality, and patriarchal structures.

Rafter observes that by the 1970s, it became difficult for writers and directors to create stories in which good guy cops were entertaining.[49] That formula had become simplistic, transparent, and cliché as more complex plots emerged throughout entertainment. Television also began depicting some police "with very real personal flaws, . . . recover-ing alcoholics, . . . racists, . . . sexists."[50] Conversely, street crime began to be depicted in the context of the deprivations and hardships of urban life in ways that focused on social and racial inequality, thus implicating larger social problems in the representation of crime problems.

Most emblematic of this shift from simplistic to complex portrayals is HBOs *The Wire*, which aired from 2002 to 2008 and had consider-able impact not just on crime-related entertainment but on television drama more generally. It received wide critical acclaim for its depiction of the lives of police, institutional and political demands on law enforce-ment, complex social and interpersonal themes from sexism to racism and inequality and intimate-partner violence, and the deprivations and human toll of some urban living conditions. *The Wire* became a cultural phenomenon in its own right, inspiring college level-courses at several prestigious American universities including Johns Hopkins and Harvard, where it was taught in a sociology class on urban inequality. Importantly, created by the seasoned crime reporter David Simon, *The Wire* was widely praised for its realistic portrayal of crime and policing. More recently, TV series with multifaceted and intricate story lines lend themselves to multiple interpretations and include critiques of capitalism, state power, racism, and misogyny.[51]

Legal dramas make an important backdrop to the new series, many of which closely follow trials. These provide information about various facets of the legal system. They typically focus on either the prosecutor or defense counsel as a justice figure, and often the legal system itself can be seen as a character, an overarching American hero or villain depending on who is telling the story and to what purpose. American audiences' familiarity with trial procedures can be attributed in part to TV legal dramas and feature films that depict, in varying degrees of technical detail and accuracy, the role of the judge, the structure of opening and closing statements, objections, rulings on the admissibility of evidence, protocol for questioning witnesses on the stand, and so on. Legal-drama box-office hits tend to focus on a single case, with films featuring the little guy fighting "the system" or huge corporations often selling the most tickets. Civil-suit films such as *Erin Brockovich* and *The Rainmaker* were popular in the 1990s. Others concern the plight of a defendant and their attorneys fighting for their innocence against a seemingly iron-clad case. These include the classic *To Kill a Mocking-bird* and the thriller *Presumed Innocent*. Legal dramas have also long been a staple of television, from Perry Mason in the 1950s, to *LA Law*, *The Practice*, and *Ally McBeal* in the 1990s. The 1990s also saw the rise of *Law & Order*, a procedural drama with emphasis on technical aspects of the law. The original series ran for twenty years and spurred a whole franchise, including the even more popular *Law and Order: SVU*. In the past ten years, notable legal TV dramas have included *Suits*, *The Good Wife*, and the latter's spin-off, *The Good Fight*.

Of particular relevance to a study of new crime documentaries in the twenty-first century is the emergence of forensic-based television shows. Hit shows such as the *CSI* franchise have their roots in procedurals such as *Law & Order* and traditional mysteries. *Quincey, ME* is arguably an antecedent. This show featured a heroic justice-driven medical examiner who often breaks protocol to pursue detective work on his own. Forensic-based entertainment focuses on the body and physical detail and makes the routine investigative work seem exciting. Small everyday objects become imbued with allure, and secrets may be exposed through fast and accurate technologies. Viewers become "pseudo-experts," conversant in the practices of odontology, toxicology, ballistics, entomology, physical anthropology, and pathology.[52] Mark Seltzer observes that through forensics, the trauma of the original crime is returned to again and again and that "true crime always involves an aesthetics of the aftermath: forensic realism. The forensic way of seeing is held steadily visible. . . . Graphic horror quickly yields to research, bodies yield to information. The forensic procedures of true crime are inseparable from the self-reflexiveness of the communicative media of contemporary information culture."[53] These shows in particular are educational and even inspire people to pursue careers in the field. Although the issue is debated, many people believe that the provision of arcane knowledge has created expectations of the criminal justice system. Trial lawyers, jury consultants, and other law practitioners claim to have observed "the *CSI* effect"—the expectation of jurors for scientific evidence to be produced at trial.[54] Studies of this effect have been somewhat contradictory, but some evidence suggests both that juries are unwilling to convict if the prosecution does not produce forensic evidence and that they are more willing to convict based on forensic evidence alone.[55]

In the past two decades, the innocence movement and popular documentaries on wrongful conviction have brought attention to flaws in forensic science and the danger of relying on methods that have not been proven through rigorous scientific method. Some techniques have been labeled "junk science" and have been critiqued more and more in recent years. A 2012 investigative piece for PBS's *Frontline*, *The Real CSI*, investigated several important examples of this, and more recently, Netflix's four-part series *Exhibit A* (2019) demonstrates how "hard evidence" can be manipulated and misinterpreted.

Innocence issues and wrongful conviction have been the subject of popular feature films, often based on real-life cases. In addition to *To Kill a Mockingbird*, films such as *In the Name of the Father* and *Conviction* dramatize the plight of the innocent and evoke strong emotional reactions. In 2019, Bryan Stevenson's memoir about advocating for wrongfully convicted Black men on death row, *Just Mercy*, was made into a feature film of the same name.

Other crime genres include heists (*Ocean's 11*, *Lupin*), traditional Agatha Christie–style whodunnits, stories about financial and corporate crime (*The Wolf of Wall Street* and *The Big Short*), spy thrillers, gambling stories, and of course, organized crime. These are generally less relevant to the conventions of contemporary true-crime documentary. However, although it may seem an unlikely backdrop, political conspiracy thrillers can be seen as playing a part in shaping an American imagination that is receptive to some of the arguments in the new documentaries. Political conspiracy thrillers present intricate, ominous stories of organized malfeasance, involving powerful actors secretly pulling strings behind the scenes to control reality and distort its appearance. They offer a cynical portrait of corrupt authority. American conspiracy films (from classics such as *Three Days of the Condor* and *The Parallax View* to the more recent *The Constant Gardener*) are charged with populist sentiments and resentments and express a kind of resistance. These stories "ideologically address real structural inequities, constituting a response to a withering civil society and concentration in the ownership of the means of production."[56] Familiarity with conspiracy films and story lines, and the sense of transgressive pleasure they bring, may lay the groundwork for audiences to see as plausible some claims in the new series about coordinated, intentional official misconduct.

True-Crime Literature

True-crime stories have evolved from magazines and penny papers to full-length book treatments of a single case, usually a murder. True crime tends to "claim journalistic authority while creating fictional, hyperreal landscapes, events and characters."[57] Seltzer proclaims that true crime is fact that looks like fiction.[58] Although true crime is always constructed through techniques of minimization, exaggeration, speculation, and point of view, both consumers and creators believe it to depict "just the facts."[59] Murley thus defines true crime as "a murder narrative whose truth-claims are unchallenged by its audience."[60]

The true-crime books of the latter part of the twentieth century are descendants of true-crime magazines that proliferated in the first part of the twentieth century. In the 1920s, "pulp nonfiction magazines" emerged, such as the widely read *True Detective Mysteries*, *Master Detective*, and *Real Detective Tales*, which dominated the market and were "the primary form of American murder narration."[61] The primary sources were usually law enforcement and, like other forms of crime narrative, were seen as informative: "Readers learned about the intricate working of the criminal justice system and the complex, often tedious procedures of good (and bad) police work. Every issue also included articles and advertisements and how-to manuals on becoming a private detective."[62] They disseminated law-and-order messages, contributing to a generalized fear of crime and forming a basis of support for policies of containment and social control.[63] These magazines were in print for eighty years and enjoyed a heyday between the 1930s and the 1960s, when book-length true-crime stories came into vogue.[64]

By the 1980s, true crime had become "a consumer-driven publishing industry category, garnering huge profits for mass-market paperback publishing houses that have continued to grow."[65] Typically, these stories focused on a single murderer, often a single crime, but by the 1980s, there emerged a greater interest in serial killers. Book-length murder narrations generally do not focus on contracted hits or murder for hire, felony murder, or organized crime (which makes for its own subgenre). They also do not for the most part focus on the trials or aftermaths of cases. They fetishize detective work, forensic technologies, and psychological explanations for criminal behavior. They very much focus on the backgrounds and makeups of their murderers—not social context—and the criminal profiler is often an important character.

The entire ecosystem of true-crime stories, including film and television as well as books, is white-dominated. Not only are the writers and producers usually white, but the victims, their communities, and the genre's audience are usually white as well. White writers tell the stories of white victims and white criminals through media controlled by white producers and sold to white audiences. Murley notes that publishers did not attempt to appeal to Black audiences and "apparently imagined an all-white world."[66] One of the few Black true-crime storytellers, Wesley Lowery, explains that "it matters a great deal that most true crime focuses on white police officers and detectives, white victims, white prosecutors working to avenge them—aimed . . . at a presumed white audience."[67] Elon Green notes in his article "The Enduring Pernicious Whiteness of True Crime" that in a recent anthology of true-crime writing, only one nonwhite author was represented.[68] Murley and others observe that the overrepresentation of white victims in true-crime literature, like crime news, obscures the reality that Black Americans face much higher rates of victimization than white people do. She argues, "true crime's intense focus on the intersection of whiteness and violence is at odds with statistical reality, where in 2006, African Americans made up 12.5 percent of the total US population, but 49.5 percent of its murder victims."[69]

The underrepresentation of Black victimhood is a consequence of white editors choosing which crimes and which criminals are worthy of storytelling, which Green observes has the deleterious effect of skewing "some people's perception of what even *constitutes* a crime."[70] Traditional true-crime literature, like other forms of crime stories, takes place in white arenas devoid of social or racial conflict and rarely articulates a critical or sociological perspective. It does not lend itself to criminal justice reform movements. During the era of the early true-crime magazines, horrific, racially motivated lynchings were common, yet these cases were not featured in true-crime reportage. The absence of racial conflict, oppression, and inequality in these stories continues to indicate "that crimes against people of color [are] not considered crimes by the larger society."[71]

Audiences of true-crime books are largely composed of white women, who have been described as obsessive in their devotion to the genre.[72] Like crime news, true-crime literature tends to focus on victims who are young, white, female, and attractive.[73] Data on readership is difficult to come by and often anecdotal, but some corroborate the generally held assumption of a female fan base; and true crime is consistently described by insiders as a predominantly female market.[74] In addition to television executives, "writers, forensic scientists, and activists and exonerees all agree: true crime is a genre that overwhelmingly appeals to women."[75] Rachel Monroe explains in her book on women and true crime that publishers package their products to appeal to what that presumed audience wants, which may in turn cultivate that very audience.[76] The Oxygen network is geared toward female viewers, and the popularity of its true-crime programming is based on its understanding of its audience.[77] At a 2018 "CrimeCon" conference hosted by the network, Monroe observed that attendees were almost all women, and the few men she spoke to said they were there because of their girlfriends' interest.[78] The gendered dimension of audiences is understood in the larger culture as well. A 2021 *Saturday Night Live* skit, "Murder Show," mocks the gendered dimensions of true-crime audiences, depicting women consuming the seemingly endless array of multipart true-crime documentaries produced by Netflix, as they settle in cozily on their couches ready for ever more lurid, bizarre, and violent murder stories. This is then countered with their boyfriends presenting their obsessive love of "cult shows," which presumably has a larger male audience.

The gendered dimension can in part explain and be explained by the rise in the 1970s of true-crime stories depicting extreme violence against women and children and violence within the household, which found a place in the American imagination a century before, when accounts of domestic murders became more common.[79] Halttunen refers to this as a "cultural nightmare of the new sentimental domesticity, terrible tales of transgression against the emerging norms of companionate marriage, 'true womanhood,' and loving child nurture."[80]

It has been argued that women are drawn to these stories in order to feel control over the threats of violence in their lives and to educate themselves to better protect themselves from victimization. Ann Rule, acclaimed author of thirty-five true-crime books, often said that she considered her work "to be a kind of public service for women, warning them against sociopaths and dangerous romances."[81] Since her death, she continues to have an enormous fan base that is mostly women, as evidenced by responses on her website's guestbook.[82] The educational value that women believe true crime offers them is confirmed in Laura Browder's study of a small sample of avid true-crime readers. These women expressed that they saw true-crime books as providing "a secret map of the world, a how-to guide for survival."[83] Because true crime invariably focuses on female victims, these readers looked for their "mistakes" and "failures to read obvious clues."[84] Additionally, they found that true crime provided them with a "good explanation of personality traits."[85] Interestingly, because of the way these books build on character, they allowed for empathy with both killers and victims.[86] While there were stories about mothers killing their children and children killing their parents, most of the true crime that these women read featured women deceived, and murdered, by romantic partners, and their responses suggested that these stories helped them cope with experienced and feared patriarchal violence in their own lives.[87]

In the glut of true-crime books in the past fifty years, a few titles stand out for their significant contribution to the genre and their lasting popularity and continued influence.[88] Originally published in four installments of the *New Yorker*, *In Cold Blood* marked an enduring shift in true-crime literature, which had been regarded as trash up until then. It offered "a new way of understanding murder—one more sensitive to context, more psychologically sophisticated, more willing to make forays into emotional identification with killers through novelistic techniques."[89] It is seen as a "prototype of the entire genre of modern book-length true-crime narratives."[90] Capote famously called it "a non-fiction novel," in which he developed complex characters and evoked compassion for one of the two perpetrators, even as he was unsparing in his graphic portrayal of their horrific crimes: the slaughter of four members of a Kansas family during a robbery. Capote developed an intimacy with the killers, which was an innovation at the time but which has since become a hallmark of many true-crime books. This "writer/ killer relationship" has been described as the "single most important narrative innovation in modern true crime."[91] *In Cold Blood* suggested that one of the killers, Perry, had committed all four murders, although each perpetrator had been convicted of just two.

Capote's disavowal of Perry's account has been seen as a betrayal and has become a controversial feature of some true crime, most notably the 1980s book by Joe McGinnis, who developed a seemingly deep friendship with his subject, Jeffrey R. MacDonald, over several years. In *Fatal Vision*, McGinnis made an ardent case for MacDonald's guilt, and MacDonald then sued him in a civil suit that became famous in its own right. In the period between the publication of *In Cold Blood* and *Fatal Vision*, true-crime stories had shifted from focusing on threats from without, like the "drifters" whom Capote profiles, to crimes like MacDonald's, committed within the family "usually by respectable men, pillars of society."[92]

Ann Rule was one of the first female true-crime writers and arguably the most significant. Her contribution to traditional true crime has been enormous and lasting, and her large fan base continues to grow. Rule was one of few authors writing about female murderers and has been critiqued for linking their crimes to gender pathology and failures to successfully perform female roles.[93] Her first book, *The Stranger Beside Me*, chronicled her relationship with the serial killer Ted Bundy. She had worked with him and formed a friendship, utterly unaware of who he really was. In this book, she brought the concept of the sociopath into mass consciousness, someone with the ability to "mimic human emotions, to appear psychologically 'normal,' to uphold a façade of ordinariness."[94] Her work on Bundy elevated her status from crime writer to expert, and her career included projects educating law enforcement and criminologists.[95]

True-Crime Documentaries

Emphasizing the disturbing behavior of murderers and explaining that behavior through recourse to characterizations of individual deviance, true-crime books have done little in the way of social critique: "There is no social reform impulse in true crime, just a vast, sometimes sordid and graphic demonstration of the inexorability of evil."[96] While traditional true crime generally ignores racial and class issues, power structures, social conflict, and cultural contexts, documentaries are notably different in this regard, and the most famous among these have openly challenged the criminal justice system and led to social advocacy. Some feature-length documentaries released in theaters are the direct antecedents of contemporary serialized true-crime docuseries. Stella Bruzzi states in her book on documentaries that even more so than true-crime books, documentaries are for the most part received as accurate representations of "unadulterated truth."[97]

Documentarians purport objectivity and generally do not reveal the filmmaking and editing process or their role in what they depict.[98] While some documentarians may recognize that their work "can never offer a representation of real events indistinguishable from the events themselves," documentarians following the trials of defendants whom they believe are wrongfully convicted are building a case and present events in service of truth—a hopefully knowable truth, which they think has been obscured in the unjust course of events.[99] The documentaries discussed here were created in pursuit of justice.

Errol Morris's landmark *The Thin Blue Line* (1988) tells the story of Randall Dale Adams, who was tried and convicted in Texas in 1976 for the murder of a police officer. Using dramatic reenactments based on differing witness testimony, *The Thin Blue Line* exposes holes in the case and implicates several witnesses for lying and framing Adams. It also makes a case for the guilt of another man, David Harris, whom Adams picked up on the road the day of the murder. This was possibly for a sexual encounter, although this is left unclear, in an "epistemological closet" where queerness is both suggested and concealed.[100]

Morris, billing himself as "director-detective," tracked down witnesses, including Harris, who made a shocking statement that Adams was innocent. *The Thin Blue Line* is noted for its stylistic innovation, but it was also exceptional in that it led to Adams's release from prison. It depicts the criminal justice system as a closed, provincial, and vindictive network of bad-faith actors. As a documentary about wrongful conviction that directly impacted the case, this film laid the groundwork for contemporary true-crime documentaries, some of which are intended to have similar impact.

In a 2014 article in *Cultural Studies*, Kristen Fuhs discusses the Academy Award–winning *Murder on a Sunday Morning* (2001), directed by Jean-Xavier de Lestrade and chronicling the plight of a wrongfully accused Black teenager, Brenton Butler, who did not match the initial eyewitnesses description but was still identified as a suspect. Butler had an alibi that law enforcement never checked. At trial, he was acquitted, and Lestrade's film highlights the tireless and heroic work of his public defender. With two cameras that the judge allowed in the courtroom, Lestrade closely followed the trial while showing reactions to opening statements and witness testimony. Although "framed by points and counterpoints" intended to mirror the structure of the adversarial process, *Murder on a Sunday Morning* advocates for the innocence of the defendant and provides an in-depth look at the work of the defense team.[101] Butler's public defender becomes the "de facto narrator . . . that guides our understanding of the case and the trial."[102] The film questions the integrity of the law enforcement officer who questioned Butler and implicates another in the writing of a false confession.

Capturing the Friedmans (2003), directed by Andrew Jarecki, recounts the circumstances around the convictions of Arnold Friedman and his son, Jessie, drawing on a trove of footage that the family had created over the years. The Friedmans lived in an upper-middle-class Jewish town in Long Island where Arnold taught computer classes in his home to neighborhood boys. The FBI raided the family's home in 1987 after learning that Arnold was mailing and receiving child pornography, stacks of which the raid uncovered. Interviews with several of his students led to harrowing accounts of repeated sexual assault, in groups and in front of other kids, committed by both Arnold and Jessie. Jarecki presents the state's case with a degree of skepticism and includes interviews with the father of one victim who is certain nothing happened and does not think the many alleged sexual abuses could have been perpetrated over time without there being some indication. The media frenzy around the case was influenced by a national panic around child sex abuse and recovered memories.

In the course of the trial and investigation, Arnold wrote a letter wherein he insisted he did not touch those boys but confessed to fantasizing about children and molesting two boys a number of years previously at his vacation home. While maintaining his innocence, he pled guilty, hoping the state would be lenient with his nineteen-year-old son, whom he repeatedly asserted had nothing to do with any of it. Nonetheless, Jessie was convicted. While Jarecki's film has been seen as advocating for Jessie's innocence, some people have criticized it for being contemptuous of Arnold (who committed suicide in prison) and uninterested in his innocence for the crimes with which he was charged.[103] Jessie was released from prison in 2001 and has continued to work to clear his name.

Sarah and Ken Burns's 2012 documentary *The Central Park Five* is about the aftermath of the famous 1989 Central Park jogger assault and the quick trial and conviction of five boys, ages fourteen to sixteen. The documentary tells the story of their innocence in the context of the social climate of New York City during a period of high-profile racial incidents and rising crime. Within this culture of fear and blame, the Black and Latino teens were seen as guilty the moment they were arrested. *The Central Park Five* features tabloid pages and the inflamed rhetoric of politicians and community members, who come across as rabidly racist, but it neglects that other, more reputable papers also jumped on this bandwagon and that, as mentioned earlier, few journalists at the time questioned the teens' guilt. Footage of their coerced confessions reveals how vulnerable and powerless the teens and their parents were against law enforcement's authority and the racial rage of the community. The boys were later exonerated (in 2002) after the perpetrator admitted his guilt, which was corroborated by DNA testing. *The Central Park Five* was released ten years after the boys' exoneration, so the details of this case were already well-known to many people. It stands out for its analysis of events and its indictment of the judicial system and the national culture of racism.

In addition to these feature-length documentaries that were first screened in theaters, it is important to note the significant work that PBS's *Frontline* has done exploring an array of criminal justice issues in a number of powerful reports that focus on innocence. The role that faulty forensics play in wrongful convictions is investigated in *Death by Fire* (dir. Jessie Deeter, 2010), about the execution of a possibly innocent man for murder arson, and in *The Real CSI* (dir. Tim Mangini, 2012), which looks critically at problems inherent in a number of forensic methods. *What Jennifer Saw* (dir. Ben Loeterman, 1997) looks at troubling issues that influence eyewitness (mis)identification. The director Ofra Bikel produced a significant and impactful body of award-winning reports for *Frontline*, many of which focus on innocence issues. These include *Innocence Lost* (1991, 1993, 1997), her three-part chronicle of the trials and convictions of workers at Little Rascals Day Care during the height of the panic around child sexual and satanic abuse; *The Case for Innocence*

(2000), which examines a case of wrongful conviction that led to the involvement of the Innocence Project and a DNA exoneration; *An Ordinary Crime* (2002), which looks at problems with the plea-bargaining process and eyewitness testimony in wrongful conviction; *Requiem for Frank Lee Smith* (2002), which follows the postconviction appeals of an innocent man on death row (who died of cancer just before his name was officially cleared); *The Burden of Innocence* (2003), which follows the struggles of five exonerated men after their release from prison; *The Plea* (2004), which looks at prosecutorial power and the pressure that plea bargaining puts on defendants to plea to crimes they did not commit; and *The Confessions* (2010), which looks at coerced confessions in the "Norfolk Four" case. Bikel is credited with playing an important role in the exonerations of thirteen wrongfully convicted men and women and has raised awareness of key criminal justice factors that contribute to wrongful conviction, including racism, coerced confessions, and abuse of prosecutorial power, all of which contributed to the convictions of the men featured in the new serialized documentaries on wrongful conviction.[104]

2

The New True

Watching a streaming series is even more like reading a
book—you receive it as a seamless whole, you set your own
schedule—but it's also like video gaming. Binge-watching is
immersive. It's user-directed. It creates a dynamic that I call
"The Suck": that narcotic, tidal feeling of getting drawn into a
show and letting it wash over you for hours.
—James Poniewozik, *New York Times* (2015)

THERE was a time when television viewing was a guilty pleasure.
People were not proud of the amount of time they spent watching
it, and it was likened to empty calories, a kind of junk entertainment that offered no substance. But all that changed in the twentieth
century. What the Frankfurt School once characterized as a strategy to
encourage "mindless capitalist consumption" has undergone a transformation; we are now comfortably in the age of prestige TV.[1] In the
early 2000s, the subscription cable service HBO began producing original content that was widely seen as elevating the television genre, and
The Sopranos has been credited with making HBO a highly desirable
"designer label," heralding the new golden age of television.[2]

Traditional true crime evolved along with the new aesthetics and
rapidly developing communications technologies that have dramatically shifted the way Americans consume entertainment, whether that
be drama, comedy, or documentary. In contrast to what is now referred
to as "linear TV," in which viewers had to plan to be home to watch or
schedule to record shows, today's audiences have enormous content li-
braries readily available to them at all hours through video on-demand
streaming subscription services such as Netflix, Amazon Prime, Hulu,

and HBO Max.[3] The new technologies brought with them new marketing strategies. Streaming services do not rely on traditional Neilson ratings, since it does not matter how many people watch a specific show at one time.[4] They are instead concerned with maintaining subscribers, which has entailed catering to (and creating) niche tastes. The result is multiple, segmented, specialized target audiences.[5] Documentaries have been affected by this change, as early on, Netflix executives learned that people who might not go see a documentary in a theater are often interested in watching at home.[6]

The "the post-network era" has introduced a significant change in entertainment consumption behavior, including the phenomenon of "bingeing"—watching or listening to multiple episodes at a time.[7] This term is now frequently used by the television industry, the popular press, and the general public, and in 2017, 70 percent of viewers said that they had binged television.[8] In fact, data suggests that viewers prefer to binge TV.[9] No longer low-brow fare on the "idiot box," quality or high-end TV is characterized by "high budgets, critical acclaim, and . . . a programming and marketing strategy to pitch television to a desirable, high-income audience."[10] Series are now often perceived as having the novelistic quality of "one epic text," and binge-watching itself encourages writers to create complex narrative arcs.[11] Not only do we no longer feel guilty about our TV consumption; we often flaunt it. It has come to be seen as an activity as worthwhile as any other, and I have noticed that people getting together will ask, "What are you watching?" just as much as "What have you been up to?"

The rise in binge-watching was part of the technological transformation known as Web 2.0, which also facilitated the rise of another new medium: the podcast. Podcasts emerged in 2004 and brought audio files, the internet, and portable media devices together (primarily Apple's iPod).[12] They are inexpensive to produce and distribute, and although far less profitable than the streaming video services, many are commercially viable.[13] As with services like Netflix, users enjoy a more individualized experience over which they have more control than with linear radio.[14] Podcasts have a variety of formats and a seemingly endless variety of topics, such as the entertainment industry and celebrity culture, sports, cooking, politics, fitness, and, of course, true crime.

New Documentary

Technological, cultural, and aesthetic transformations have directly impacted true crime. Early on, Netflix executives realized that there was a wider audience for documentaries than was previously assumed. One reflected that "just because a person doesn't go see a documentary on a Friday night, it's not a reflection on the film; it's just a reflection that maybe a documentary isn't a film that a couple is going to want to see on date night."[15] Today documentaries of all kinds are highly popular with Netflix subscribers, including those on celebrities and business leaders, social problems, and politics. Netflix has become "a home for breakout docuseries," and among its offerings are a wide array of true-crime titles.[16] Many of these share the features of prestige TV that distinguish them from traditional true crime: "they have subtle senses of theme and character, and they often feel professional, pensive, quiet—so far from vulgar or sensational."[17]

A cursory list of Netflix's most well-known crime series includes *Night Stalker: The Hunt for a Serial Killer* (2021), about a notorious serial killer convicted in the 1980s; *Crime Scene: The Vanishing at the Cecil Hotel* (2021), which initially presents its subject as an unsolved mystery but concludes with a clear theory and closed case; *Tiger King* (2020), about an eccentric zookeeper currently in prison; *Jeffrey Epstein: Filthy Rich* (2020), about the infamous sex offender and his decades-long sexual abuse operation; *Wild, Wild Country* (2018), about a 1980s cult and the alleged criminal conduct of its leader; and *The Keepers* (2017), about an unsolved murder that explores recovered memory and sexual abuse in the Catholic Church. In addition to these are three of the subjects of this book, *The Staircase* (2005–2018), *Making a Murderer* (2015, 2018), and *The Innocent Man* (2018). HBO/HBO Max has also distinguished itself in the documentary field, with a number of popular titles covering a range of topics. One of its most acclaimed documentaries is also among the subjects of this book, the three feature-length films known as the *Paradise Lost* trilogy (1996, 2000, 2011).

True crime has thrived on podcasts as well, and critics periodically offer lists of top ones.[18] *Serial* (2014) is credited with pioneering the genre. The number of true-crime podcasts is too vast for me to enumerate, but among the most popular are *Up and Vanished* (2016–2018), which investigates unsolved missing persons cases; *My Favorite Murder* (2016–present), in which two comedians discuss different cases each week; *Undisclosed* (2015–present), which explores a different (possible) wrongful conviction each season; *Women and Crime* (2019–present), in which two criminologists discuss a case each week; *In the Dark* (2016–2020), which delves into a different case each season; and *Crime Junkie Podcast* (2020–present). The true-crime podcasts *Serial* and *Atlanta Monster* (2018), about the 1979–1981 child murders, as well as two HBO documentary series on the same cases, are among the subjects of this book.

The New True

This book provides a close reading of a subgenre of true-crime documentary series that I am calling the New True. They differentiate themselves from traditional true crime in a number of ways, most importantly as critiques of the criminal justice system that to various degrees and somewhat radically side with the accused.[19] The documentarians, "dissatisfied with the outcome of a criminal case, conduct their own investigations."[20] Acting as innocence advocates, they present critical analyses of cases and trial processes that "are a kind of legal intervention. . . . They function as an alternative appeals process . . . designed to effect a change in the legal outcome."[21] Since 2014, these new series have been "gaining cultural prominence and resonance," and they have recently elevated the status of the true-crime genre.[22] Their cultural significance is evidenced by the "whole ecosystem of comment, conjecture and investigation from viewers" that they have inspired.[23]

I look at six cases presented in eight series. They have been selected as representative of the New True because each meets most of the following criteria.

Multiepisode Documentaries

The New True are documentary films and podcasts. They are not scripted and do not feature actors, except for brief dramatic reenactments. Scripted treatments of actual cases, such as the 2010 film *Conviction*, about the wrongful conviction of Kenny Walters in 1980; the Netflix series *When They See Us* (2019), about the five boys convicted in the Central Park jogger case; and *Just Mercy* (2019), about Bryan Stevenson's work exonerating Walter McMillian in Alabama, do not fit this category, although they present strong critiques of the justice system and are important parts of the cultural landscape within which the New True exists. While the New True may have moments when they "sacrifice reality for drama" in their attempts to create narrative, they nevertheless document actual people and events.[24]

With the exception of the *Paradise Lost* trilogy, the New True were produced as multiepisode series. The trilogy is an important precursor to the New True and is included here because of its impact on the viewing public and on the outcome of the cases. Netflix has produced some important episodic series on wrongful conviction issues, most notably *The Confession Tapes* (2017), *Exhibit A* (2019), and *The Innocence Files* (2020). These series cover different cases in each episode, illustrating crucial problems in the justice system, and I draw on this work in my analysis of the New True, which tell singular stories over a long narrative arc.

Newsworthy Murder Cases

The New True cases are about murder convictions with long prison sentences. The series do not address the most common forms of crime and victimization, and in this regard, they conform to the conventions of traditional true crime. All the cases meet the threshold of newsworthiness discussed in chapter 1. They were all high profile and received a great deal of media coverage, which itself becomes a character in the documentarians' storytelling. Amazon Prime Video's *Free Meek* is an important true-crime work but is not included in my analysis because, although the series critiques the justice system, it focuses on minor crime and oppressive features of probation.

Convictions and Innocence Issues

The New True focus on cases of (possible) wrongful conviction. All the trials ended in guilty verdicts, and as far as the state is concerned, the cases are closed. The documentarians present arguments for the subjects' innocence, often following the defense's preparation and/or following postconviction efforts. Each series explores some of the recognized contributing factors to wrongful convictions, including eyewitness misidentification, coerced false confessions, state misconduct, and faulty forensic science.

Documentarians as Advocates and Their Activated Audiences

Because the documentarians question the validity of the convictions, their work elaborates defense theories, and they act, to varying degrees, as advocates for their subjects' innocence. The prosecution rarely participates in these docuseries. While traditional true crime relies heavily on institutional sources and does not see the accused as a source of truth, these new series do the opposite: they foreground the accused's version of events and challenge the institutional narrative.[25] In some ways, they are a form of journalistic exposé. The popular HBO series *The Jinx* (2015) is not included in my analysis because the director does the opposite of the New True documentarians by exposing what he believes to be his subject's guilt. Also not included is *Murder in Alliance* (2021), in which the journalists and investigators end up more convinced of their subjects' guilt than innocence.

These docuseries have all inspired audiences to act on the subjects' behalf, creating online forums, starting petitions, and staging protests. Their efforts in turn become part of the narratives, as most of the New True include follow-up episodes or new series that chronicle the impact of the documentarians' work on the stories they have been telling. The New True, then, exist simultaneously as metanarratives about the process and consequences of researching high-profile crimes, in which aspects of criminal justice become entwined and "confounded with its own representation."[26]

Ambiguity and Uncertainty

Although the New True documentarians in some ways act as innocence advocates, they also present the prosecution's case. Their investigations point to holes in it, raising many questions about truth. At the same time that they challenge the verdicts, they leave some room for doubt. New True viewers and listeners come away from the series divided in their opinions, in part because the documentarians explore multiple perspectives on the facts in evidence and present a variety of interpretations. The absence of absolute, incontrovertible certainty is a destabilizing and compelling feature of the series.

The New True Synopses
The *Paradise Lost* Trilogy (1996, 2000, 2012)

Paradise Lost: The Child Murders at Robin Hood Hills is about three teenagers who were convicted of the sadistic sexual murders of three young boys in West Memphis, Arkansas, in 1993. Directed and produced in 1996 by Joe Berlinger and Bruce Sinofsky for HBO, the film had a limited release in theaters while being aired on cable. The three eight-year-old victims were last seen together after school, and their bodies were eventually discovered decomposing in the woods. They came from middle-class, suburban families, while the three teenage suspects—Damien Echols, Jason Baldwin, and Jessie Misskelley—were from the lower class. The accused did not fit the town's normative, white, evangelical Christian culture and wore dark clothes, read horror books, and listened to heavy-metal music. Echols, who received the most attention from local media and the documentarians, particularly stood out for openly practicing Wicca and exploring the occult.

There was no direct physical evidence linking the teens to the crime, and there were no leads until Misskelley confessed under what the filmmakers present as a highly pressured interrogation. Misskelley, who had an IQ of 72, said that Echols and Baldwin participated in the murders while he was with them. Echols and Baldwin were immediately arrested, and because Misskelley's confession had been leaked to the press, the teens were already seen as guilty before they were formally charged. Misskelley soon recanted and refused to negotiate a lesser sentence in exchange for testimony against the other two. He was convicted and sentenced to life plus forty years in prison, in spite of the fact that he was out of town at the time of the murders and had a solid alibi. Baldwin and Echols likewise were in school at the time of the boys' disappearance. The three teenagers were tried together, and the substance of the prosecution's case rested on character evidence, including testimony from students at their high school who had heard rumors of Echols's involvement and from an occult expert who promoted the prosecution's satanic-ritual theory.[27] After they were convicted, Baldwin was sentenced to life without parole and Echols to death by lethal injection.

Berlinger and Sinofsky produced two sequels that HBO aired in 2000 (*Revelations*) and 2011 (*Purgatory*). Both devote more attention to physical evidence than the original film does, particularly the state of the victims' bodies and the crime scene, and they explore a few alternative theories. They point the finger at John Mark Byers, the stepfather of one of the victims, as well as at another victim's stepfather and an unnamed stranger who was reportedly seen bloodied in a bathroom near the highway.

The films have been described as "tastefully lurid Southern-gothic-meets-heavy-metal."[28] *Paradise Lost* follows the teenagers, the victims' families, the defense team, and the course of the trial. The prosecution declined to participate. During the film, we see the pain and suffering of the victims' families, expressed as ire and hatred for the defendants, along with an unquestioning and absolute belief in their guilt. Byers features prominently, preaching in church and offering fire-and-brimstone rhetoric in multiple interviews. He is Echols's "equal in terms of sheer creepiness."[29] Although particularly "melodramatic," he speaks to the general religiosity of the community.[30]

Echols, in contrast, conspicuously lacks expression and seems unconnected to the gravity of the situation. It is unnerving when he speculates, with apparent awe, that he will be known for years as the bogey man. *Paradise Lost* does not seriously explore the prosecution's theory of the crime and spends more time presenting the defense and documenting the character of the community. Echols, Baldwin, and Misskelley became known as the "West Memphis Three" (WM3), and following the release of *Paradise Lost*, groups of viewers publicly took up their cause and advocated for their innocence.

In *Revelations*, we see Byers fall from grace. He reports that his wife, the mother of one of the victims, became addicted to heroin after the murders and that they lost their business and their home. She died in her sleep from an undetermined cause, and the film suggests that Byers might in some way be responsible. The filmmakers make a case for Byers as a suspect, presenting evidence that his stepson was abused by him and questioning a link between marks on the bodies and Byers's teeth. We learn that he is on a tremendous amount of psychotropic medication, and his fervent belief in the WM3's guilt is presented as almost maniacal.

In *Purgatory*, the filmmakers address accusations that they themselves had exploited circumstantial evidence to paint Byers as guilty in the same way the community demonized the WM3. At the same time that they raise questions about the ethics of doing so, they make a case that the stepfather of another victim was the perpetrator. In this final film, we learn that the evidence analyzed in the second film convinced Byers of the WM3's innocence, and in an unexpected twist, he became an ardent supporter of them.

Purgatory is a bit more of a legal procedural, as it follows the post-conviction teams' work on securing DNA testing and their petition for a new trial. When no DNA at the crime scene matched any of the WM3 (or Byers), their lawyers filed for a new evidentiary hearing for a new trial. This was denied and then appealed based on a statute requiring that all other evidence be considered if there is no DNA match. This would include all the evidence analyzed in the films. In 2011, an unexpected circuit court hearing was convened, which was a surprise to the filmmakers and viewers, as well as to the WM3's supporters. The WM3 were able to negotiate *Alford* pleas—a legal mechanism that allows defendants to accept a sentence without acknowledging guilt. It is essentially a guilty plea without an allocution or admission; those who enter *Alford* pleas still have their criminal record and are barred from filing civil suits based on wrongful convictions. This presented a difficult compromise for the defendants, but since it allowed them to go free, whereas a new trial would take years to resolve, they entered the pleas. Baldwin was the most deeply reluctant, but he explains to Berlinger and Sinofsky that the state was going to execute Echols (on death row) and that he could not let that happen. They were released from prison in 2011.

From the outset, this case received a great deal of media attention. *Paradise Lost* highlights footage of the victims' families venomously denouncing the WM3 to reporters and casts a critical lens on the media's amplification of rumors of satanic ritual abuse and how "sensational television news" interacted with "religious fervor" in cementing belief in the WM3's guilt.[31] The documentarians particularly focus on the parents' profound rage, exhibited in front of the cameras, in a way that casts them as savagely craving vengeance. The filmmakers contrast the parents' behavior before the news cameras start to roll with their on-camera demeanor, calling into question their authenticity.[32] The films feature footage of the news crews setting up that provides a glimpse into how news is constructed and how the town reacted to the media attention. In all, Berlinger and Sinofsky illustrate "the way people modify their behavior in an attempt to project one image or another."[33]

The response to *Paradise Lost* in 1996 was unprecedented. Audience members were deeply roused by the injustice it portrayed, and a group of friends in Los Angeles who could not stop thinking about it took advantage of the still-new web technology.[34] They created a website with chat rooms for supporters and began to raise funds and organize protests. This was before Facebook and Reddit, where "crime-centric groups" would eventually proliferate.[35] It marked an early instance of a documentary generating an "ongoing research project, . . . a sort of Internet-centered criminal justice cottage industry."[36] Mark Seltzer describes the WM3 support group as "the sociality of the wound, . . . a public gathering around the scene of the crime."[37] After seeing *Paradise Lost*, celebrities such as Tom Waits and members of Metallica publicly endorsed their innocence. The impact of the film on the actual case was profound. The advocacy it inspired brought heightened attention to the convicted teens and supported actual postconviction processes. When a young Brooklyn-based landscape architect saw *Paradise Lost*, she was so affected by the story that she wrote to Echols. They quickly began an intense correspondence and eventually married. Her legal advocacy for Echols was financially supported by the director of *Lord of the Rings*, who also hired forensic experts for the WM3 cases.[38]

Revelations particularly focuses on the process of a "viewing public transformed by the film from passive spectator to engaged citizen."[39] In *Revelations*, we learn that one member of the support group was inspired to register for classes on forensic analysis and then put one of her professors in touch with Misskelley's attorney. The professor then became a consultant for the defense. Berlinger and Sinofsky realized that they themselves were part of the story they were telling when Byers gave them a knife he believed was evidence, and they had to turn it over to the courts. The film shows the way documentaries "can affect matters being observed."[40] Throughout their films, the documentarians negotiate dual roles as journalists and advocates.[41] Depicting "violations of the boundary between players and spectators," *Revelations* and *Purgatory* work as metanarratives wherein the filmmakers explore the role of documentary in the solving and prosecution of the case.[42]

The Staircase (2005, 2018)

Directed by Jean Xavier de Lestrade, *The Staircase* originally aired on the Sundance Channel in 2005 with eight episodes. This was unique for documentary storytelling at the time, when feature-length was still the norm.[43] Two follow-up episodes aired in 2013, and Netflix produced three additional episodes in 2016, releasing the entire thirteen-episode chronicle in 2018.

Lestrade was drawn to the then-unfolding criminal drama concerning a wealthy crime-fiction writer charged with murdering his wife in North Carolina. In 2001, Michael Peterson called 911 claiming to have discovered Kathleen's body at the bottom of the stairs. When police arrived at the scene, there was so much blood that they doubted it was a simple fall, and Peterson was soon arrested. The initial eight episodes of *The Staircase* closely follow Peterson, his family, and his defense team preparing for and going through the trial. In spite of a very expensive defense and a dedicated attorney (David Rudolf), Peterson was convicted in 2003 and sentenced to life without parole.

The series begins with Peterson re-creating his and his wife's movements through their nine-thousand-square-foot home the night of her death. He explains that after dinner, they sat out by the pool drinking wine. This scene establishes their comfortable lifestyle and their warm relationship. Throughout *The Staircase*, Peterson describes his marriage as happy and ideal, and his wife as his soul mate, a claim supported by his children, friends, and other family members. They had a blended family that included two sons from Peterson's first marriage and two daughters he adopted with his first wife when the girls were very young. When he married Kathleen, she had a daughter from a previous marriage. By all accounts, everyone got along, and Peterson's sons and two daughters actively participated in the documentary.

The assistant medical examiner determined that Kathleen died of blunt force trauma to the head, not an accident. Law enforcement seized Peterson's computer and found gay pornography and explicit emails with a male escort. The prosecution argued that Kathleen had not known about Peterson's bisexuality and that a huge fight had ensued when she discovered it, resulting in Peterson beating her to death. *The Staircase* closely follows the battle of experts, with both sides analyzing the blood spatter in support of their theories. Complicating matters, his friend and the mother of the girls Peterson later adopted had also been found dead at the bottom of the stairs. At the time, it was attributed to a brain aneurysm, but the district attorney in Peterson's case got permission to have her body exhumed and sent to North Carolina from Germany for a new autopsy. The same assistant medical examiner determined that she too had died of blunt force trauma to the head. Of the similarities in the two cases, one of Peterson's daughters says that it is "interesting" that both women were found at the bottom of the stairs but that "what they have in common is that dad loved them both very, very much and would never have hurt them."[44]

The first eight episodes were filmed in real time, and as Lestrade was filming, he did not know how the case would turn out. He intended the film to be a companion piece to his *Murder on a Sunday Morning* (2001), to "show how the justice system functions for wealthy white men compared to black teenagers."[45] Yet he was shocked by the verdict. Eight years later, after all Peterson's appeals had been exhausted, a prisoner in North Carolina was exonerated because the state's blood-spatter expert had given false testimony at his trial. The same expert had testified against Peterson.

Lestrade then returned to film the hearings for a new trial. These episodes cover the conviction being overturned and the state planning a new trial, possibly without the evidence of Peterson's bisexuality or the previous death of his friend, the mother of his adopted daughters. Peterson, whose wealth was now depleted and who had aged greatly in prison, was released on house arrest with an ankle monitor and $500,000 bail. Two and a half years later, he was still waiting when Lestrade filmed the final three episodes, which concern the negotiation of an *Alford* plea, which Peterson eventually entered.

The first eight episodes are a classic courtroom drama, establishing clear protagonists and villains. Working closely with the defense, Lestrade seeks to present Peterson in a flattering light, giving him room to share his personal history and worldview, at times philosophizing on the criminal justice system. In the follow-up episodes, we see Peterson broken and frequently emotional. In fact, *The Staircase* has been critiqued for casting him as the victim.[46] Rudolf emerges as a hardworking, traditional justice figure advocating for the innocent. The prosecutors, particularly the assistant district attorney, are cast as villains, as are Kathleen's sisters, who, learning of Peterson's bisexuality become convinced of his guilt. As in *Paradise Lost*, news media are also an important character in *The Staircase*, which opens with local news stations' aerial shots of the Peterson home and the initial coverage of the case. News teams followed the trial closely, reporting on it each day. Rudolf's team in turn closely followed the coverage, using it as a feedback loop for how to proceed. Newscasters are often shown off camera, setting up shots, which highlights the produced nature of information.

As Lestrade frames the news media as a player in the narrative that influences the case, he is producing another form of media that will have its own impact on the case. After the first eight episodes aired, viewers debated the case and researched details, developing theories of what happened, including the "owl theory": that the lacerations on Kathleen's skull were caused by an owl or raptor.[47] Kathleen's sisters were outraged at how they are portrayed. One sister publicly complained that Lestrade made "a pseudo-documentary about [her] sister's murder without [her] family's cooperation or consent. Michael Peterson had a movie made where he could pontificate and tell everyone how bad the criminal justice system is."[48]

The Staircase also impacted court proceedings. In the final episodes, Peterson says that if it were not for Lestrade, he would not even be back in court. Similarly, Rudolf told a *Rolling Stone* reporter that Lestrade's footage was a crucial supplement to the trial transcript because it allowed him "to show the judge the actual testimony where the judge is sitting on the bench and [Duane] Deaver [the prosecution's investigator] is lying right in front of the judge and lying to the jury": "You pick up his facial expressions and his demeanor and his certitude in saying certain things that were just false. All of that really, really helped me in immeasurable ways to convince the judge that Michael needs a new trial." The filmmaking also affected the lives of producers, as one of the editors of *The Staircase* became romantically involved with Peterson while working on the documentary.[49]

The Staircase has been praised as "an evenhanded, empathetic look at the human toll of the machinery of justice" and seen as "the modern template for true-crime TV," which established "a booming subgenre" that "never relies on an exploitative tone or a prurient approach to achieve its goals."[50] The relationship between Peterson and Lestrade is understood as crucial to the film and the casting of Peterson as a protagonist. Because the prosecution did not participate in the filmmaking, the edited trial footage is all we have to counter his claims of innocence, yet Lestrade manages to build tension "between Peterson's apparent openness with the camera and crew—the outgoing performativity of someone who has nothing to hide—and the frequently graphic documentation presented, principally by the prosecution, which undermines directly his version of events."[51]

Serial (2014) and The Case against Adnan Syed (2019)

While the *Paradise Lost* trilogy and *The Staircase* follow the trials of their subjects in real time, the podcast *Serial* investigates an older case. *Serial* started as a spin-off from the popular NPR show *This American Life*. Its first twelve episodes aired in 2014, with three follow-up episodes in 2016. It reached five million downloads faster than any other podcast and earned status as the most popular podcast in the medium's history.[52]

The first episode begins with producer Sarah Koenig asking listeners to consider the vagaries of memory, before describing the facts of a 1999 murder case in the Baltimore area. A teenage girl, Hae Min Lee, disappeared after school, and her body was found six weeks later in a park. The cause of death was manual strangulation. Her ex-boyfriend, Adnan Syed, became a suspect when another teen, Jay Wilds, implicated him, claiming that Syed had killed her and that Wilds had later helped him bury her body. Importantly, Wilds was able to tell the detectives where Lee's car was. The prosecution's case focused heavily on Syed's whereabouts during an unaccounted-for twenty-one minutes on the day Lee disappeared, when Wilds had Syed's phone and car for at least some key hours. In addition to Wilds's testimony, the prosecution had records from Syed's cell phone. Wilds had told detectives a few different versions of what happened, and the prosecution used the narrative that best fit the phone records. This was the first trial to use cell-phone data to establish location. The prosecution also pointed to Syed's Pakistani heritage and his Muslim religion in framing parts of its case, specifically his motive. When first interviewed by detectives, all Syed and Lee's friends were trying to recount events from an ordinary day six weeks before, and Syed could not account for the crucial twenty-one minutes when the state claimed the murder took place. Syed was tried and convicted for the crime and received a sentence of life plus thirty years.

The story touches on race and class issues in the United States. Lee and Syed both came from immigrant families. Lee was Korean American and described by everyone as smart, beautiful, responsible, and cheerful, a great student and athlete who took care of her siblings. Syed is Pakistani American, and his family was part of a tight-knit mosque community. Like Lee, he was a good student and played sports. While the prosecution emphasized his cultural heritage, his attorney went to lengths in her opening statement to describe him as American. Both teens attended a magnet program together inside a larger high school, and they had a large, diverse group of friends. Wilds, who is Black and had recently graduated, often smoked marijuana with Syed. Wilds explained to detectives that even though they were not that close, it made sense that Syed would choose him as an accomplice, because he was regarded as "a criminal element." He also expressed fears about being blamed for the murder because of his race and the police harassment he was already accustomed to experiencing. It was important for the defense that Wilds did not seem credible, and perhaps the attorneys hoped that negative racial associations would work in their favor.

In *Serial*, we hear Koenig trying to understand the complex dynamics of the teenagers' social world amid inconsistencies in and between everyone's statements. That day there were thirty-four calls on Syed's phone, which Wilds had with him. The prosecution, defense, witnesses, and Koenig all tried to untangle who was calling whom, when, and why, and multiple timelines exist from one person's narrative to the next. Koenig realizes that both Wilds's and Syed's stories are partial, and she has to solve for what is missing. She believes that the details of Wilds's account got squeezed into the constraints of the phone records, distorting things. She spends a lot of time mapping out where cell-tower pings came from and who was where. In the course of her investigative work, she tracks down old floor plans for the Best Buy that had long since closed and records of AT&T billing policies from 1999. She and her producers re-create Syed's alleged movements during that twenty-one minutes to determine if Wilds's account is plausible. In her efforts to reconcile the discrepancies and points of view, she enlists experts, including a detective, a forensic psychologist, and an innocence lawyer.

Unlike the visual documentaries, *Serial* is narrated, and Koenig's voice is a main character in the podcast. We are immersed in her experience and hear extended audio clips of her phone conversations with Syed. She invites us to follow the clues with her. We are not seeing events through a camera lens but hearing them constructed through Koenig's thought process. She continually questions and assesses, Does she agree with Syed's mom that the jury was prejudiced, that his lawyer blew it? Could a key outgoing phone call have been a butt dial? What version of events does she think is possible? Probable? Her narrative style draws out "inconsistencies and doubt," as she weighs each facet of the case.[53] To assess the motive that the state attributed to Syed, she interviews family, friends, and teachers and reflects, "Not one person says he was acting strangely after they broke up. . . . By all accounts he and Hae were still friends, and he was interested in other girls and headed to college. . . . I don't think he was some empty shell of a kid who betrayed his family and religion and was now left with nothing and conjured up a murderous rage for a girl who broke his heart. I simply don't buy it."[54] But she also argues that this does not mean that he did not do it, and she explores other ways of framing his motive.

For many people, *Serial* is experienced as "a story about storytelling," an account of a producer's investigation.[55] In one phone call, Syed tells Koenig that she does not have to take a side but can just go down the middle, point for point, and let listeners make their own decisions. Throughout, Koenig highlights her difficulty coming to conclusions, displaying "a sort of agonized pleasure in not be able to make up her mind."[56] When *Serial* ends, Koenig has not come to a conclusion. She remarks that at the beginning of the project, "certainty seemed so attainable": "We just needed to get the right documents, spend enough time, talk to the right people, check his alibi. . . . And now more than a year later, I just feel like shaking everyone by the shoulders. . . . We didn't have the facts fifteen years ago, and we still don't have them now."[57] The podcast's unfinished nature is characteristic of the New True, embodying the "precocity and uncertainty of the later modern era."[58]

Serial was first made available in weekly episodes, as Koenig and her team continued their research. While it was airing, listeners called in who attended the high school and knew Lee, Syed, and Wilds. One listener, Asia McClain, was a friend of Syed's who remembered seeing him at the library at a crucial time on the day Lee disappeared. McClain had written a letter for him when he was first in jail attesting to this fact, but his attorney did not use her as a witness. *Serial*'s impact on the case, including motivating this alibi witness to come forward, was unprecedented. This impact and subsequent events are chronicled in a four-part series produced by HBO, *The Case against Adnan Syed*, which revisits the evidence and follows Syed's hearing for a new trial. Directed by Amy Berg, *The Case against Adnan Syed* was released in 2019. It follows Syed's new lawyers and investigators as they work with evidence and arguments presented in *Serial* and get their client a new trial. In this show, some evidence that went unexplored in *Serial* is more seriously considered, such as Lee's boyfriend at the time, Don, as an alternate suspect, the lividity of her body when it was discovered, and the state of the grass under the car. The motion for Syed's new trial was based in large part on McClain, who did not know that she was Syed's alibi until she heard *Serial*. The podcast had over 175 million downloads, and Berg shows us the impact that the media sensation had on the case. Syed's new lawyer explains its significance: "*Serial* brought obsessed people on Reddit to the case and the obsessed people brought new evidence."[59] He claims that it was the first ever "open-source investigation" and that because of *Serial*, he "had essentially thousands of investigators."[60] A lawyer and *Serial* listener blogged about the case and developed theories that were helpful to Syed's lawyer preparing his new appeal.

In *The Case against Adnan Syed*, Syed's lawyer attributes his ability to get a new trial to *Serial* and the public attention it brought to the case, as well as to the evidence Koenig produced. While the state was appealing the ruling for a new trial, it offered Syed a plea deal. He would have reluctantly considered an *Alford* plea with time served, but the state only offered a full guilty plea, with admission during allocution, and four additional years. It was a very tough decision, and Syed recognized that if he turned it down and lost in the appeal, he would remain in prison for the rest of his life. In the end, he did turn down the offer, the state won its appeal, and Syed remained in prison until an unexpected turn of events.

In September 2022, "a stunning reversal" caught Syed's supporters by surprise.[61] After twenty-three years, he was suddenly released from prison when prosecutors asked a Maryland judge to vacate his conviction and grant him a new trial. For a year, the state's attorney's office had been investigating juvenile convictions that had resulted in life sentences, in tandem with a new Maryland law that allows people convicted as juveniles to request a reduced sentence after serving twenty years. In the course of going through old cases, the office came upon problems in Syed's file, including evidence of other possible suspects. Prosecutors no longer had "confidence in the integrity of the conviction."[62] The state allowed for additional DNA testing that ruled him out as a suspect, and a month after his emotional release, all charges were finally dropped.

Many of the New True docuseries have been criticized for neglecting the victims and the suffering of their families.[63] Lee's brother vehemently objected to *Serial*, which he believed presented her murder as "crime fiction" and viewed "his sister as public property."[64] In *The Case against Adnan Syed*, Berg highlights Lee's life through animation sequences of her diary entries and provides background on the Korean community, which came together to advocate for her, protesting what community members perceived as neglect on the part of law enforcement and the larger community. Berg does a better job than Koenig at amplifying the tragedy, and the visual medium lets us see Lee and Syed's now-adult classmates as well as Syed's family and provides more breadth than Koenig's intimate and self-reflective narrative.

Making a Murderer (2015, 2018)

Making a Murderer, directed by Laura Ricciardi and Moira Demos, first aired on Netflix in December 2015 with ten episodes. It concerns the case of Steven Avery, a Wisconsin man who was convicted in 1985 for sexual assault and who was later exonerated by DNA evidence after serving eighteen years in prison. When he was released in 2003, he filed a suit against the county relating to his wrongful conviction. Then, in 2005, he was charged with the murder of a missing woman who was last seen on his family's property, a salvage yard whose squalor is much featured in the documentary. During an intensive interrogation, Avery's sixteen-year-old nephew, Brendan Dassey, who has a low IQ, confessed to being with his uncle when Avery raped and murdered the woman.

Like Misskelley's confession in *Paradise Lost*, Dassey's confession is seen by some experts as an egregious example of a coerced false confession.[65] Dassey was convicted in 2007 and sentenced to life in prison, with the possibility of parole in 2048. Avery was sentenced to life without parole. *Making a Murderer* received widespread attention, and celebrities who expressed outrage over the case include Mia Farrow, Ricky Gervais, and Alec Baldwin.[66] Meanwhile, over 350,000 viewers petitioned for Dassey to be pardoned, and President Obama issued a public statement about his inability to grant pardons to state prisoners.[67] Journalists have noted an increased interest among the general public in exoneration cases as a result of this series.[68]

The first season of *Making a Murderer* was ten years in the making.[69] After seeing it, the high-profile attorney Kathleen Zellner decided to represent Avery. Her exhaustive work and subsequent appellate filings are the subject of Ricciardi and Demos's ten-episode follow-up, *Making a Murderer*, season 2, which aired at the end of 2018. Both Avery and Dassey remain in prison.

When Avery was convicted of rape in 2005 and sentenced to thirty-two years, the only evidence against him was the testimony of the victim, who had picked him out of a photo array. He was considered a suspect because the Manitowac County Sheriff's Office was already familiar with him from his relatively minor run-ins with the law. The Wisconsin Innocence Project petitioned for DNA analysis of the pubic hair in evidence, and the testing, which conclusively excluded Avery, matched a man now in prison.

The exoneration had immediate repercussions in the sheriff's office. It emerged that the witness was shown a composite sketch before the photo array, which the sheriff's office had created based on a photo of Avery on file. Avery did not fit the witness's original description, and officers had been told by nearby law enforcement about another possible suspect (the actual perpetrator), whom they chose not to pursue. Nor did they turn this information over to the defense (a *Brady* violation). Avery's exoneration and Wisconsin's subsequent investigation received national media coverage. He was frequently in the news, posing for photo-ops and giving interviews, and there was a great deal of public sympathy for him.

Avery filed a civil suit against the county for $36 million. His attorneys claim that during the depositions, the county district attorney and local officers knew they were in serious trouble and were facing a likely prospect of a verdict in Avery's favor, which insurance would not cover. The case was still pending when news broke about a missing young woman.

Teresa Halbach, a photographer for a local publication, had last been seen on Avery's property, where she had been called to photograph a car he was selling. Avery lived in a trailer on his family's vast salvage yard, where a private search party led by Halbach's ex-boyfriend discovered her vehicle hidden behind some branches.

Avery's nephew was interrogated by detectives and confessed to being in Avery's trailer when Avery raped and shot her. In a video that is painful to watch, we see Dassey struggle to come up with details as the interrogators prod him. Following this confession and Avery's arrest, law enforcement officers discovered the key to Halbach's RAV4 in Avery's trailer on their seventh search. They also found human bone matter, including skull fragments, in a burn pit outside. Halbach's DNA was nowhere in the trailer. There was no blood on the mattress or bedding or in the bathroom (except for small drops of Avery's blood on the sink, which he claimed was from a cut). Even though Manitowac County law enforcement officers were recused from the investigation, they were at these searches and were alone when the key was discovered. Avery's defense included expert analysis of the physical evidence, arguing that the county planted it and framed him in retaliation for the lawsuit. The prosecution prevailed, and the directors returned four years later, in 2011, to follow his appeal, which was denied.

Making a Murderer is replete with villains. Dassey's court-appointed attorney, Len Kachinsky; the Manitowac County district attorney, Ken Kratz; and a number of Manitowac law enforcement officers, particularly James Lenk and Andrew Colburn, are portrayed as an entwined malevolent force. Kachinsky stands out most prominently for betraying the interests of his client, a sixteen-year-old with a low IQ. He is shown preening for the camera with ill-concealed pleasure at the attention. He does not believe in or advocate for his client's innocence, as evidenced by a scene with his investigator in which he pressures Dassey for details and tells him he will feel better if he tells the truth. Like Kachinsky, the district attorney, Kratz, also seems to revel in the media attention and improperly provides information to the press about Dassey's confession that has potential to influence jury members. At the end of the documentary, we learn that Kratz became embroiled in a sex-texting scandal when five women whose criminal cases he was handling came forward. They claimed that he pressured them sexually in exchange for leniency.

Manitowac County is populated by working-class farmers, and Halbach and her family are presented as middle class. The Averys, however, are poor, deal in junk, have little education, and are not seen as part of the community but rather as an isolated entity unto themselves. A cousin says that when Avery was charged with the 1985 rape, "people believed he did it because he was an Avery." Avery's family is presented as helpless and naïve, without material or social resources to aid their son.[70] Avery observes, "poor people lose all the time."[71] One reviewer describes the series as an almost "Dickensian account of the tragedy of the Averys. . . . [His] parents [are] as movingly bewildered and terrified as any fictional creations."[72]

The press coverage of Avery's exoneration in 2003 was intense, and the investigation launched by Wisconsin innocence lawyers received national attention. Once Avery is accused of murder, the directors cast the media as aggressive vultures contributing to the family's victimization. The directors critically distance themselves from the media and its "lurid voyeurism."[73] We see the news hounding Avery's girlfriend, who is simultaneously being harassed by the state to testify against him. The press is seen amplifying Kratz's and Kachinsky's claims, and one of Avery's lawyers observes that the gory details of Dassey's confession give the media "a horror story they can't get enough of."[74] As other New True directors do, Ricciardi and Demos show news crews setting up and make visible the theatricality of news production. After the Dassey verdict, the press descends on his mother as she leaves the courthouse, and she becomes highly agitated. The filmmakers emphasize her defenseless position as they show a man who screams at the reporters, "Give the lady some peace. . . . You give the Halbachs respect, but you won't give her some respect? What the fuck's wrong with you?!"[75]

Ricciardi and Demos made a second ten-part season that picks up the story in 2016, nine years after Avery's verdict and a year after the release of the first season. They recognized immediately that the story had changed because of the impact of the first season, making it "very meta."[76] We see the enormous impact that the series had. The Averys received enormous support from viewers, expressed in petitions, cards, letters, and gifts, for which they are grateful and proud. Avery says that he receives forty letters a week in prison. A number of women begin correspondence with him, and his relationships with two new girlfriends are chronicled.

Viewers responded "with near-universal outrage about the verdicts," and the media attention impacted Teresa Halbach's family, who are outraged at how their suffering was minimized and express anger at the portrayal of the Averys as victims.[77] District Attorney Kratz received death threats.[78] Although he resigned amid the sexting scandal, we see him continuing to bask in the media attention. He also expresses outrage, arguing that the documentary left out a lot of key evidence. He has a book about the case coming out, and we see him make media appearances promoting it, including appearances on *Dateline*, where he comes across as opportunistic and seeking to benefit from the media attention.

Kathleen Zellner, an attorney with a track record of having exonerated seventeen innocent clients, decided to represent Avery after she saw the first season of *Making a Murderer*. She says she made it clear to him that she would discover whether he was guilty and that he ran the risk of her proving it. We see her come to firmly believe in his innocence, as he enthusiastically agrees to various honesty tests, such as "brain fingerprinting," which records his response to certain stimuli. The documentary follows Zellner's investigation, which includes purchasing the same model RAV4 as Halbach's, working with experts on ballistics and blood stains, removing the sink from Avery's trailer, and interviewing a number of potential witnesses. She leaves no leaf unturned in her efforts to accomplish two goals: take apart the state's case and find out what really happened.

Zellner develops a theory of the crime that implicates Dassey's half brother, Bobby, after she learns that the state had Bobby's computer and knew that it contained thousands of searches of violent "death porn" and how to handle dead bodies.[79] She investigates Halbach's personal life and discovers conflicts with an ex-boyfriend, Ryan Hillegas, who had moved into her place after she disappeared, giving him access to all the evidence there. She discovers another sexual relationship that potentially points to another suspect. Investigating the ex-boyfriend as a potential suspect, she ties together a theory that involves Bobby killing Halbach, and Hillegas and law enforcement framing Avery. Zellner is presented as heroic and tireless, and the footage of her on location, testing various evidence, makes for great viewing.[80] She petitions for a new evidentiary hearing, which is denied. At the end of the season, she files a motion to reconsider the decision.

Season 2 of *Making a Murderer* also closely follows the postconviction work on Dassey's behalf. The Center for Wrongful Convictions took on his case in the aftermath of the series's first season. The series shows the "tortuous process of filing appeals and re-examining forensic evidence" in both cases.[81] We learn that Dassey's lawyers have used the footage of his confession to educate the public about false confessions and the psychology of interrogation techniques. In the series, we see them win a habeas corpus motion for Dassey, but the state appeals it. His lawyers also petition for Dassey to be released on bail, but that too is denied. They conduct exhaustive preparation work for their circuit court case, although unfortunately the state prevails in the appeal, and Dassey remains in prison.

In both seasons, Ricciardi and Demos create "a mood of melancholic Americana."[82] *Making a Murderer* has been described as "immersive, compulsive, and unpredictable, but also exhausting."[83] It has been critiqued for its bias in favor of Dassey and Avery, as well as for its neglect of the Halbach's experience of victimization.[84] One reviewer sees Zellner's hands-on efforts as "televised theatrics" that inadvertently show "how easily a story about unjust interrogation can turn into a salacious quest to uncover the remains of another dead woman."[85] The same way that Berlinger and Sinofsky paint damning portraits of guilt with two of the victims' stepfathers, Ricciardi and Demos give Zellner a platform to mount a case against Dassey's brother and stepfather, seemingly unconcerned with the additional anguish this brings to the family.[86]

Atlanta Monster (2018) and *Atlanta's Missing and Murdered: The Lost Children* (2020)

Atlanta Monster is a ten-episode podcast hosted by Payne Lindsey. It was released in 2018 and enjoyed status as the number-one podcast on iTunes during that year.[87] Like *Serial*, *Atlanta Monster* delves into an old case. Between 1979 and 1981, a number of Black boys in Atlanta disappeared and were found murdered. Two adults were found murdered as well, and all twenty-eight murders were attributed to the same suspect, Wayne Williams. He was tried and convicted for the murders of the two adults, although the prosecution used fibers found on some of the child victims (whose deaths he was not charged with) as evidence against him. The judge allowed this evidence in to establish a pattern, even though it had not been proven that Wayne committed those murders. Lindsey narrates the story in a style similar to Koenig's, inviting listeners into his thinking process, revealing his doubts, and chronicling his investigative efforts. In 2020, HBO aired a five-part documentary on the case, *Atlanta's Missing and Murdered: The Lost Children*. Williams remains in prison serving a life sentence.

The Atlanta murders are the most famous of the cases explored in the New True. They received national attention at the time. President Ronald Reagan and Vice President George H. W. Bush made public statements about them and enlisted the FBI. State and local authorities were under enormous pressure to solve the crimes, convict the perpetrator, and close the cases. Both *Atlanta Monster* and *Atlanta's Missing and Murdered* delve into the trauma of the United States' racial past, and no telling of this story omits the role of race. Local authorities' initial neglect of the murder of Black children from the city's poorest neighborhoods was seen as a civil rights issue, and families of the victims mobilized against the injustice. Entwined in the case was the tension between Atlanta's history of racial inequality and its emerging status as a city with a thriving Black middle class and destination business hub. The city's police chief and mayor were both Black, which created an expectation of equitable treatment at a time when mistrust of the largely white police force was entrenched in the community. Leaders in the Black community and public figures like Bill Cosby and Muhammed Ali took up the cause. James Baldwin observed in his book about the case, *Evidence of Things Not Seen*, "Black death has never before elicited so much attention."[88] The local community had difficulty believing that a Black person would commit these crimes, and many people believed that authorities feared the fallout if the perpetrator was white. Theories of the crime included Ku Klux Klan involvement and racial terror.

During the two-year period, one child after another was discovered murdered, by a variety of means, in a variety of locations. The Atlanta police, the Georgia Bureau of Investigation (GBI), and the Federal Bureau of Investigation (FBI) had no suspects. After an adult victim was found in the river, law enforcement conducted a stakeout on the bridge. On the last night that they had resources for the surveillance, at around two in the morning, they heard a car slow down and stop, and then they heard a splash. When they pulled the car over, the driver was Wayne Williams, who offered an unconvincing account of himself, saying he had an early-morning appointment and was checking out the address. They searched his car and found some twine and gloves and, without enough evidence to arrest him, let him go.

A couple of days later, a body (of an adult) was found in the water, and Williams was arrested. The search of his home yielded a number of different fibers, including those from a carpet, a bedspread, and the family dog, which matched those found on the two adults. Williams was charged with those two murders. In addition to the fibers, the prosecution presented circumstantial evidence that included his shaky explanation for being on the bridge and the fact that he was a local talent scout for youth entertainment acts, which buttressed a theory that the victims went to him willingly. Baldwin explains the impossible situation his lawyers were in, with their client being held responsible for twenty-eight murders but only being able to defend against two. Once Williams was convicted of the two murders, twenty-three of the child murder cases were closed. The families of these victims felt devastated and betrayed. One mother cried, "Why, they just done forgot about Timmy!"[89] The Atlanta murders are unique among the New True in that the victims' families did not believe in the guilt of the defendant and many believe that their child's case remains unsolved. Lindsey reports that 90 percent of the Black community believes Williams is innocent.

Wayne Williams was a small, mild-mannered twenty-three-year-old Black man living with his parents in a middle-class neighborhood. As a child, Williams excelled in some academic areas, and by fifteen, he had built his own radio station. At the time of the murders, he was a freelance crime-scene photographer who followed police bulletins, and he was building a career as a talent scout. He organized talent shows and had created a youth band. Because of his quiet nature and somewhat-unusual pursuits, Williams was seen as peculiar. On the stand, he was composed for the first few days but lost his temper at one point, revealing hauteur and aggression. The FBI, however, characterized him as nonthreatening, which they believed had made it easy for him to interact with the victims. The defense presented him as physically slight and incapable of lifting and handling the dead weight of the adult bodies. Lindsey conducts phone interviews with Williams in prison, during which he repeatedly asserts his innocence and, unlike Adnan Syed in *Serial*, is at times agitated. His explanation for key details changes several times, and Lindsey questions his reliability.

After Williams was convicted, an investigative journalist discovered that the GBI had had evidence on alternative suspects, which they never turned over to the defense. These included some men associated with the Ku Klux Klan. After this reporting, Williams was represented in his appeals by high-profile civil rights attorneys, including William Kunstler and Bobby Lee Cook. Lindsey goes to lengths exploring the alternative theories. He interviews an expert on white-supremacist groups who reviewed the GBI transcripts of interviews with an informant. These describe a group of brothers who were investigated for the murders and who were notorious Klan-involved racists. They were described as having a number of official uniforms, such as police and postal workers, which Lindsey and others note would have allowed a white person to go unnoticed in a Black neighborhood. Another theory that Lindsey investigates concerns a local pedophile ring. There was a home of known sex offenders in one of the neighborhoods, and some of the boys who were murdered were rumored to have gone there for paid sex or were seen near the house on multiple occasions.

Lindsey, acting as a "citizen sleuth," interviews a number of witnesses, including some who came forward as *Atlanta Monster* was first airing, who remember incidents they had experienced.[90] One person feels certain that Williams once approached him and that he was almost a victim. Lindsey talks to an old friend of the group of Klan-involved brothers and enlists a number of experts for their opinion on various facts and theories. He does not present himself as an authority but rather, like Koenig in *Serial*, adopts an "improvisational approach."[91]

Some people believe the considerable air time that Lindsey gave Williams exposed his "narcissism and dishonesty," complicating the narrative.[92] After Lindsey has conducted his own experiments, such as re-creating the night on the bridge, he is left without certainty about Williams. He is unable to prove either his guilt or innocence and concludes the podcast by offering his opinion that Williams probably did not murder *all* the victims. "I think your monster is probably a group of some of these white supremacists who were involved in some of the killings. I think your monster is probably people involved in some of these sex and drug rings that no doubt killed some of these victims. And I think your Atlanta monster may well be the streets of Atlanta where the victims were victims of street crime. . . . Atlanta monsters . . . put a plural at the end of it."[93]

HBO's *Atlanta's Missing and Murdered: The Lost Children*, directed by Joshua Bennett, Maro Chermayeff, Jeff Dupre, and Sam Pollard, opens with shots of a 2019 Atlanta community meeting where Mayor Keisha Lance Bottoms announces reopening some of the cases that were closed when Williams was convicted. The visual documentary adds greatly to the story, allowing us to see the neighborhoods where the children lived and were found, the grief-stricken families at the funerals, the tenor of news coverage and press conferences, and the Black community's activism. We see Atlanta's mayor at the time call on the president to take action, pointing out, "The Lindberg baby was one white child. I have fourteen missing or murdered Black kids. I want the Feds."[94] Likewise, we hear Lance Bottoms decades later comparing it to the attention Jon-Benet Ramsey's murder received. We learn more about Williams's defense and appellate teams and their theories, as when William Kuntsler tells reporters that the government wanted a Black man to be the perpetrator, which they believed would prevent a race war, and that the mayor did not want the economic progress in Atlanta destroyed by racial violence.

The series succeeds in portraying the terror of the Black community and grassroots organizations' push for racial justice.[95] The bleak graveyard footage, the scenes of abject urban poverty, the mournful, gasping Joan Armatrading vocals over the opening titles ("Save Me"), and the wailing of the children's mothers at "funerals with child-sized caskets being lowered to the ground" create a profound sense of tragedy, with depth and social complexity not matched in the other New True.[96] The final scene of the 2019 community meeting ends with the now-aged mother of one of the victims standing up shakily and declaring, "Curtis was very important. He was a Black America child."[97]

The Innocent Man (2018)

Directed by Clay Tweel, the six-episode series *The Innocent Man* was released by Netflix in 2018. It tells a more complex story than the other New True, because it concerns two sets of two codefendants. Ron Williamson and Dennis Fritz were convicted of the 1982 murder of Debbie Carter in Ada, Oklahoma. The young woman was found raped, stabbed, and strangled in her apartment. When a witness claimed to have seen Williamson arguing with her earlier that night, he was arrested. He then relayed a dream in which he murdered her, and this was taken as a confession. The Innocence Project exonerated both Williamson and Fritz with DNA evidence eleven years after their conviction. The perpetrator turned out to be the eyewitness from the bar where Carter was last seen, who was serving time in prison for other crimes.

Two years after Carter was murdered, another young woman disappeared in Ada. Denice Haraway was last seen at work at a highway convenience store, and a witness claimed that she was led out by a man who drove her away in a truck. A waitress at a nearby diner said that earlier that night, two men had come in and were acting strangely. Her description of them was the basis of the composite sketches that were posted throughout town and featured on the local news. Law enforcement received calls about a number of possible suspects who resembled the drawings, including Tommy Ward and Karl Fontenot.

Like Williamson, Ward relayed a dream while in custody that was taken to be a confession, and Fontenot, who had a low IQ, quickly confessed under interrogation. Their accounts differed in a number of important details, but both described a stabbing, a floral blouse, and a third person. This third man had a solid alibi, and the prosecution argued that Ward and Fontenot were unconsciously ascribing to him their own heinous deeds. Their confessions were played at trial, and they were convicted and sentenced to life in prison. After their trial, Haraway's remains were found, in a different location than indicated in the confessions, and it was determined that she was shot in the head, not stabbed. The men were retried and, in spite of contradictory evidence, were convicted and resentenced.

Williamson's Innocence Project lawyers were struck by the similarities between the cases. In both, law enforcement officers had received information about other suspects whom they had not pursued (including Debbie Carter's actual murderer). The cases featured the same cast of characters: the same prosecutors and investigators and even the same jailhouse informant. And both included strange dream confessions. *The Innocent Man* puts forward a theory that members of Ada law enforcement were involved in the local drug world, where some of the other suspects were active. They did not pursue these leads because the suspects could expose their criminal conduct. The documentary presents evidence that prosecutors and investigators blackmailed an informant, staged improper eyewitness procedures, coerced false confessions, and committed *Brady* violations by not turning over information about alternative suspects. Both Fontenot and Ward had pending cases in the courts at the time Tweel was filming, and in the year after *The Innocent Man* aired, both their convictions were overturned based on new evidence uncovered in the series. Fontenot was released in 2019, and at the time of this writing, Ward remains in prison awaiting an appeal decision.

The Innocent Man is based on a nonfiction book of the same name by the crime novelist John Grisham and uses source material from *The Dreams of Ada*, by the journalist John Mayer. Like these works, the documentary series centers Ada itself as a main character. It is described as a pleasant small town that has "a church on every corner" but has a sinister underbelly of corrupt law enforcement and poor, underemployed men prone to violence and domestic abuse.[98] Like many of the New True, the opening sequence features aerial footage of empty landscapes and worn structures: open fields, a lone cow, a large cross, and the cement plant, which is an economic center of the town and the place where Ward dreamed Haraway was taken. Tweel presents the dream confessions in blurry, "surrealistic and impressionistic" dramatic reenactments and seems to insinuate something sinister about the similarities between Williamson's and Ward's confessions.[99]

In the course of *The Innocent Man*, we learn of five alternative suspects, all white men with violent records. As one reviewer observes, Ada is "the kind of place where, when a woman is murdered, there are a disproportionate number of plausible suspects with a documented history of violence against women."[100] *The Innocent Man* argues that gendered abuse is perpetrated by law enforcement as well, as it investigates a witness's disturbing accusation related to it. She claimed that she was blackmailed by Ada officers and that the district attorney had tapes of her having sex with multiple people in jail.

Haraway's family was reportedly outraged by the "one-sided" portrayal of Ward and Fontenot. Just as Michael Peterson's sister-in-law railed against *The Staircase*, the Haraway family asserted, "Denice doesn't have a famous, wealthy, author/film producer or people seeking five minutes of fame to stand up for her."[101] However, Tweel does provide a close study of how the murder and subsequent exonerations devastated the Carter family. We see her mother's anguish as we learn of her spiral into alcoholism and depression, and we follow her cousin Christy's work on behalf of the wrongfully convicted. After Williamson's and Fritz's exonerations, Christy became an innocence advocate and throughout the series voices a critique of the criminal justice system. We learn about Williamson's mental illness and the ruinous impact of his incarceration. His illness went undertreated in prison, and he deteriorated physically and mentally. He drank himself to death five years after he was released. During that time, he and Carter's mother formed an unlikely and deeply moving friendship. We also learn of the suffering of Fritz's family. In all, *The Innocent Man* is a story of multiple and generational tragedies wrought by state corruption and failed justice.

An Imperfect Category

What I am calling the "New True" is an imperfect category. For example, some of the defendants are less ambiguously guilty; two cases ended in *Alford* pleas, but the others did not; the *Paradise Lost* trilogy is not serialized; *The Innocent Man* has not been as popular as some of the others. In addition, other series I have not included may meet these criteria, such as one podcast by two criminologists, *Direct Appeal* (2019), which questions the innocence of a woman convicted of murdering her husband, or HBO Max's *Mind Over Murder* (2022), which explores the aftermath of an exoneration and the consequences of wrongful conviction on an entire community. In the end, I chose these six cases (eight series) because overall they have had the most cultural impact and they have enough shared unique characteristics to warrant analysis.

Table 2.1. Series Overview and Key Persons

Title and years	Director/producers	Defendants	Victims	Other notable persons
The *Paradise Lost* trilogy (1996, 2000, 2011)	For HBO: Joe Berlinger and Bruce Sinofsky	Damien Echols, Jason Baldwin, Jessie Misskelley	Steve Branch, Michael Moore, Christopher Byers, all eight years old	John Mark Byers: the stepfather of one of the victims
The Staircase (2004, 2013, 2018)	For Sundance and Netflix: Jean Xavier de Lestrade	Michael Peterson	Kathleen Peterson	David Rudolf: Peterson's attorney; Candace: Peterson's sister-in-law
Serial (2014)	Sarah Koenig et al.	Adnan Syed	Hae Min Lee	
The Case against Adnan Syed (2019)	For HBO: Amy Berg	Adnan Syed	Hae Min Lee	
Making a Murderer (2015, 2018)	For Netflix: Laura Ricciardi and Moira Demos	Brendan Dassey, Steven Avery	Teresa Halbach	Ken Kratz: the prosecutor; Len Kachinsky: Dassey's first attorney; James Lenk and Andrew Colburn: county law enforcement; Dean Strang and Jerome Buting: Avery's trial attorneys; Kathleen Zellner: Avery's appellate attorney.
Atlanta Monster (2018)	Payne Lindsey	Wayne Williams	Twenty-eight Black children and two young men in an impoverished section of Atlanta	
Atlanta's Missing and Murdered (2020)	For HBO: Pollard et al.	Wayne Williams	Twenty-eight Black children and two young men in an impoverished section of Atlanta	
The Innocent Man (2018)	Clay Tweel	Tommy Ward, Karl Fontenot	Denice Haraway	Ron Williamson and Dennis Fritz: two men wrongfully convicted in Ada around the same time as Ward and Fontenot; Debbie Carter: the victim in the Williamson/Fritz case

Exhibit A

I was more and more astonished reading the episode synopses from Netflix's *Forensic Files* collection: "When a woman's body is found in a burned-out house, microscopic clues on a piece of pipe help determine whether her death was an accident or murder." "When a woman is raped and murdered on the beach, investigators track down the killer through a pair of shoes left near the body." . . . It's clear we love the Dead Girl, enough to rehash and reproduce her story, to kill her again and again.

—Alice Bolin, *Dead Girls: Essays on Surviving an American Obsession* (2018)

THE year I moved to Boulder, Colorado, was the same year the body of six-year-old JonBenet Ramsey was found in the basement of her family's large, upper-middle-class home. This case caught national attention, and images of the girl, a child pageant star, quickly became iconic. That year, in my circle of friends back east, I acquired a small degree of status by virtue of my proximity, as if I had some insider knowledge about the case, and friends visiting me wanted to drive by the house. It was an unofficial tourist attraction in Boulder. JonBenet is the quintessential American victim: young, white, blond, and middle class—an "angel betrayed."[1] Her death gave rise to a media frenzy and conspiracy theories. Her strangled and bruised body and the results of her autopsy report became objects of fascination. Was she sexually assaulted? Did someone clean her before she was found? This is typical: the victim's body and the possible clues it contains are always center stage in crime stories. It is what draws us in.

Crime-scene photos of the murder victim are typically a focal point in crime stories, repeatedly returned to as a narrative anchor; the image of the victim frozen in an unnatural, jarring position is revisited in the hopes of seeing something new, seeing something one did not notice before. These images rivet us in spite of the fact that they are such a predictable staple of the genre, such a familiar cliché. The victim's body is a central element in the murder trial. Gruesome events are sensationalized at the same time that they are flattened by laws of procedure and evidence. Excitement and spectacle are produced by fetishistic attention to certain details imbued with the power to illuminate mysteries and reveal secrets.

Practiced attorneys well understand their role as storytellers and the importance of building compelling narratives around images. In preparing Michael Peterson for his trial, his attorney, David Rudolf, tells him how important it is that they give the jury a story about his marriage so jurors can imagine the good relationship he had with the victim, Kathleen. Trials lend themselves well to entertainment because they have built-in dramatic features, including characters, plots, and performances by attorneys, witnesses, and judges. The courtroom drama has appeared in classic literature, such as Dickens's *Bleak House* and Dreiser's *An American Tragedy* (and its film version, another classic, *A Place in the Sun*), and Americans have obsessively watched many real-life trials on television, such as the O. J. Simpson trial and the civil trial between actors Johnny Depp and Amber Heard. Trials are inherently performative, with attorneys and witnesses conscious of how they come across to the jury. Trial movies dramatize the processes of law and the production of legal truth, and documentaries about them become "both a platform and a structuring device to contest the evidentiary value of testimony [and] bear witness to the performance of law in our culture."[2] Trials and films share a number a features, including "their mutual manufacture of truth through strategies of representation and storytelling.[3] Narrative conventions shape trials just as much as the law does, and while constrained by legal procedure, building a case draws on the same "laws" of storytelling that novelists use.

A criminal trial is an arena of competing narratives where prosecution and defense vie over the definition of the situation, with the jury's verdict declaring the winner. To achieve this, attorneys must demonstrate fluency with elements of dramaturgy, rhetoric, and literary devices that taken together are intended to assert authority over what happened and why, in a way that is comprehensible, meaningful, logical, and persuasive to a jury. The attorneys' "dominant narratives" are "interpretive strategies tailor-made to emphasize points" that are beneficial to their side.[4] Because the prosecution has the burden of proof, its storytelling must meet a high standard of rational and emotional plausibility. Putting forth items of evidence (exhibits), the prosecution weaves each strand of its case together to create a portrait of irrefutable guilt that establishes the what, how, who, and why of the crime. The defense then must highlight flaws in the state's logic, undermine the credibility of its witnesses, and offer alternative interpretations of facts, all to unravel the prosecution's narrative and reveal the defendant's true innocence. Both sides rely on literary-like "devices that make novelistic narratives seem real or plausible . . . in the legal retellings of the 'facts' of a case in the US law courts."[5] Facts, however, can be interpreted differently. For example, as the defense team prepares its case for Michael Peterson, it makes a list titled "good fact / bad fact" to illustrate how, on the one hand, prosecutors can use Peterson's bisexuality as evidence of guilt while, on the other hand, as Rudolf explains, the defense can claim that they are "gay-bashing" and point to their prejudice to discredit that argument.[6]

In the New True formula, we see three accounts of events: (1) the prosecution's, (2) the defense's, and (3) the documentarians', which offer what can be seen as a metanarrative, stepping out from and above the courtroom. While the prosecution needs to persuade the entire jury beyond a reasonable doubt, the defense only needs to sway just one member. Thus, the objectives of the defense's storytelling are fundamentally different, with the prosecution mounting a case and the defense poking holes in it. As for the documentarians, the goals of their narrative efforts are often less clear. The New True are stories about the stories told at trial and use "forensic rhetoric, . . . the persuasive language used in true-crime texts about trials."[7] At the same time, these series chronicle the continued life of the case beyond it.[8]

Most of the New True display an excessive attention to minute detail, examining each facet of every piece of evidence from multiple perspectives and analyzing and questioning the significance attributed to it. These details—the objects—are narrative elements, foundational to the three different accounts. They move events from point *a* to point *b*, signifying means and motives of the crime. Blood-spatter patterns, cell-phone-tower pings, green carpet fiber, and bone fragments are interpreted multiple times by different actors and forensic processes, telling different versions of the story.

The defense, the prosecution, and the documentarians all depend on experts to make the objects of evidence meaningful and to communicate to audiences and jurors what the objects really say. Scientific method, reasoning, and vernacular are imbued with awesome powers to reveal otherwise-inscrutable truths. The defense uses experts to make its truth visible by shifting the perspective on objects, showing what the "hard facts" do not say, and highlighting how the objects lose their import once they are properly deconstructed. Legal innocence, founded on "beyond a reasonable doubt," is a contrast to and contradiction of the prosecution, a negation, or the empty space created once the facts are proved to be mirages. But the defense must often build its own substantive narrative when negating the prosecution's may not be enough. It presents alternative theories and its own exhibits, at times introducing new characters and plots.

The cases hinge on pieces of evidence without which the narratives fall apart. In the New True, documentarians are able to show much more to audiences than the juries see (although they leave things out as well, in service of their own storytelling). Through interviews, media footage, and their own investigations, they provide a broader, more layered story about the trials while furnishing new evidence and strategies for future appeals. In contrast to the prosecution and defense, the documentarians at times present their stories as puzzles, not striving for a definitive conclusion, instead allowing audiences to figure out for themselves how they want to make sense of the cases. The clues they provide make the New True fun, and they are a jumping-off point for audiences to do their own research, creating a form of entertainment that activates rather than pacifies, providing a chance for audiences to assume the role of detective or "websleuth" and develop their own possibly usable theories (such as the owl theory to explain *The Staircase*).[9]

The Body of Evidence and the Life of the Corpse

The victim's body in crime-scene photos establishes that an act of horrifying violence has occurred. It is a necessary component of the rhetorical style meant to inspire horror that dates back to the earliest true-crime magazines.[10] Its lurid and gruesome presence hangs over the New True and is returned to again and again; it is usually part of the prosecution's opening and closing statements and forms a recurrent motif in the visual documentaries. Images such as these can "powerfully affect jurors."[11] These photos can supersede probative evidence and logical arguments with the emotional power of their stark and shocking drama. They are integral to the cultural life of the trial, as they contribute to "a visual culture saturated with 'reality' images of punishment and suffering."[12]

A dead body is out of the ordinary range of experience, not seen in daily life and usually seen only at the most somber of times, such as a funeral. The victim's body is a centerpiece of true crime that can seem endlessly fascinating: "True crime is obsessed with full-on visual body horror: autopsy footage, close-ups of ligature marks and gunshot wounds on bodies, bruises of lividity on flesh, and blood pools, stains and spatters in the physical space where murder has occurred are all depicted in the genre, . . . causing some critics to refer to true crime as 'crime porn.'"[13] The bodies of New True victims are an example what the anthropologist Mary Douglas famously referred to as "matter out of place"—previously a person, now an object of revulsion signifying a deeply unsettling breakdown of important boundaries, such as between the living and the dead and the self and other.[14] In early American culture, the dead body was commonplace, but by the late eighteenth century, Americans began to "segregate the dead from the living," privatizing death and concealing it from public view.[15] As they began to see pain as "intolerable and death repulsive," a pornography of death and violence emerged and took shape in the gothic imagination that informs the true-crime aesthetic.[16] One cannot deny the fact of death when looking at either an actual corpse or a graphic image of it, and this is one reason the prosecution enlarges these photos for the jury, providing close-ups of various body parts from different angles and forcing the jury to behold the unnaturally defiled life. Whatever theories of what happened, whatever arguments about fibers or blow pokes or call records, the central fact that a life was horrifically and prematurely extinguished is beyond debate. The victim's body is a necessarily consistent feature of the New True and true crime more generally, which Marc Seltzer describes as part of "wound culture" and the "mass-mediated spectacle of torn bodies and torn persons."[17] Its image is a kind of synecdoche of the entire narrative, standing in for the person, the crime, ensuing events, the quest for truth, and the fate of the accused.

The victim's body is performative in the New True. Although a static image, it has a dynamic role; while a starting point for building the case and constructing the crime, it also directs viewers backward into the past. It is the powerful signifier of the life that was lost. Crime-scene photos of a dead body contain within them the life of the victim, who is always a central character in the New True (though, importantly, never *the* central character). They are all the more powerful juxtaposed with photos from the victims' lives that depict vibrancy and potential. Crime news and crime entertainment are usually built around "ideal victims," those in whom innocence and virtue, in the broadest most stereotypical strokes, can be imbued.[18] These are usually young, white, middle-class women, or they are children, also white and middle class.

In addition, the New True usually focus on rural or suburban victims whose environments can most easily be conflated with the American Dream and mainstream lifestyles and values. The overrepresentation of ideal victims in crime stories elevates the suffering of the white middle class as interesting and dramatic while obscuring realities about the relationships between inequality and victimization. Some New True stories are tinged with nostalgia for an Americana embodied in the posed high school photos of a smiling white girl. This is how innocence is first contoured in the docuseries—given shape in the life and characters of the blameless victims who are incontrovertibly worthy of our sympathy.

Status as victim has a legitimizing effect that confers unassailability and righteousness, enshrined in the victims' rights movement and legislation named after mostly white, middle-class children, usually victimized by strangers.[19] Constructing a narrative around a flawed or unsavory victim is a more difficult task, one that we have begun to see more recently in films and prestige television such as *The Wire*, in which both heroes and victims are multidimensional, conflicted, compromised, and imperfect. But moral complexity is not a hallmark of typical true-crime stories. People who have done bad things, who are stigmatized and on the margins of society, make appearances as suspects and/or as their family and friends. In choosing stories that lend themselves to this formula, documentarians have made their task easier and make fewer demands on their audiences. Thus, the crime stories presented in the New True "reinforce culturally rooted norms and expectations."[20]

Hae Min Lee was Korean and is depicted as a "model minority" from a hardworking immigrant community. She is represented in both *Serial* and *The Case against Adnan Syed* as a typical middle-class teenager. Sarah Koenig says of Lee's diary, "It is *such* a teenage girl's diary," describing the breathless writing and heart doodles. While Lee was not white, she is drawn as a variation on the convention of the ideal female victim. She was "not living a high-risk existence at the margins of society.”[21] She attended a magnet school, was active in sports, and even had a part-time job at the local mall. Her junior-year prom photo evokes elegance and promise; that photo and photos of her beaming with her friends convey a healthy, energetic, robust spirit. In fact, victims in the New True are often described as "loving life."

We see Kathleen Peterson in *The Staircase* beaming in front of a sunset on a mountainous lake, waving goofily and exuberantly with a friend in a white convertible, smiling mischievously behind a coffee mug, and gazing dreamily at herself in her wedding gown. School photos are frequently used in stories about young victims, whom we see looking to the future, about to turn to a new chapter of their promising lives.

In *Making a Murderer*, cameras zoom in on Teresa Halbach's dark and shining eyes in the photo printed in local papers, as if the answer to her whereabouts lies in the pixels. She had made a video of herself talking to the camera about her views of the world. We see her in makeup looking sophisticated and adult as she tells us how she wants people to think of her after she dies. Hearing the now-dead girl speak of her own death comes as a shock. This part of her home video is a kind of *punctum*, a word that the literary theorist Roland Barthes uses to describe a surprising, unintended element, a poignant accidental pinprick, that gives her otherwise-banal words an otherworldly power.[22] Taking a deep breath and searching for the right words, she says, simply, that she wants people to know that she was happy.

In *The Innocent Man*, Debbie Carter's high school photo shows a questioning, expectant glint in her eyes and a demure smile. She is in a frilly, white-lace blouse. The photo hangs framed in her mother's kitchen in the exact spot the picture was hanging the day her mother got the call informing her of Carter's death. Carter is described as a "people person" and "a good girl with a lot of morals."[23] The newspaper photo of missing Denice Haraway is also from a high school album, and as the filmmakers do with Halbach in *Making a Murderer*, the camera in *The Innocent Man* zooms in on Haraway's shining big, brown eyes. A professor she worked for describes her as "just a pretty little girl that was in college," and we see reenacted crime-scene photos of her opened textbook on the counter in the convenience store where she was last seen.[24] Conjectural reenactments like this serve to reinforce generalized ideas about victims and perpetrators.[25] In this case, the textbook signifies Haraway's potential and the unrealized future she was striving for.

Paradise Lost repeatedly shows the school photos of the three eight-year-old boys, and the expression on each face seems like a different version of innocent boyhood, from the laughing, satisfied smile of Steve Branch and playful, trickster grin of Chris Byers to the vulnerable, puppy-dog eyes of Michael Moore. Byers's stepfather refers to them as "angels," dramatically articulating a true-crime precept that sanctifies victims.

Unlike the angelic boys in rural America in *Paradise Lost*, the young Black victims in the city of Atlanta are not bestowed with the same mantle of innocence. They are devalued as "street kids," their mothers disparaged as drug users and prostitutes, and their murders met with delayed, almost reluctant concern. James Baldwin reflected that the children came from "Atlanta's lowest economic stratum . . . and were strangers to safety, for, in the brutal generality, only the poor watch over the poor. The poor do not exist for others, except as an inconvenience or a threat."[26] Often school photos of the victims shown in *Atlanta's Missing and Murdered* appear stained and wrinkled, perhaps suggesting neglect and lack of proper care. The comparative minimization of the suffering of these children and their families is consistent with a racist view in US society that depicts Black people as less sensitive to pain. The historian Robin Bernstein argues in her book *Racial Innocence: Performing American Childhood form Slavery to Civil Rights* that images of Black children in the nineteenth century were so "grotesque" that "only white children *were* children" and that it was commonly believed that Black children did not feel pain.[27] This callous view of Black suffering is a feature of the cultural response to the Atlanta murders and the subject of critique in both the *Atlanta Monster* podcast and the HBO Max series *Atlanta's Missing and Murdered*.

Photos of ideal victims outdoors, at parties, and with family members are used in the New True in stark contrast to crime-scene photos. The life photos give dimension to the victims' innocence, which becomes sacred when contrasted with images of their corpses. The camera lingers over each corpse, captivating the viewer's gaze as an object that is not really an object because it was previously animate. It is de rigueur in "the age of forensic noir," in which "the corpse becomes a prop that helps the science-as-detective narrative to unfold at the crime scene or in the morgue or autopsy theater."[28]

In *The Case against Adnan Syed*, we are shown the initial photos of Hae Min Lee's body when it was discovered in the park six weeks after her disappearance. The body is covered in leaves, and small parts of her are just barely visible. We are shown views of clothing wrinkled and caked in dirt, but the leaves obscure her body in a confusing, ominous way. It is hard to tell what we are looking at. Yet an element of one photo is clear: a close-up of her toes peeking out from under the soil, twigs, and leaves. They are small, vulnerable, female, and undeniably human, another *punctum*, disturbing the otherwise-unremarkable scene. These photos are important to Sarah Koenig and the other producers of *Serial*, who we learn pored over them and concluded that because the body was so concealed, it would have been hard for the man who discovered her body, "Mr. S.," to just happen upon it, as he claimed. Here the photo plays an important role in recasting Mr. S., who transforms from witness to suspect when his entire story about innocently stopping to relieve himself comes under suspicion.

Before we are shown Kathleen Peterson's body at the bottom of the staircase, we see the cops' crime-scene video slowly scanning the hallway and zooming in on blood stains on the doorway. We then see her legs, in blood-spattered white sweatpants, unnaturally splayed on the floor. She is strangely slumped, with her head turned up and her bloody hand limp on her lap. The black-and-white photo of Debbie Carter naked on the floor speaks of the horrifying violence of her last hour: face down in the midst of the chaos made of her living room, with a cord around her neck and threatening words scrawled on her back.

Paradise Lost opens with the police crime-scene video of the boys' bodies being pulled from the creek. Their thinness reads almost as skeletal, an impression heightened by the bright sunlight on their pallor. The boys are bent strangely because they had been hog-tied before rigor mortis. The camera lingers on one of their faces. A few green leaves have been left on the frail chest of another.

The photos of the many Atlanta victims show them in the range of settings in which they were found: one in an alley with a bike lying behind them; another in tall grass with bare feet; a boy in shorts and a T-shirt in the woods. These torn and wounded Black bodies are also discarded bodies, evoking refuse and waste and the contempt of the broader society.

These grisly crime-scene photos mark the violent end of innocent lives and attest to the manner in which those lives were taken, evoking horror and establishing the depravity of the perpetrator. The photos are the prosecution's needed reality check against the granular details that will be the focus of much attention at trial and that may absorb jurors in such a way that they lose sight of the fundamental tragedy. Crime-scene photos reinforce the sense of tragic loss and outrage that the prosecution needs from jurors, whom it must steel against the defense's attempts to elicit sympathy for the accused. Foundational to the prosecution's narrative, the body of the victim demands justice. The crime-scene photos are the starting point for the righteous work of the state. As an investigator in the murders attributed to Robert Durst explains in *The Jinx*, "As a homicide investigator, you work for God. Because the victim is not there to tell [their] story. You're there to represent the victim. You're there to tell [their] story. You're doing that for God."[29]

Blood at the scene can take on significant narrative and forensic importance. It represents a leaky excess of the body that blurs the boundary between sacred and profane and contains information that can further case-making. Blood is an active, dynamic storytelling feature in the New True. Peterson's guilt or innocence rests on the explanation for the extreme amount of blood at the crime scene. While true of all "forensic realism," in these photos we most vividly see "the sudden eruption of violence from beneath a deceptively normal surface of things."[30] Kathleen Peterson's blood—her spilled life force—splattered on her clothes and walls is shocking and gory. It is a crucial problem for the defense, as its argument that she was alone and fell down is belied by the nightmarish crime scene. It just does not seem possible that someone would bleed that much from slipping and falling. The investigating officers and prosecution team see no other explanation than that she was beaten, which is confirmed by the medical examiner, who concludes that she died of "multiple inflictions of blunt force trauma."[31] Peterson's statement that he called 911 immediately when he found her is also contradicted by the blood, which was already dried on the floor and walls when police arrived, leading them to deduce that she had been there for hours.

As powerfully gruesome as the crime-scene photos are in *The Staircase*, it is the lack of lurid images that takes on significance in *Making a Murderer*. The absence of blood is a narrative element because Dassey's coerced confession accuses Avery of raping, stabbing, and shooting Halbach in his trailer before butchering her body and burning her in a pit. His trial attorneys explain that it would have been impossible for Avery to have sanitized his trailer so thoroughly that no trace of her blood could be found. The premises were searched and tested multiple times. As the defense attorneys point out, even professional cleaners would not be able to do such a thorough job, particularly since there was so much clutter in the trailer. The utter lack of Halbach's blood renders Dassey's account preposterous. That no spray or droplet or trace of Halbach was anywhere, including the mattress, defies common sense in the same way that attributing the copious blood to a fall in *The Stairway* does.

Meaningful Items and Objects of Evidence

The New True features cornerstone objects—crucial physical evidence that is repeatedly analyzed and explained and on which the case against the defendant is built. Imbued with meaning by different case-makers, storytellers, experts, and processes, these objects take on almost talismanic importance. They take on such significance that they can be seen as characters in their own right, with relationships and backstories. Audience attention fixates on them, as they contain the key to unlocking the confounding central mystery of the series.

Audience members' opinions consistently gravitate to one object or other, as do trial attorneys. The objects are the mental and cognitive hook that audience members latch onto in their efforts to solve the cases. Innocence, it is supposed, can be revealed through the objects' proper reading. It is performed through their analysis. Objects in *The Staircase* include blood-stained walls, bloody clothes, a "blow poke," family films, audio of Peterson's 911 call, and pornography on the computer. In the Atlanta case, they include red fibers, green fibers, lavender fibers, dog hair, and a Post-It note; in *The Innocent Man*, a message in blood, a palm print, a belt, pubic hair, remains, and a blouse; in *Paradise Lost*, a knife and drawings; in the Adnan Syed case, phone records, cell-tower records, architectural plans, the car, a note, a palm print, and Lee's diary; in *Making a Murderer*, Halbach's vehicle (the RAV 4) and car key, bullet fragments, bone fragments, an evidence box, the crime-scene log, Halbach's day planner, and pornography found on another suspect's computer. In this section, I look at examples of two types of exhibits: physical objects and documentation. Both establish key elements of the crime in question and are central to storytellers' narratives.

The Blow Poke

The prosecution of Michael Peterson is built on the theory that he beat Kathleen with an object. Prosecutors have to infer the properties of the object from their reading of the long, narrow lacerations on her skull. The skin is broken, and the marks are bloody; but the skull itself is not fractured, nor is her brain bruised or damaged in any way. Looking at these injuries, the prosecution infers the qualities the object must have had; it must have been blunt and long but light enough that it would not have fractured the skull. While nothing in the Petersons' home fits this description, they learn from Michael's sister-in-law Candace that she had given the family a "blow poke" from a set of four she had. While many viewers were initially not familiar with the item, we learn that it is a long and hollow fireplace tool you can blow through as you tend the fire.[32] Kathleen's sister furnishes her own for the prosecution team while it searches the Peterson house looking for the missing one, which has become the de facto murder weapon, a central character with its own history, furnished by Candace, and featured in the memories of other family members. The mystery of the blow poke's whereabouts becomes an important plot point. At trial, the prosecution is able to enter into evidence one from the original set furnished by Candace. Arguing that the blow poke was not the murder weapon and that Kathleen was not beaten, Peterson's attorney confronts the medical examiner with the fact that in 250 beating deaths, not one occurred without either a skull fracture or brain injury. He enlists experts, discussed in the next section, to narrate an alternative sequence of events explaining the lacerations.

No one, however, disputes that the Petersons had at one point owned the blow poke that Candace had given them, and his family is confounded by its disappearance. Just as the prosecution believes it would prove his guilt, Peterson and his team think it could exculpate him. Peterson is upset and expresses a wish that he could find it and have it examined to prove that it was not used in Kathleen's death. To help determine when it was last seen, his daughter Margaret reviews home videos she had been making of her family since 1994. She painstakingly goes through the footage of the living room and observes that in the photo of their fireplace that the prosecution used, their dog is still a puppy, which means the photo is several years old.

In this way, the blow poke is a vehicle for revealing more about the family. It leads the filmmakers to Margaret's videos, which serve their narrative purpose by depicting the Petersons' family unity and happiness over time. Such scenes include the unwrapping of presents and Kathleen goofing around in yoga attire. Then, suddenly, in episode 7, toward the end of the trial, the blow poke makes a dramatic entrance after being happened upon in the garage by one of Peterson's sons. It has possibly been there the whole time—a stunning fact, given that the premises had been searched thoroughly and more than once. When the son discovers it in a dusty corner, covered in cobwebs, he and his father immediately call their lawyer, who comes right over to video it. Presumably it had been there long before Kathleen's death a year before. Furthermore, it is damaged and, when inspected, shows no signs of having been used in a crime. The defense feels this exculpates Peterson, while the prosecution, suspicious and mystified, does not concede that it may have been wrong.

The RAV4

Making a Murderer is cluttered with evidence in ways that distinguish it from some of the other series, and forensic analysis makes up the bulk of its second season. Just as the blow poke takes on talismanic significance in *The Staircase*, so does the RAV4 in *Making a Murderer*. This one object carries several distinct forms of evidence: (1) its location on the Avery property, (2) its missing parking light, and (3) drops of Avery's and Halbach's blood found around the dashboard and other parts of the car. In addition, the key to the RAV4, found on the seventh search of Avery's trailer, is part of the prosecution's case, while to the defense attorneys, it points to state misconduct (because they believe it was planted). In the other docuseries, the defendants' innocence hinges on the interpretation of one main piece of evidence, but Avery's rests on the meaning attributed to several (bullet fragments, bone fragments, blood tests, etc.).

The RAV4 stands out for a few reasons. For one, it is constantly referred to as "the RAV4" by just about everyone, rather than "Teresa's car" or "the victim's vehicle" or "Toyota RAV4." This is also seen in media reviews and subReddits. "RAV4" functions as a synecdoche that signifies several plot elements such as where Halbach was the day she disappeared, who saw the vehicle where and when that day, where her vehicle was found and by whom, who had access to it after it was found, how blood got in the car, when the parking light was damaged, and how the key ended up in Avery's trailer. Days after her disappearance, as part of a wide search led by her ex-boyfriend, the discovery of the RAV4 on Avery's property sets the investigation against him in motion. Law enforcement immediately seals off the area and creates a log to mark everyone who comes to the scene. Since Avery was the last person known to have seen Halbach, the RAV4 now indicates that she never left the property. Drops of Avery's blood near the wheel are particularly damning for him, as he has claimed that he had not been in her car. On the other hand, drops of Halbach's blood actually complicate the prosecution's narrative, which has Avery murdering and burning her on the property, and its sequence of events does not account for her being in the car.

The Flowered Blouse

The case against Tommy Ward and Karl Fontenot for the kidnapping and murder of Denice Haraway was built on the two men's confessions. By the time of their trial, her body still had not been found, and the eyewitness who saw her escorted out of her workplace had only seen her from a distance and at night. The witness did not describe what Haraway had been wearing, nor did anyone else. However, both Ward and Fontenot in their confessions described her as wearing a white blouse with blue flowers and lace trim. This blouse, or its description, has enormous significance in *The Innocence Man*, and Tweel presents drawings and images of it that are returned to throughout the series. It is so crucial because it is one of the only elements in the two men's confessions that match. Some elements of the two confessions even contradict each other. The white blouse with blue roses becomes central to the state's case, emphasized by prosecutors for the jury as proof that both men were there. How would they both have known what she was wearing? Their confessions must be true! Her sister even confirmed that she owned a blouse of that description and that it was missing from her closet. The blouse helped convict Ward and Fontenot by corroborating information in the confessions, which the defendants claimed were coerced.

Months after Ward and Fontenot were found guilty, Haraway's remains are discovered (in a different location from the one that one of the men indicated in his confession), along with remnants of the top she had been wearing. There is no white blouse with blue flowers and lace; instead, she is found in a striped red shirt. The blouse was not only key to the prosecution's case; now that it is revealed to be false, it becomes part of the defense's narrative: it proves that law enforcement planted the information. Law enforcement officers claimed that they knew nothing about Haraway's wardrobe at the time the men confessed, but it emerges later that they had an inventory from her sister and were aware of a missing white blouse with blue flowers. The blouse that the victim was not wearing but is repeatedly visualized in the series is as important as any other piece of evidence in the New True. In one narrator's hands, it signifies guilt; in the other's, it points to innocence.

Documentation

Documentation figures prominently in several of the series. The crime-scene log on the Averys' property becomes evidence of potential law enforcement misconduct; a Post-It note left by Wayne Williams could possibly support his alibi. In *The Case against Adnan Syed*, the class schedule of one of his former classmates, Kristi, becomes critical. However, Koenig's "story about storytelling" in *Serial* makes the most use of documentation, centering it as a catalyst for action.[33] Physical evidence from the crime scenes can establish the basic elements of what happened and can link victim and offender. But other artifacts are used by attorneys and detectives to fill in gaps and corroborate different theories. In the case against Adnan Syed, there was no forensic evidence directly linking him to the murder. The prosecution relied heavily on cell-phone records and cell-tower pings to corroborate Wilds's testimony and cement the case against Syed. In so doing, it squeezed parts of his narrative into the timeline dictated by the records. Syed's 1999 trial was the first time a cell phone was used in court to establish location, which proved to be, and continues to be, controversial in claims of Syed's innocence. Koenig, who herself spends a good amount of the podcast devoted to these cell-phone records, reflects that the defense's thorough examination of them might have numbed jurors, boring them with minute details in a plodding manner that may have made it harder for them to grasp their overall import. Like the jurors in 1999, *Serial* listeners have become familiar with the distinctions between call logs (which indicate which phone numbers calls came from) and cell-tower records (which indicate where the specific tower was that pinged when a call was received). Koenig explains that the prosecution needed to work to align these with Wilds's narrative, since he had Syed's phone the day Lee disappeared. The call log is particularly crucial because it is what first brought the detectives to Wilds: After receiving an anonymous tip about Syed, police subpoenaed his call records; they contacted a friend of Wilds's, Jenn, who had received a call from Syed's phone, and in her second interview, she claimed Wilds had told her that Syed murdered Lee. Of the thirty-four calls on Syed's phone that day, one from an unknown number at 3:36 p.m. is the one the prosecution said was Syed calling Wilds from Best Buy after allegedly murdering Lee. This call, then, establishes the timeline the prosecution uses, against which all testimony has to be reconciled. The timeline is returned to again and again in *Serial* as Koenig and her producers create a narrative by fixating on minute-by-minute accounts of the day from the perspective of each actor (Syed, Lee, and Wilds).

In addition to establishing the timeline, the call log establishes the interactions that took place within a complex teen social network. All tellers of this story insist that in order to understand the log, you must understand the relationships. A call to one girl's number (Jenn) had to have been made by Wilds, because he was her friend and Syed hardly knew her. Similarly, a crucial call to another girl, Nisha, had to have come from Syed, because he was the only one who knew her. This call would place Syed with Wilds at a time that he said he was at school. Investigators, attorneys, and podcaster all need to determine what transpired in these calls.

In an example of how important understanding social dynamics is to the case, in one iteration of Wilds's story, he asserts that one of the calls to Jenn was to find out where their mutual friend Patrick was; Jenn, however, says that would never have happened. Interviewed in *The Case against Adnan Syed*, she simply states, "It's just not a thing that would have happened," asserting her authority over events on the basis of her knowledge of nuances in relationships that cannot be adequately explained to outsiders.[34] The mystery of "the Nisha call" is critical to Koenig, for whom it is the most direct evidence against Syed. She manages to find Nisha, who says that Wilds never called her. She does have a memory of a call from Syed at some point, when he did put his friend Wilds on the phone, but she remembers him as having been working at the video store at the time. Koenig believes only Syed could have made the call on that day, but it is logged at a time that Syed insists Wilds had his phone. Determined to do all that is possible to reconcile Syed's story with her understanding of the social relationships and the call log, Koenig tries to find out if it is possible that it was an unanswered butt dial. Nisha did not have an answering machine at the time, and AT&T claimed that it did not charge for unanswered calls, which means the length of the call on the log could not be accounted for. This troubling bit of evidence nags at Koenig, and she manages to get hold of an AT&T user agreement from a 2003 trial. It comes as a dramatic revelation when it is revealed that if a call rings for an "unreasonable" amount of time, it might be billed, even if never answered. For Koenig, this changes everything, and she no longer interprets the call log as pointing to Syed's guilt. It is possible that it was a butt dial that rang and rang.

Documents in *Serial* tell several stories. A characteristic feature of the podcast is the work Koenig and her producers do to procure obscure documents. The story becomes about a fact-finding detective mission, and they take listeners along for the ride. The AT&T user agreement establishing that unanswered calls could be charged was a particularly exciting find, along with an infamous fax coversheet that went unseen by the state's expert at trial and that states that incoming calls on the log do *not* reliably establish location. The expert who had testified about the call logs later says that he would have made different conclusions had he seen the coversheet. Indefatigably, the producers also track down the architectural plans for the infamous Best Buy where Syed allegedly called Wilds after the murder. They want to determine if there had in fact been a phone booth there, as Wilds claimed but that another teenager tells Koenig did not exist. In the end, the producers concede that the existence of the booth on the plans does not unequivocally establish that it had in fact been built. These documents and others are so intrinsic to Koenig's story that the *Serial* website has a page on which listeners can inspect them themselves, along with Syed's potential alibi witness, McClain's handwritten letters to him in jail, both of her affidavits, and the map of Best Buy that Wilds had drawn for the police.

Let the Evidence Speak

Evidence does not speak for itself; at trials, making sense of evidence requires expert testimony. Professional and popular discourses about crime have been shaped by the development of the field of criminology, which evolved from the study of disciplinary techniques and power relations to create a range of experts who define and explain the criminal.[35] Crime events require interpretation and translation. Facts are not knowable on their own, and specialized knowledge is required to make truth visible. Crime expertise can be divided into two categories: criminology, which relates to people who commit crimes; and forensic science, which relates to physical evidence.

In this section, I look at how objects and images in the New True are rendered legible by experts and how their implications are disputed by each side's attorneys.[36] In addition to direct scientific analysis of physical evidence (conducted by medical examiners and biologists and chemists), we have experimental re-creations of events, conducted by investigators and forensic analysts (as opposed to scientific testing). In an article for the *New Yorker* on what is often referred to as "the *CSI* effect," Jeffrey Toobin explains that most types of tests featured on popular crime shows cannot be statistically verified and were developed by police-department investigators rather than scientists. These tests include "analyses of bite marks, blood spatter, handwriting, firearm and tool marks, and voices, as well as of hair and fibers."[37]

Since the availability of DNA analysis, many people have argued that other tests are not reliable enough for court.[38] Nevertheless, juries and audiences remain fascinated by these other tests, which continue to be very persuasive. A 2019 Netflix series, *Exhibit A*, examines the ways various forms of forensic evidence seem irrefutable to juries and exposes a number of standard methods, such as video evidence that leads to seemingly obvious conclusions, cadaver dog discoveries, and blood-splatter analysis, as flawed and unreliable. Graphic images that appear to unequivocally show truth can in fact easily mislead, something that wrongful-conviction cases have proved time and again.[39]

The New True are heavily populated with forensic authorities, in whose hands a defendant's innocence may rest. In addition to medical examiners who conduct autopsies on the victims and render conclusions about the cause of death, the New True feature FBI profilers, hair and fiber analysts, biomechanics, forensic anthropologists, cadaver dogs, ballistics specialists, "turf physiologists," and even psychics and occult "experts." In addition to medical exams, laboratory blood tests, and DNA analysis, the New True series include analysis of fingerprints, polygraphs, blood spatter, bite marks, and brain activity (a test referred to as "brain fingerprinting"). The importance of experts in case-making is emphasized by Avery's appeals attorney, Kathleen Zellner, who argues that his original team did not have enough experts—only two, compared to the state's fourteen. In this section, I look at some examples of how experts shape the prosecution's narratives in the New True and how defense teams counter with their own interpretations of evidence.

Fiber

The most compelling physical evidence against Wayne Williams in the 1980s Atlanta murders was the unique green carpet fibers found on some of the child victims, which linked the victims and pointed to the same suspect. Although Williams was not charged with any of the child murders, the fibers matched the carpet in his home, and the prosecution was able to use these victims against him as evidence of a pattern. State experts learned in the course of their research that the green, manmade fiber had a specific shape and composition that was only produced by one company and sold to only 820 homes in ten states. The jury heard days of testimony about this, focusing on how fiber is manufactured and how this particular fiber was distributed. The statistical likelihood of its coming from another home would be "an astronomical coincidence," according to one FBI investigator.[40] The jury was shown huge blown-up images of translucent green and pink fibers matching the carpet and a lavender bedspread in Williams's home.

These images convey the power of technology to show laypeople otherwise-inaccessible microscopic details. The defense argued that Atlanta was in "cloth country" and explained that up and down the river where the adult victims' bodies were found, textile companies dump all sorts of material. To demonstrate, the defense team took clean pillowcases and washed them through the river, pulling out thirty-five different types of fiber. The state argued that none of those fibers included the green carpet fiber and that never before and never since had their experts seen that type of fiber. For the prosecution, the green fibers were crucial in grounding circumstantial evidence, anchoring it to something more concrete that had the irrefutability of fact, and elevating its case beyond speculation, inference, and assumption. For the defense, dismantling the argument that the fibers came from Williams's home was necessary to draw him as innocent for the very same reason.

Blood

Small amounts of Avery's blood were found in Halbach's RAV4, leading to the seemingly obvious conclusion that he had been in her car. The prosecution maintains that Avery had cut himself before getting in the car and that the blood dropped from his hand. However, the story the defense tells is one of state corruption and misconduct. The defense argues that this evidence was planted from samples the prosecution had from Avery's 1985 case. The prosecution, on the other hand, uses the blood as proof that Avery got in the RAV4 after he murdered Halbach and drove to hide it in a far corner of his property. At his trial, his attorneys argue that the vials in state evidence had been tampered with and showed photos of a messily taped Styrofoam box with the original seal cut and a small hole in the top of a test tube that could have been made with a syringe. The vial has a purple top, which means that it had a chemical, EDTA, added to it as a preservative. This chemical is not found in the human body. The defense wanted the blood found in the RAV4 to be tested for EDTA, but the prosecution resisted. There was a prolonged disagreement and legal battle over procuring the specialized test.

When the test was finally conducted, the defense was disappointed with the lab's results. That EDTA was not found has dramatic significance. But while its presence would incontrovertibly have proven that the blood came from a stored sample, its absence does not definitively mean anything either way. Science was expected to solve a mystery, but instead the meaning of the results is differently interpreted by both sides. In researching for Avery's appeals, Zellner argues that the blood was indeed planted by law enforcement but that it did not come from the stored sample and was instead taken from Avery's sink, where he had always maintained he had cut himself the morning of a search of his trailer. Zellner enlists experts, discussed in the following section, to narrate their version of events.

As we have seen, blood-spatter analysis was crucial in the Michael Peterson case, and the stains on the walls, the stairs, and Kathleen's clothing were analyzed by experts for both sides. The blood had dried by the time law enforcement arrived at the scene, indicating to the prosecution that Peterson had not called 911 immediately following the incident. As a reporter outside the courthouse clarifies for the cameras, "They said the blood *appeared* dried. No one touched it." He then elaborates, "What we really need in this case is for experts to tell us how long does it take for blood dry," expressing a need for professional expertise to make sense of phenomena; the layperson cannot trust their untrained impressions. The defense team latches onto discrepancies in photos developed by the prosecution, such as stains in the kitchen that were taken on two different days. In one instance, a photo from the first day shows a droplet that is not in the photo taken later, and in another instance, something appeared on the later set of photos that is missing in the first. The prosecution explains that this was a glitch in processing the photos, a fact the defense then uses to discredit the claims. Furthermore, the defense argues that the problems with the photos indicate contamination of the crime scene and refers to a textbook on the subject, *North Carolina Justice Academy Blood Spatter Interpretation Manual*, focusing on a section about the need to preserve the scene: "Even the movement of a single blood-stained object at the scene can significantly alter the interpretation of the spatter patterns."[41]

Blood at the scene contains the history of what happened to Kathleen Peterson on the stairs. The prosecution's investigator, Duane Deaver, had videotaped experiments of his team using a blow poke to whack a Styrofoam head covered in a saturated sponge. It takes many tries for them to reproduce spatter similar to that at the Petersons'. The defense's DNA expert watches this video and explains that the investigators distorted the scientific method by starting with the results and working backward to get the outcome they wanted, rather than starting with a re-creation of the conditions to test the hypothesis and exploring alternatives for achieving that result. The defense's blood-spatter expert comes to the Peterson house in preparation for his testimony and spends time at the scene. He concludes that it would be impossible for a blow to the head to generate those cast-off patterns, as Deaver had testified. Calculating Kathleen's height and weight and measuring each step, as well as the distance between walls and door frames, the defense's expert shows how Kathleen could have slipped on one step and hit her head hard on the molding, which would have created some of the lacerations. He argues that she tried multiple times to stand up, each time slipping and creating more spatter and lacerations. He explains the possible direction of her fall and shows how she would have struggled with her hands for support to get up, leaving prints on the wall, and how she could have coughed and spit blood that created more spray patterns. The expert's run-though makes the fall seem plausible and makes it easier to imagine a horrible accident. It makes the theory seem real.

Deaver, the state's blood-spatter expert, was later crucial to Peterson's postconviction motion for a new trial, when it emerged that he was implicated in the wrongful conviction of another man in North Carolina. This man was exonerated in 2017 after it was proved that Deaver had falsified results. In that case and Peterson's, he had concealed results unfavorable to the state and performed convoluted experiments attempting to get the facts to match the state's theory. One juror later told Lestrade that Deaver's testimony had been instrumental in his decision and that the blood-spatter evidence convinced the holdouts. Misapplied forensics accounted for 52 percent of exonerations in 2020.[42]

The experts populating the New True are not limited to those presented at trial. The documentarians rely on a variety of experts throughout their series to narrate theories and voice perspectives from an authoritative standpoint, such as the Innocence Project cofounder Barry Scheck in *The Innocent Man* and the law enforcement consultant Jim Trainum in *Serial*. Some of the same experts are featured across series. The legal scholar Richard Leo is featured in *Making a Murderer* and *Paradise Lost*, among other documentaries on wrongful conviction, and the forensic expert Werner Spitz makes appearances in *The Staircase* and *Paradise Lost*. The same private investigative firm that the filmmakers use in *The Case against Adnan Syed* is used in the series *Free Meek*.

Rather than convince a jury, these experts are employed by the documentarians to frame their narratives of wrongful conviction, offering meta perspectives on the trials that support alternative truth claims.

Other Experimental Re-creations

In the New True, attorneys, investigators, and documentarians conduct experiments to re-create events in order to test and confirm different assertions. These can be particularly persuasive because they allow theories to come to life and take observers step by step through a sequence of events that demonstrate how things must surely have happened or surely could not have happened. They have a simplicity and logic that is easily conveyed to the layperson, whether to a jury or to a New True audience. These experimental re-creations begin with a premise, a claim that one side or the other is making, and either return to the actual setting or simulate the alleged environment and conditions. They then act out or set in motion the events in question. The re-creations create action; they are kinetic performances of truth. For example, early on in Peterson's defense, his attorneys want to establish the likelihood of his not having heard his wife's screams for help. He had been by the pool at the time that he claimed she must have fallen down the kitchen stairs. To ascertain how the sounds might have traveled, his attorneys bring a tape recording of a woman calling, "Help! Help me!" and place it in the stairwell, where it is played at a volume loud enough to reasonably approximate someone's distressed pleas. Meanwhile, another attorney sits by the pool. This re-creation confirms for them that her cries would not have been heard and lend credibility to their client's version of events.

Audio simulation is similarly used by Payne Lindsey in the *Atlanta Monster* podcast when he seeks to prove whether it was possible for police to hear the events-changing splash in the river from where their car was conducting surveillance. Payne and his producers use a large, weighted dummy, designed to approximate the proportions of the adult victim Williams was accused of murdering on that night. Listeners hear the difficulty they have maneuvering the dummy, a fact that casts doubt on the claim that Williams, a slight man, could have done so. However, from the way Lindsey plays the recording, we can distinctly hear the sound of it splashing, which supports the prosecution. The experiment does not yield definitive results; listeners are left believing that it could be possible that things played out as law enforcement claimed, but it is not certain.

In the second season of *Making a Murderer*, Zellner indefatigably revisits all the evidence in the original trial in an attempt to prove that none of it meant what the prosecution purported, bringing far more resources to bear on the case than Avery's trial attorneys. She explains to the filmmakers that they should have used a blood-spatter expert to analyze the drops of Avery's blood found in the RAV4. He claimed that he had never been in the vehicle, and according to Zellner's expert, the small amounts did not make sense for someone who was actively bleeding, as the prosecution claimed (arguing that the blood came from a cut on Avery's finger). Because so much evidence concerned the car, Zellner realizes that she has to buy the same vehicle in order to properly understand the scene. With photographs of precisely where each of the six drops of blood were, Zellner simulates the conditions to demonstrate how blood would actually drip. She uses a researcher whose hands are similar to Avery's and puts some drops where Avery's cut had been. The researcher then opens the door, gets in, and puts the key in the ignition. We see no droplets, but there is a big smear on the gear shift. The prosecutor had argued that the stain near the ignition happened when Avery turned the key, but Zellner demonstrates that the hand is two inches from that area. Not only does this experiment contradict the state's assertion; it is also critical to Zellner's belief in Avery's innocence and contributes to her proceeding with his case: "What does this tell me? Once I uncover one lie, like, then I know there's a whole bunch more lying going on. Because no legitimate, honest prosecution would ever resort to that. . . . All of this blood testimony is just a complete lie."[43]

Many of the New True concern cases in which truth hinges on an especially tight timeline. While in *Serial*, Koenig seeks to find out if the prosecution's timeline is feasible, in season 2 of *Making a Murderer*, directors Ricciardi and Demos follow Zellner as she seeks to prove if her own alternative theory is possible. Both involve specific and timed drives, and the re-creations of both have an exciting quality, as audiences are taken along with them. Zellner's theory is that Avery's other nephew—Bobby, not Brendan Dassey—had followed Halbach when she left the property and had gotten her alone on the side of the road. Zellner's time frame depends on when Avery says he last saw her and the time she received a call on her cell phone.

Zellner and her investigator determine where each person would have been when Halbach drove on the property, and from these positions, they reconstruct events. One of her team is at Avery's trailer, one at Bobby's trailer, and one, who looks like Halbach, in Zellner's replica RAV4. The vehicle approaches the property and drives its vast expanse to Avery's trailer, having her arrive at 2:35 p.m. At that moment, the Avery stand-in is inside, initiating a call to Halbach, but hangs up when he sees her pull up. He walks out to give her the money for photographing, and when she gets back in the car, she gives him an auto-trader magazine. When she drives off, it has been about five minutes of contact. He goes back in the house for a moment and then walks over to see the Bobby stand-in and is told that he just left; he notes that Bobby's truck is now gone. From there, he can see the RAV4 make a left turn in the distance, and he returns to his trailer. Following the RAV4 is the investigator playing Bobby, who had gotten in the truck right after Halbach left Avery's trailer. He is thirty seconds behind her but is not visible to the Avery stand-in because that part of the road dips. Both vehicles are driving a little over the speed limit when the investigator playing Bobby signals and Halbach's 2:41 p.m. call comes in, which she sends to voicemail. Zellner's theory is that at this point, Halbach pulled over and Bobby met up with her to talk, possibly about photographing another vehicle, and the crime was set in motion.

The prosecution's case against Adnan Syed, based on Wilds's account, holds that Lee was murdered during the twenty-one minutes between when Syed was last seen at school and the 2:36 p.m. call to his phone, presumably Syed at Best Buy calling Wilds, who had his phone that day. The timeline of events varies depending on who is explaining them. Koenig and her producers seek to confirm these accounts by driving through each side's version. The state had Syed in Lee's car. Koenig and her coproducers go to Woodlawn High School and wait for the last announcements and bell. They allow two minutes for Lee to get to her car, giving the state the benefit of the doubt on the possibility that she could do this so quickly. They have to wait for the buses to clear at the bus loop, which Syed had said takes a long time. They then drive to the circle near the gym, where Lee was last seen getting a snack. Koenig's coproducer gets out, runs in, and runs back. They then drive through large intersections to get to the back of the Best Buy parking lot where Wilds had said the car was. It takes a total of eighteen minutes, which Koenig explains leaves "three minutes for the actual horror of the thing: an argument maybe, then strangulation, then he's got to put her body in the trunk, somehow without anyone seeing." They allot for "the quickest imagining of such a thing." Whereas Koenig and her producers inform us that manual strangulation usually takes a few minutes, they allow just one and half minutes—again giving the state's theory the benefit of the doubt. They then go to the pay phone and mime getting out a quarter and dialing. The whole thing takes a total of twenty-two minutes and two seconds. Koenig reflects that this is very farfetched but still is technically not *impossible*, which Syed had insisted. Like many important instances in the New True, this is a frustratingly inconclusive conclusion. It does not support Syed's claim, and yet it does not refute it.

* * *

In the New True, images, exhibits and reenactments are all performative, dramatizing the battle of good versus evil, guilt versus innocence. Evidence can be a truth-creator or a truth-destroyer. Images of the victims tell the story of their lives and the tragedy of their death and are returned to throughout the series to underscore the reality of these people, human beings who were violently murdered. Exhibits presented by prosecution as the building blocks of its narrative link the defendant to the events and irrefutably mark him as guilty. Experts bring these objects to life through their scientific analysis, translating them in a way that draws innocence as a reinterpretation of phenomena that must be made meaningful. In furtherance of their narratives, defense, prosecution, and documentarians create portraits of the defendants' characters, allowing personality and psychological dispositions to make sense of the facts.

Where the Devil Truly Resides

Monsters . . . stand in for what endangers one's sense of at-
homeness, that is, one's sense of security, stability, integrity,
well-being, health, and meaning. They make one feel not
at home at home. They are figures of chaos and disorienta-
tion . . . revealing deep insecurities in one's faith in oneself,
one's society, and one's world.
—Timothy Beal, *Religion and Its Monsters* (2020)

Be wary of the construction of the monster and monstrosity. . . . The monster is a distorted mirror image or screen
projection of our collective fears and desires.
—Roger Lancaster, *Sex Panic and the Punitive State* (2011)

THE monster is something humans made up, a mythological,
magical figure who is at once human and not human; who is
depraved in ways we are not; who is more animal, more preda-
tor, and less civilized; who does not share the qualities that separate
us from beasts; who does not belong; who should be cast out. "The
monster" is frequently necessary to our construction of the perpetrators of heinous crimes and our justifications for punishing and
banishing them.

"West Memphis is pretty much a second Salem," explains Damien
Echols in the first installment of the *Paradise Lost* trilogy, painting a
picture of the social dynamics of his town, where all the families are
churchgoing and a high premium is placed on conformity.[1] He is also
alluding to irrational sentiments, the danger and risk that come with
transgression, and the looming potential of violence.

In the modern era, the power to define and punish is ultimately held by the state, but this is achieved through social processes and the harnessing of collective beliefs about offenders.[2] Social deviance is always a factor in denunciation and punishment, as often someone's criminalization is related to a marginalized status, and conviction usually cements that marginalization. State punishment by definition confers it.

In *The Exclusive Society*, Jock Young examines the relationship between crime and identities and the demonization embedded in our punishment practices, arguing that "the imputation of criminality to the deviant other is a necessary part of exclusion."[3] Punishment operates through beliefs about human behavior and why some people transgress. Heinous crimes raise the problem of explaining depravity, and casting the perpetrator as nonhuman is often the go-to solution. "Ascribing an essentialist other is to suggest that the deviance is a product of some deviant essence inherent in the individual."[4]

In the New True, poverty and race are critical factors in dehumanizing some of the subjects, while others are deemed subhuman by recourse to theories of psychopathology. Monster theory explores the ways that ideas of monstrosity inform aspects of culture, particularly our understanding of human difference. The concept of "the sociopath" is often invoked as a way of categorizing essential deviance, as it disconnects monstrosity from physical appearances and is operative in some contemporary anxieties inherent in the Othering of defendants.[5]

This modern monster is "invisible and potentially ubiquitous" and inspires stories imbued with anxiety and dread.[6] Once someone is stripped of their status as fully human, "fantasies of aggression, domination, and inversion are allowed safe expression."[7] They can then be excepted from the protections of civil society; they may be cast out. In addition to relying on the factual evidence, prosecutorial narratives and argumentation build on tropes of normativity, based on facile markers of race, heterosexuality, middle-class status, and Judeo-Christian culture, that structure inequality across US society. The New True pose as problematic the existence of "true" identity, calling into question the relationship between appearance and reality and destabilizing our trust in the knowability of the people around us.

The way deviance is signaled and exploited has consequences not just for the specific cases but also for the way the public consumes crime stories. Jurors, of course, are members of the general public, and exploring how deviance is given meaning through reliance on beliefs about evil and/or lay understandings of the clinical category of sociopathy can inform our understanding of factors that influence verdicts. Jurors' experiences, like everyone's, are shaped by broad cultural assumptions; they bring their understandings of the social world—its people, its groups, its beliefs, its logics—into the courtroom, which prosecutors and defense attorneys then play to in framing their narratives. This crucially affects who goes to prison and who does not. It also affects how audiences view the subjects of the docuseries and the extent to which they see the verdicts as social injustices.

The public trial is our visible degradation ceremony, a ritual that assigns a demoted status to a citizen, stripping them of civil rights.[8] The New True docuseries cast a critical lens on these processes by questioning the deployment of broad deviance categories in determining who is (and is not) deserving of punishment and who can be cast out as *homo sacer*, no longer eligible for civil protections or full civil status.[9] In the series, deviance renders the defendants as beings without full humanity who never truly belonged in the social order in the first place because of essential and monstrous natures. The series cast a critical lens on these processes by questioning the deployment of broad deviance categories and the ways they are used to exclude those who fail to conform.

Deviance and Guilt

True crime has traditionally portrayed criminals as "monstrous, deviant, and other."[10] In each of the specific New True cases, as in all criminal trials, the prosecution and defense present two contrasting views of the defendant that engage such constructs in relation to guilt or innocence. The prosecution tries to show that the defendant is deviant and contends that this deviance is evidence of guilt, while the defense argues that the defendant is not deviant or that the deviance in question is not in fact evidence of guilt.

Furthermore, the defense argues that associating deviance with guilt demonstrates prejudice, irrationality, or provincial thinking. On the other hand, the prosecution presents deviance as a necessary part of a plausible narrative that undermines claims of innocence. It has an explanatory power related to but in some ways larger than motive. In addition to the prosecution's reliance on these familiar tropes, in the series, we at times see the filmmakers themselves highlighting their subjects' deviance. Rather than contradicting their support of their subjects, their refusal to simplify their narratives brings nuance to their texts. At times, the subjects themselves will explain to the cameras their understanding of how they are seen as deviant. Thus, prosecution, defense, filmmakers, and defendants all engage ideas of deviance in their definitions of the situation and their versions of truth.

The *Paradise Lost* Trilogy

News coverage of the West Memphis child murders featured victims' families, who declared that the teen defendants in *Paradise Lost* were obviously guilty because they looked like "punks"—a reference to their goth style, wearing black clothes and nail polish. This case was part of a cultural panic around satanic cults that was easily employed to explain the crimes in West Memphis. At the time, media reports about ritual abuse had been sweeping through the nation, leading to arrests, trials, and convictions of completely innocent people, while in fact cult activities never existed.[11] With no evidence at all, the West Memphis Three were said to have engaged in "satanic cult orgies" and animal sacrifices, where they ate the animals they had allegedly ritualistically killed.[12] These were among several disturbing rumors that had been circulating in the high school, where the teens were alienated from the mainstream milieu.

The backdrop of Americana amplifies the gothic horror of the crimes and the characterizations of the defendants. The prosecutor pointed to the fact that Echols had deliberately changed his name from Michael to Damien during his brief interest in Catholic saints. Unfortunately, Damien is also the name of the devil's spawn in the 1970s cult movie *The Omen*. In addition, it did not help Echols's case when he explained to the jury that his practice of Wicca was celebratory of nature. While he tried to make it seem less sinister, it highlighted his unusual interest in obscure religions and practices. The prosecution presented his library copy of *The Book of Shadows*, a text about rituals, along with a pentagram that was found in his room. The prosecutor also referenced the lyrics of the heavy-metal music the teens listened to as evidence of their dangerousness and perversity. Echols explains to the filmmakers that he was seen as guilty only because he stood out and rejected the town's norms, pointing to the fact that he was not into sports or other popular activities.

Poverty was a significant part of what marked Echols and the other two defendants as deviant and therefore guilty. Speaking to the filmmakers in the second installment of *Paradise Lost*, Echols states, "We were absolutely poverty-stricken white trash. I really believe these people would have gotten away with murdering me if it weren't for you [Berlinger and Sinofsky]."[13] Echols attributes the entire case against him to what the novelist Dorothy Allison has described as "the inescapable impact of being born in a condition of poverty that this society finds shameful, contemptible, and somehow oddly deserved." As Allison puts it in reference to her own experience, Echols "knew [himself] to be despised."[14] Advocates of the WM3 often observed that they were vulnerable to prosecution because of their poverty. Their vulnerability and disadvantage elicited sympathy from the filmmakers and audiences, as opposed to the contempt expressed by their community.

Affect also plays a role in the way deviance is constructed by prosecutors and presented by documentarians. The directors of *Paradise Lost* emphasize moments during the trial when Echols seems detached, letting the camera linger on his blank and enigmatic gaze, his self-absorbed grooming in the courtroom, and the way he does not seem to take the proceedings seriously. Demeanor is often linked to guilt and is a factor in many innocence cases, and Echols's unusually aloof manner at trial was called into question, furthering the idea that his outward appearance reflects culpability.[15] Except for the defense attorneys and the filmmakers, all involved—the media, the victims' families, the community, and the jury—seemed to accept social difference as proof of guilt, and this portrait worked with the jury.

Making a Murderer

Steven Avery's poverty is closely associated with his alleged aberrant behavior. The Averys made their living as junk dealers and lived in trailers amid the debris on the sprawling property. Their occupation and living conditions contributed to their social marginalization. Avery had a number of run-ins with local law enforcement in his youth, and officers emphasized that in the past, whenever they brought Avery in following arrest, they found him dirty and needed to give him a shower. One officer was aghast and expressed outrage at the fact that Avery allegedly did not own any underwear. Numerous times, Avery is referred to as "an Avery," both by law enforcement and by others, as they explain why the community seemed so hostile to and disgusted by him.[16] On the news, in court, and in interviews with the filmmakers, it is clear that the Averys were widely viewed with contempt.

Making a Murderer has been described as "a familiar tale of social class and provincial small-mindedness, with the middle-class denizens and institutions of Manitowac County united in scorn against the Averys."[17] The filmmakers underscore this view of the Averys with relentless, bleak aerial footage of their yard, highlighting rust and disrepair. Extended shots of the Averys in their homes seem to linger on disarray in the same manner as the video taken by law enforcement officers during their first search of his trailer, evoking waste and hopelessness in a space that "lives where people do not want to live."[18] Drawing on familiar associations between poverty and perversity, the filmmakers show Avery and his family as "white trash, . . . lower-class smokers, . . . failed citizens self-medicating in the face of poverty and exclusion."[19] The prosecution implicitly hold up squalor as evidence of guilt, and defenders—Avery's attorneys, the documentarians, and viewers—invoke it explicitly as evidence of prejudice. As with the *Paradise Lost* trilogy, the filmmakers present the Averys' poverty to evoke sympathy for them and to highlight their powerlessness.

The Innocent Man

Bleak aerial footage devoid of people is a consistent feature of the docuseries that focus on the poor, white defendants, in *Paradise Lost*, *Making a Murderer*, and *The Innocent Man*. *The Innocent Man* provides a history of Ada, Oklahoma's 1909 lynching of white ranchers who had murdered local cattlemen, underscoring brutality and cultural isolation. The filmmaker Tweel posits this cultural legacy as relevant to Ward's and Fontenot's stories. It pertains to the social context in which the violence against Carter and Haraway took place and perhaps additionally suggests that Ward and Fontenot are victims of a heartless and punishing mass sentiment. This docuseries relies on reenactments that are dark and shadowed, moody and sinister. Ada is described by some residents as a tight-knit community with "a church on every corner," yet *The Innocent Man* depicts a violent underbelly of poor, substance-abusing men.[20]

As in *Making a Murderer*, the victims here are young, middle-class, white women. However, while Echols and Avery are presented as outsiders on the margins of middle-class communities, Ada itself—the whole town—is presented as harboring a network of dangerous and underemployed, drunken, thrill-seeking men. And, as I quoted earlier, the town has been described as having "a disproportionate number of plausible suspects with a documented history of violence against women."[21] Ward's brother-in-law offers his explanation of the case: "They looked at

Tommy as a ruffian, a lower-class person."[22] A friend similarly explains, "The police had it in for him because they were dirt poor. The police tried to blame everything on them. . . . It's their social standing, because they were poor. And in Ada, if you're poor, you're nothing."[23]

The Staircase

The prosecutors of upper-class, suburban Michael Peterson argued that he murdered his wife because she discovered his bisexuality and learned of his sexual liaisons with men he met online. To support their theory, they presented evidence of gay porn on his computer, as well as explicit emails with a male escort about anal sex. One prosecutor in this case expressed outrage and disgust at his behavior, saying to the jury, "These things are filthy! We can't even show them on TV!" sensationalizing his sexuality to inflame irrational emotions in jurors and to demean Peterson as an outsider while simultaneously depicting his extramarital bisexual relations as de facto discrediting.[24] For the prosecution, his sexuality is where deviance and motive meet and mesh. The overt argument is that his wife would never have condoned this behavior and that the idea that he had the marriage he and others described as "wonderful" and "so happy" ("never saw any problems," "never fought") is absurd in light of it.[25] There was no direct evidence to either support or refute the prosecutor's claims—merely assumed community standards and beliefs. The prosecutor invokes these when she asks, incredulously, "Do you believe Kathleen would have been okay with him being bisexual . . . ? It's not *common sense*."[26] One critic observes that it is likely that "the jury couldn't handle [the] possibility" that his wife knew about and condoned the relationship, noting that "the prosecutor, Jim Hardin, couldn't even say the word 'bisexual' without choking."[27] The filmmaker Lestrade believes that Peterson was only on trial "because of the type of man he was, . . . [a] bisexual who sought the company of male escorts."[28]

The prosecution also claimed that Michael Peterson was different from the majority of people in North Carolina because he is a crime writer whose lurid fiction describes violent behavior and heinous acts. The filmmakers show Kathleen's sisters reading excerpts from his writing that depict the inner workings of an imagined criminal mind: "You cannot kill and be unaffected. Like an animal who first tastes blood, so is a man who kills. He is forever disposed to that thirst."[29] The prosecutor stated in her closing, "Keep in mind we are not dealing with an average individual here. We are dealing with a *fiction writer*," not only pointing to the fact that he specifically wrote crime fiction but also framing all writers as suspicious and essentially different from the average everyman juror.[30]

Peterson's relative sophistication was used to paint him as dangerous. Peterson himself claims that he was viewed as questionable in this community because he was a writer, but he specifies that he was targeted because in the past he had written a piece in the local paper critical of the district attorney's office. He explains to Lestrade that this made them hostile to him and led to a vindictive prosecution. He sees himself as an outsider who tried to expose the insular, provincial world of the local authorities. Presenting him as more articulate, well read, and erudite than the larger community, Lestrade suggests that these assets rendered him deviant in that social context. He underscores the way Peterson might be seen as pretentious and odd by including extended shots of him listening to classical music and smoking a pipe.

Serial

The trial of Adnan Syed was less structured around his outward deviance. Producer Koenig argues that in many ways, he seemed a typical middle-class teenager to the people around him. But to support the case against him, prosecutors emphasized anything they could possibly use to frame him as different, to then argue that these differences indicate guilt. They stressed that he had stolen from his mosque when he was younger, that he often smoked marijuana, and that he had written poetry that his teacher found dark and disturbing. For Koenig and her listeners, these facts seem innocuous and in keeping with common teen angst. Drawing on deep-seated fears, the prosecutor presented a theory of honor killings in Muslim culture to explain why Syed would feel justified in killing his ex-girlfriend. They banked on the jury's willingness to believe that a teenager of Middle Eastern descent is capable of patriarchal and religious violence. In a bail hearing, the prosecutor additionally linked Syed's religion and heritage to danger when she argued that he belonged to a strong mosque community that might collude to protect him and help him flee to Pakistan. Given that he was in fact denied bail, this seems to have been an effective strategy.

Atlanta Monster

Like Peterson and Syed, Wayne Williams was middle class. But this case stands somewhat apart from the rest of the New True because both Williams and the victims were Black, and the case concerns serial murders. As a Black man, Williams has contended with widespread cultural fears that de facto cast him as a dangerous and criminal Other, a point that the podcaster and directors of *Atlanta Monster* and *Atlanta's Missing and Murdered* explore throughout both series. Not only is Williams seen as guilty because he is Black, but the death of the children, their families' anguish, and their community's suffering are slow to get the public attention they deserve. American culture has a long history of denying the suffering of Black bodies, which are often depicted as not experiencing pain, and as previously noted, the mantle of victimhood was not so readily bestowed on the Atlanta victims.[31] Williams is also framed as deviant because of his various hobbies and occupations. Like Peterson, he is seen as suspicious because he stands out from the norms of predictable middle-class behavior and takes an active and studious interest in relatively unusual pursuits.

While it is impressive that Williams built his own radio station when he was a teenager, this fact also marks him as nerdy, a loner with perhaps too much time on his hands. His attorney describes him as a "whiz kid," yet his intelligence was one of his characteristics that flagged him as suspicious to the FBI, which argued that he "wanted to show the world that he was smarter than everyone else" by getting away with crimes that so many officials were struggling to solve.[32] He was an amateur photojournalist and a talent scout, two pursuits that indirectly linked him to the murders. Because he frequently showed up to document crime scenes and was characterized as an odd "police groupie," he had familiarity with local police officers and procedures.[33] The prosecution argued that he was able to use this knowledge to his advantage and to help him elude detection. His work as a talent scout was also discrediting because it supported the state's view that the victims were not abducted but knew the perpetrator and went willingly when approached.

* * *

Taking these series together, we see deviance constructed around several axis of social oppression in order to buttress arguments of guilt: class, religion, race, and sexual norms. It took little to tap into these and access mainstream anxieties about the Other. These broad, overreaching concepts do the work for the prosecution, making their job easier. They have less to prove if they can use the shorthand for guilt that is readily available in the larger culture. Echols, Avery, and Ward, all accused of murdering strangers, are from the rural poor, which makes them vulnerable to the criminal justice system in a number of ways. Not only do they lack the resources to fight the state, but their poverty is itself discrediting. The conditions of their lives are used against them. Their economic inability to conform to middle-class lifestyle expectations is taken as indicative of the danger they pose to the community. In contrast, Syed and Peterson, accused of murdering romantic partners, are able to claim middle-class suburban respectability. Rather than being framed along class lines, Peterson's deviance is presented in terms of conventional heterosexuality and monogamy. His extramarital encounters with male escorts are not only used to account for motive; they do damage to his character in light of jurors' presumed homophobia.

The prosecution in Syed's case casts him as suspicious through reliance on white Christian fears of Muslims and people of Middle Eastern descent. In each case, social deviance marks the accused as culpable murderers. Williams, like Peterson and Syed, was middle class, but his victims were strangers. Still, his intelligence, manner, and unconventional interests made him seem odd for a Black man in the 1970s, and this difference was read as dangerous. In Williams's case, his Blackness was used to further mark him as criminal. In all of the New True, the prosecution prevailed, successfully achieving guilty verdicts by relying on general fears about the deviant Other.

It is important to note that the defendants are not the only ones for whom deviance theories are employed to paint a picture of guilt. Theories of alternative suspects, posed by defense attorneys and documentarians, do the same thing. John Byers, the stepfather of one of the boys murdered in West Memphis, is portrayed as maniacal in his religious fervor, and the second season mounts a circumstantial case against him, based in part on the unraveling of his middle-class life since the murders, some instances of bizarre behavior, and his treatment for mental illness. Pornography is central to Zellner's theory that Avery's other nephew was the murderer. The podcast and the HBO series about the Atlanta murders both point to sexual deviants and rabid, committed racists linked to the KKK as responsible for some of the murders.

Deviance and the "True" Self

In the modern world, the distinction between someone's true inner identity and who they outwardly appear to be is taken for granted, a recognition of both the performative nature of social life and a belief in authentic selves. This is at the heart of the dynamic process of "getting to know" someone and the adage that "looks can be deceiving." We navigate the social world with an understanding of this potential discrepancy. There is also a shared understanding of the social norms around revealing oneself and the need for trust to be established before showing a more private version of self. This can be seen in fears about losing the regard of others, having our accomplishments undermined, or being judged for inappropriate displays of emotions or oversharing.

Erving Goffman brought attention to the performative nature of the self in his work *The Presentation of Self in Everyday Life*, in which he argues that our performances are maintained through collective social behavior organized in different spheres and settings. Anthony Giddens also explains that there are norms and structures around disclosures of self. Successful presentation of self is necessary for social bonds with intimates, friends, family, and colleagues, as well as with weaker ties. Goffman shows that not only do most people understand the facts of impression management, but they know that others understand them as well. Navigating what he refers to as front- and backstage areas is second nature, and I would argue that this creates an unease about which version of self is "true" and to what extent performances of self are merely performances. We try to experience ourselves and others in terms of one self, our "inner core," and an "ideal self," which represents how we would like to be seen, with an awareness that each of us can be strategic in how we present self.[34] With the "over-all objective . . . to sustain the definition of the situation," most social performances involve managing secrets that can threaten it.[35]

The prosecution in each case needs to posit a "true" self to advance its theory of motive. The crime has to make sense given who the defendant *is*: Is their guilt plausible given who they are—or seem to be? All of these cases are examples of convictions based on little (or no) direct physical evidence, where interpretations of the defendants' "true" natures undergird the verdicts. The prosecution argues that particular deviance points to guilt because it is evidence of the defendants' actual and disturbed essence. That is, it suggests the essence of the kind of person who would commit such an act. These series explore the nature of one's real self, play on anxieties about how we can know the people around us, and raise uncertainties about the relationship between appearance and reality.

On the surface, Peterson, Syed, and Williams led lives consistent with middle-class norms, and in *The Staircase*, *Serial*, and *Atlanta Monster*, the prosecution argues that the defendants have been hiding their true natures behind the façades of respectability, successfully concealing their dangerous and sinister attributes. Outwardly, all three are usually mild in their manner, well spoken, and articulate; they are polite and agreeable in their recorded interactions with the documentarians (although Williams is less so). Syed and Peterson demonstrate a capacity for self-awareness and self-reflection that makes them seem reasonable and reliable. Williams comes across as more enigmatic and harder to read; on the one hand, he is highly intelligent, yet on the other, he offers no version of self that makes a convincing portrait of innocence. Peterson is often shown as a warm and engaged father with each of his four children, who supported him throughout the entire process. Syed was an exemplar of the American teen: popular in a diverse group of friends, involved in sports, high achieving, and helpful and respectful within his family.

It becomes the job of the prosecution to prove that these defendants are not who they appear to be—to prove that the articulate, popular, and respected self is a sham concealing the ugly and dangerous real person. This task was a bit easier in the case of Williams because he was a quiet loner who fit FBI profiles "to a T" and popular imagination's idea of a serial killer.[36] Because of deep-seated racist stereotypes, as a Black defendant, Williams could be constructed, without much work on the prosecution's part, as inherently criminal.

In Peterson's case, the prosecutor went to great lengths to prove that his bisexuality was hidden and that the concealment indicated both a problem in his marriage and Peterson's sinister and untrustworthy nature. The prosecutor argued that being discovered for who he really was threw him into a homicidal rage. As mentioned earlier, to further the argument that he harbored perversity and suppressed rage, the prosecutor pointed to his crime fiction. After reading a particularly extreme excerpt from one of his novels, his sister-in-law states that only a deviant mind could have written it and then concludes, "I have no idea who Michael Peterson really is."[37] The true self, revealed through the guise of fiction, is the guilty self. Grappling with the question of his identity, Peterson's stepdaughter Caitlyn states, "The person I knew didn't kill my mom."[38] Unlike her four stepsiblings, she actually does think he did it, but to reconcile the discrepancy between her experience of him as kind and loving and her understanding of the evidence against him, she speaks about him as two different people. That is, she does not articulate that his core authentic self is more real than the self he presents. Rather, she grants them each a reality and, by bifurcating Peterson, enables herself to keep the person she "knew" intact.

Significantly, Koenig similarly states that many friends of Syed said, "I can't say for sure if he's innocent, but the guy I knew, there's no way he could have done this," expressing belief in the possibility of two distinct selves.[39] In Syed's trial, the prosecution argued that he felt deeply humiliated by the breakup with his girlfriend. There is little testimonial evidence to either support or refute this. While a few friends said he continued to be upset about it, others pointed to the fact that he had started dating other girls. The state's case would be too weak if it did not offer jurors some theory of motive, so it argued that he had everyone fooled. As we will see in the following section, the fact that he was able to successfully fool people is presented as itself proof of how disturbed he is.

To make the stereotypical claims about honor killings in Syed's Muslim culture, the prosecutor employed a consultant to lend credibility to the idea that his middle-class suburban, American lifestyle was a front for the angry and culturally specific misogyny that the expert could attest to. The idea that foreigners with malign intent are hiding behind a generic Americana façade, pretending to be "real Americans," is a paranoid undercurrent in the popular imagination, seen in the past decade in fictional series like *The Americans* and *Homeland*. Unlike the documentary films, *Serial* (and *Atlanta Monster*) is narrated, so we get more direct insight into how the producers understood Syed and the case. For

Koenig, the heart of the matter rests with who Syed really is. She says, "What hooked me is him. Who is this person who says he didn't kill this girl but is serving a life sentence . . . ?" She tells him, "My interest in it honestly has been you. Like, you are a really nice guy. I like talking to you. Then it's kind of like this question, what does that mean?" Interestingly, rather than feeling flattered or validated, as some people might expect, Syed bristles at this statement, explaining that it makes him mad because the issue is not whether he is nice or not but whether there is a case. "I want to shoot myself when I hear someone say, 'I don't think you did it because you are a nice guy.' . . . I'd rather someone say, 'I don't think you did it because I looked at the case and it seems kind of flimsy.' I'd rather you think I was a jerk."[40] With this segment, *Serial* explicitly problematizes the role of the real self in cases like this, where personality trumps evidence.

In contrast to *The Staircase* and *Serial*, where middle-class status is seen as concealing invisible deviance, in *Making a Murderer*, *Paradise Lost*, and *The Invisible Man*, the white defendants are posited as clearly exhibiting their real natures. The prosecution links their visible, incontrovertible poverty to depravity that is meant to represent who they really are. The material conditions of their lives are connoted with moral filth, and we can see in these cases the idea that punishment "is about eliminating the disgusting and unruly."[41] It falls on the defense to argue that their true nature is a decent self, one that is occluded by this damaging cultural association.

The disorder and uncleanliness throughout Avery's trailer and the literal junk on his property are implicitly linked to an uncivilized, raw nature. The investigators and prosecution invoke dominant cultural attitudes and fears to portray the Averys as undersocialized, in contrast to sanitized middle-class norms, even claiming, without apparent evidence, that family members have sex with each other. They present the family as clannish, tribal, and degenerate. Avery's admitted and shocking cruelty to animals in his youth (he threw the family cat into a fire) buttressed viewers' belief in his guilt, as it is simultaneously a sign of antisocial disorder and barbarism that consequently renders him unsympathetic and inhuman.[42]

Yet when the filmmakers present the defense's perspective, Avery appears as a frightened, humble, earnest man who is powerless against the state. Both at trial and in other scenes from *Making a Murderer*, he can be seen with a vulnerable, dumbfounded expression on his face. His worry and fear regarding his aging mother's health in the second season appear sincere and make him more sympathetic and relatable. As evidenced in reviews and online forums, many viewers feel compassion for Avery and find him believable. Zellner, his appeals attorney, states that she took the case after the first season of *Making a Murderer* because of how problematic the evidence against him was and the clear bias of law enforcement, but in her work with him, we see that she also found him credible and sympathetic. On the other hand, Ricciardi and Demos complicate this portrait with segments quoting Avery's ex-girlfriends, who claim that they were afraid of him and that he harbored considerable rage and hostility. They believed he was dangerous. In this way, the filmmakers play on the knowability of their subject and present different versions of Avery for viewers to sort out.

The problem of the teens' true selves is less confounding in the *Paradise Lost* trilogy, where the evidence of their bad character is particularly thin and attributable to youth. The prosecution relies on rural poverty as a basic marker of their guilt, inflaming then-current fears about satanic worship and ritual. These, we have seen, are argued on the basis of the teens' clothing, musical taste, and opposition to mainstream norms, all of which are seen by the directors and audiences as within a well-recognized range of normal teenage expression that is absurd to equate with murder. The supporters shown in subsequent episodes say that they identified with the teens' appearance, tastes, and youthful rebelliousness.

Echols openly rejects what he sees as his community's small-mindedness and flaunts his nonconformity, and Berlinger and Sinofsky frame their documentary around the idea that the teens' real self is obscured by the ignorance of the people around him. The community—

and the jury—had to evaluate his presentation of self: at trial, he appeared "head down and hangdog, looking as if he feels ashamed or has something to hide."[43] On the other hand, the filmmakers themselves rely on interpretation of affect as they position him as someone who "doesn't *seem* like a murderer," as if being a murderer is an identity that can be recognized and is essential, rather than a description of an act, as Syed had argued.[44]

Like Koenig and Zellner, the directors have an idea of what a murderer seems like and feel confident in Echols's innocence partially because of the impression they have of him. During the three episodes produced over the course of a decade, they show Echols mature into a thoughtful, reflexive man who is able to articulate his plight through a critical lens and put his past teenage behavior in perspective. They present his true self as emerging over time from behind the teen façade and into public view, demonstrating that people are capable of growth.

Evil and True Identity

Linking deviance with claims about the defendants' real self undergirded the prosecutions' theories of motive. But this link alone does not fully or satisfactorily explain the murders to audiences. If we accept that they did it because they are truly bad, the next question is, Why are some people's true identities bad? While we all understand and negotiate the existence of private selves and public, inner selves and outer, murders such as these present the problem of extreme malice, not the kind of bad behavior people more routinely encounter. The idea that this kind of malevolence can be lurking beneath others is hard to integrate into a functioning orientation to social life and the negotiation of everyday interactions. Maintaining moment-to-moment ontological security requires "'faith' in the reliability and integrity of others."[45] Social actors believe themselves to be attuned to this reliability and are anxiously alert to what Anthony Giddens calls "misrepresentable cues" in performances.[46] Do most of us believe that everyone harbors the potential to commit such deeds? Or are the people who committed these crimes (not necessarily the defendants, of course) essentially different from the rest of us? Deviation from the norms of broad social categories employed in these series (class, sexuality, religion), because of their breadth, cannot fully account for such egregious individual violations. Thus, to explain badness, we see two concepts invoked: evil and sociopathy.

Evil, without referencing an underlying pathology, is associated with visible deviance. It is vaguely referenced in a way that enfolds that which is injurious to human life with some otherworldly malevolent force that is unexplained and usually underanalyzed. Karen Halttunen explains in her study of murder stories and the gothic imagination that a new, more secular concept of evil emerged in the nineteenth century that framed it as elusive, "not self-evident but puzzling and problematic," and that murder narratives began to affirm the darkness of crimes that violated "the prevailing understanding of human nature."[47] "Sociopathy," a diagnostic term that does not evoke a theology or grand moral belief system, is associated with hidden deviance. Both evil and sociopathy can be used to answer the question, "At what point does deviance make someone a monster?"[48]

Evil in the Docuseries

We have seen in *Making a Murderer* and the *Paradise Lost* trilogy that Avery's and Echols's rural poverty marks them as less civilized, more primitive than the middle-class residents in their counties, possessing animal natures that are premoral. As explained by David Frankfurter in *Evil Incarnate: Rumors of Demonic Conspiracy and Satanic Abuse in History*, evil has long been associated with "polluting things" pertaining to the body, such as "blood, feces, semen, corpses, incest," and we see deviance ascribed to both Echols and Avery because of animality and excess of bodily functions not contained in ways that signal the civilizing process.[49] Avery is described as dirty and having an offensive odor. As previously noted, he did not always wear underwear, and he confessed to cruelty to animals in his youth. Echols is accused of eating raw sacrificed animals in pagan rituals and of keeping one of the victim's testicles in a jar (there is no evidence of this). Neither is seen as having the sanitized containment of the body associated with progressed social evolution, and they are in this way linked with a nonhuman (monstrous) element outside the moral order. As in classic true crime, they are seen as "moral aliens."[50]

As part of the filmmakers' critique, they accentuate this view of their subjects by using aerial footage depicting vast open environments devoid of architecture or organized social life, chaotic rural conditions that lack indicators of human care. The association with primitive nature lends itself to concepts of evil. *Paradise Lost*—itself a reference to Milton's poem about the fallen angel—begins with the voice of a state investigator saying, "Imagine all the evil you can think of," with shots of the primordial West Memphis woods. The community is very religious, and Mark Byers, the stepfather of one of the victims, says of the crime, "I believe there's angels here on earth, and I believe there's demons on earth, to do the devil's will." And of course, Echols is directly accused of literal satanism. The prosecution says of him, to the jury, "You look inside him, and there is not a soul in there."[51] Speaking of the entire Avery family, a state investigator in *Making a Murderer* says, "This is where the Devil truly resides in comfort."[52] Steven Avery's entire "clan," marginalized in the community, is connected with evil. Dassey's attorney says that he was under the influence of "evil incarnate."[53] Local communities view the Averys and the WM3 in similar ways to historical beliefs about witch cults: "they eat what we find disgusting, they mock what we find sacred, . . . they abuse what we protect."[54]

In this context, the stakes for the filmmakers are high. Once a defendant is marked as evil, they are more likely to receive harsher punitive sentencing, and it is up to Berlinger and Sinofsky and to Ricciardi and Demos (as well as to Tweel) to present counterimages of their subjects, in a sense to "save" them, reclaim their status as human, debunk the idea of evil, and reveal their unseen innocence.[55] Their projects align with defense attorneys' efforts to humanize the defendants, critique the construction of them as monsters, and offer an alternative version of self. They present their subjects not as subhuman but as victims of deep and pervasive cultural beliefs about poverty being both the cause of evil and a condition that evil people deserve, justifying exclusion.

Sociopathy in the Docuseries

The malevolent forces attributed to Peterson and Syed are not outwardly evident. Instead of invoking the concept of evil, the idea of "the sociopath" is presented, drawing on a long history of "charming and enigmatic" sociopaths in movies.[56] The concept of the sociopath allows us to attribute monstrosity to those who outwardly appear normal and is operative in some contemporary anxieties inherent in the Othering of defendants.[57] This modern monster is "invisible and potentially ubiquitous."[58] Frankfurter states that "monstrous people are physically human, their monstrous tendencies *usually hidden*."[59] Once someone is stripped of their status as fully human, "fantasies of aggression, domination, and inversion are allowed safe expression," and they can be excepted from the protections of civil society.[60]

This clinical diagnostic category is overtly examined by Koenig, while the colloquial understanding of the concept is more subtly attributed to Peterson in the way the filmmakers frame him as they highlight his somewhat-macabre humor and intellectual distance from the unfolding of the case. Wayne Williams is described many times in *Atlanta Monster* and *Atlanta's Missing and Murdered* as fitting the FBI profile of sociopathic serial killers. While sociopathy gives ominous portent to the defendants' deviant aspects, it also works effectively in these instances because it presents the *conforming* aspects of the defendants in a suspicious light. It is a concept of the monster "decoupled from physical appearance."[61]

Sociopaths are the unseen dangers in our midst, and these narratives are cautionary tales against trusting the appearance of the people around us. They are uncanny in that they are simultaneously familiar and strange. Freud believed that people are uncanny "when we ascribe evil intentions to [them]."[62] The public has a general understanding of someone whose outward appearance and lifestyle are conventional yet who does not feel remorse or guilt and is capable of despicable acts. This understanding of the sociopath comes from the media, particularly TV shows, rather than from professional psychology or criminal justice, and is a feature of many fictional crime stories, such as *Dexter*.[63] This general framework informs the actual trials in the docuseries. A psychology professor explains in *Atlanta Monster* that in general "the term 'sociopath' is used very loosely": "There's no one meaning of it. It has five or six different meanings. We [experts] don't use it because it's kind of a colloquial term."[64]

The problem of identifying the real Syed or the real Peterson requires reconciling a number of contradictions, and we see the conflicts this creates most clearly in the efforts of the people around the defendants, including the documentarians, to make sense of their own impressions versus pieces of evidence that vary in their degree of persuasiveness. The prosecution argues that Williams, Peterson, and Syed are experts at manipulation. In the cases of Peterson and Syed, their intelligence, consideration, humor, and insight, as well as other social strengths, are precisely what cannot be trusted about them. Syed is seen as likeable, but even this is suspect, as Peterson and Syed may be conning their audiences.[65] Koenig and Lestrade explore this possibility, showing their subjects in both lights. In sentencing Syed, the judge directly accused him of manipulating everyone by coming across as nice, stating, "This wasn't a crime of passion. You planned it. You used that intellect. You used that physical strength. You used that charismatic ability of yours that made you the president—or, what was it, the king or the prince—of your prom. You used that to manipulate people, and even today, I think, you continue to manipulate even those that love you, as you did to the victim. You manipulated her to go with you to her death."[66]

Peterson's wry, at times sardonic reflections and dark humor can indicate either a sensitive, wise, and sophisticated nature or a creepy dissociation from the tragedy. His ability to reflect and intellectualize his situation is confusing because it "could be read one of two ways, either implying guilt (because he is just too cool and controlled) or resonating with the innocence of a man who has nothing to hide."[67] Dual, mutually exclusive readings of affect and demeanor are easily attributed to him, as he is often (though not always) controlled and articulate.

In wrongful-conviction cases, the prosecution can easily use demeanor as evidence since a defendant's reactions can either be characterized as "too calm and collected" or "too upset and over-the-top."[68] In *The Staircase*, Peterson at times openly weeps and at times intellectualizes his situation, and both his excess of emotion and his lack of it can be read as proof of guilt. Demeanor is also a factor at Williams's trial, where in frustration, under questioning, he got angry, called FBI agents "goons," and appeared combative. His attorney admitted that she bore some responsibility for his troubling impression management in court because after she thought he was seeming aloof, she advised him to show emotion. She also said that he had trouble with the jury because he was "full of himself."[69]

Like Peterson and Syed, Williams is cast as thinking he is better than everyone else, and all three of their crimes are read as expressions of arrogance. Yet James Baldwin conversely observes that "everything this creature does—smiling or not smiling, calm or panic-stricken, belching or not belching, sweating or not sweating, smoking or not smoking, shouting or not shouting—is suspect."[70] For Baldwin, Williams's demeanor and lack of "energy" indicate an inability to have committed the crime: "He impresses me as a chubby, weak, arrogant boy. . . . He impresses me, too, in spite of his seeming energy, as a profoundly lazy boy."[71]

Sociopathy is a concept that seemingly explains the invisible malevolence of people with pleasing demeanors. Describing one of the first books on sociopathy, the journalist Janet Malcolm relays that the sociopath does not seem different from others and that their "chief symptom is the very appearance of normality. . . . [They] can mimic the human personality completely."[72] The danger of casting "normal" behavior as suspicious is highlighted in precedents to the New True, such as *The Thin Blue Line*, in which Errol Morris shows how detectives concluded that "perceived normality was proof of [Adams's] lack of normal human emotions, which could cause him to 'work all day and creep all night.'"[73]

Koenig reflects that the same facts can take on opposite meanings depending on one's point of view. Can the audience trust its impression? Is certainty possible? She interviews an expert who says that most murderers are not true sociopaths, whom he describes as having no conscience or empathy but possessing an ability to read people well; they are glib and have a superficial charm. After exhaustively talking to Syed and those who know him, Koenig does not see a sociopath in him. But she muses that at the center of her story is the unsettling prospect that he may be one or that it is fundamentally unknowable. She observes, "One person's evidence of good character is another person's evidence of questionable character."[74]

Sociopathy allows this slipperiness, seemingly able to explain how good people do bad things. Or, as in these series, it can be a way of explaining the crimes of the privileged as opposed to those of the poor. It has the satisfying clinical credibility and weight of a medical diagnostic term. Yet, examined closely, it is not that different from the concept of evil. The psychologist Martha Stout writes that saying people have no conscience "isn't quite calling them evil, . . . but it is disturbingly close."[75] Neither actually explains anything. Both have the circular effect of saying that someone is bad because they are bad. Janet Malcolm explains, "The concept itself evades the problem it purports to solve. To say that people who do bad things don't seem bad is to say something we already know: no one flaunts bad behavior, everyone tries to hide it, every villain wears a mask of goodness. The concept of the psychopath is, in fact, an admission of failure to solve the mystery of evil—it is merely a restatement of the mystery—and only offers an escape valve for the frustration felt."[76]

Ian Punnett observes a lineage between true crime and the gruesome stories of "beasts and monsters" in the Grimms' fairy tales, stating that in true crime, social deviants are cast as "a psychological beast or monster."[77] For the middle-class defendants in these series, sociopathy is a stand-in for evil that reconciles the respectability attributed to the middle class with heinous acts that violate the tranquil image of suburban life. Crimes of the conventionally respectable represent "sudden eruptions of violence from beneath the deceptively normal surface of things."[78]

Raising the issue of innocence and wrongful convictions, the New True move beyond the conventions of the traditional true-crime genre, which has historically upheld many of the assumptions on which the criminal justice relies, including the essential nature of the criminal. While traditional true crime relies heavily on institutional sources and does not see the accused as a source of truth, these new series do the opposite: they foreground the accused's version of events and challenge the institutional narrative.[79] Traditional true crime has upheld conservative values and generally does not advance social reform.[80] The New True push the boundaries of the genre as they problematize the easy reliance on prejudice and stereotypes about ethnicity, religion, sexuality, and class status that are foundational to how we describe and recognize monsters.

* * *

The New True all seek to humanize subjects deemed monstrous through the demonizing mechanisms available to criminal justice. These series present dramatic narratives around the process of assigning guilt through trials—the mechanisms employed by the law to designate an individual as deserving of punishment and to legally strip them of their rights. In this analysis, we see that these series look critically at the ways deviance is leveraged in service of exclusion. The convictions in these cases are based largely on character, in essence enacting punishment not for what the defendants did but for their "nature," so that they can be "safely disposed of" as legal slaves stripped of civil rights and status.[81] Although the filmmakers do not unequivocally strong-arm audiences into a conclusion, their perspectives point to the injustice of using such patently prejudiced and biased beliefs that are counter to the ideals of our system and hinder the functioning of healthy democracy.

Wrongful convictions can potentially expose serious cracks in the system and undermine the legitimacy of punishment, exclusion, and penal harm. By making visible the manipulation of social deviance categories, the New True bring the criminal justice system into sharper focus. The enormous outcry and viewer engagement surrounding these cases, and the role both have played in the proceedings and outcomes of individual cases, demonstrate that these series have an effect in the "real world"; all have had a powerful emotional impact on viewers—some who could not sleep after watching—altered viewers' behavior, created demands for institutional action, and contributed to continued legal proceedings.[82] The series makers importantly shine light on how deviance is unjustly used in convicting the innocent and help viewers see this as inappropriate extralegal information. In this way, they expose and critique popular and sadly enduring cultural beliefs about deviance, evil, and exclusion, pushing the boundaries of true crime in an era currently being shaped by movements for criminal justice reform.

5

Conviction and Wrongful Conviction

If people *feel* powerless it is, because to ever greater degrees, they *are* powerless. Actual power proceeds from agencies and entities ever more removed from popular control or effective monitoring.

—Ray Pratt, "Theorizing Conspiracy" (2003)

 PERSON imprisoned for a crime they did not commit stirs a particular anxiety: not fear of crime but fear of government, a sense of unease related to vague feelings of helplessness in the face of unseen power. Corrupt elite organizations victimizing an ordinary individual are a consistent theme in the American imagination, one we see running through both conspiracy thrillers and innocence narratives. While the New True are instructive—explaining and illustrating the factors that contribute to wrongful conviction—they dramatize injustice through familiar archetypes that shape our worldview. The stories they tell about wrongful conviction are in some ways stories of being victimized by the state, turning our attention to unethical and possibly illegal actions of the people in power and the harms they are able to inflict on the most socially vulnerable.

Even though most exonerations and most cases of wrongful conviction do not involve DNA evidence, the public's awareness of the issue has expanded greatly since the "DNA revolution" accelerated exonerations and began sharing the stories of the wrongfully convicted.[1] Such cases are no longer seen as "anomalous, if not freakish."[2] The New True now join the small but significant true-crime literature focusing on individual cases, which the wrongful-conviction scholar Richard Leo says "poignantly illustrate the discrepancy between our legal ideals and the ongoing failures of our criminal justice system."[3] Documentarians fore-ground sympathetic portrayals of their subjects and put forward argu-ments about their innocence by posing and exemplifying established facts about wrongful conviction. Raising the possibility that the juries "got it wrong," the series look at several important contributing factors and at examples of problems in jury decision-making processes. The series look closely at forms of state misconduct and interrogation tech-niques that elicit false confession. In some of the series, these efforts cre-ate narratives about the vulnerability of the poor against the dominance of state authority and shift the criminological gaze to state actors.

Juries in the New True

Even though the vast majority of criminal convictions in the US are the result of plea bargaining and the majority of civil cases are settled out of court, the role of the jury in criminal justice is still enormous. Beliefs that people hold about how a jury would probably determine an outcome if a case went to trial drive the plea-bargaining process and influence the decisions actors make at this stage.[4]

There is a large body of research on how juries operate, which includes both mock jury experiments and analysis of actual trials. We know that when it is possible to determine that actual juries have made real mis-takes (either convicting an innocent person or acquitting a guilty one), their processes reflect established psychological principles and common forms of reasoning.[5] Real and mock jurors make "fundamental attribu-tion errors," where actions and statements are understood in terms of the individual rather than situations and contexts.[6] Thus, impressions of the defendant's character are instrumental. The defendant is often seen as the driver of events, which has explained erroneous guilty verdicts even in cases in which the state or others have been shown to have acted unethically or in bad faith.[7]

Another factor known to influence juries is pretrial publicity, which disproportionately affects high-profile cases and has become a greater problem as communications technology and social media speed up the flow of information.[8] Research has shown that jurors use information from outside sources in their deliberations.[9] The New True cases received a great deal of coverage on local news outlets, and the docuseries look critically at media's role in influencing the juries.

Jurors are not shown on camera in these series, and few of those on the New True cases spoke with documentarians. What little we do know about them indicates outside influences. Through documentarians' interviews with some jurors and their own investigation, they are able to illuminate events that went on behind closed jury doors. Of the six docuseries, half of them follow the original trials in real time: *The Staircase*, *Paradise Lost*, and *Making a Murderer*. In these, the documentarians were drawn to the story as it emerged in the media and were able to chronicle events from the defense's pretrial preparation through to verdict. In the others, the filmmakers and podcasters draw inferences about defense strategies from footage, transcripts, and retrospective interviews. Without the participation of prosecutors in any of the New True, we have only a limited understanding of their strategies and intentions.

In the third installment of *Paradise Lost*, we learn that at least one juror had their mind made up before the trial and potentially engaged in misconduct. After the release of the first film, filmmakers were contacted by a practicing lawyer in the West Memphis area who had nothing to do with the case but who remembered receiving an unusual phone call before the trial. Someone had called his office asking how they could get selected for a jury. This person explained that they were already in the jury pool for the Echols and Baldwin trial and wanted to make sure they were picked. He explained that he had been following the case closely, already knew a lot about it, and was convinced the teens were guilty. Not only did this man succeed in getting on the jury, but he became the foreman. He again called the lawyer's office, this time seeking advice on how to sway jurors. Although Misskelley's confession was not presented at the other teens' trial, we learn that the foreman had told his fellow jurors about it. In relaying these events, Berlinger and Sinofsky show how the media may have influenced the verdict and informed at least one juror's unethical conduct.

Michael Peterson was able to spend a considerable amount of money on his defense. At one point, he speculates that it will cost him over $750,000 and observes that "American justice is very, very expensive."[10] A good portion of the money was spent on jury consultants, focus groups, and opinion surveys to help his defense prepare and frame its arguments to most effectively persuade the jury. Lestrade shows us a session with a witness expert who engages Peterson in vocal exercises and physical relaxation techniques before sitting him in a mock witness box to answer intrusive questions about his sex life. His attorney explains that he hopes Peterson will be able to present to the jury in a way that will allow them to see Peterson as his wife saw him, not just likeable but also lovable. We are also shown a focus group in which participants watch a video of Peterson's blood-spatter expert and learn that they were turned off by his heavy Asian accent. They also thought he seemed like he was stretching the facts, contorting them to fit a desired conclusion. The defense's jury consultant explains that the southern jury may be more provincial than in other cities and will probably have more of a problem with ethnic differences.

As many as 90 percent of verdicts reflect positions held at the very beginning of deliberations.[11] Steven Avery's jury deliberated for twenty hours. During this time, one juror was excused for a family emergency and replaced with an alternate. We learn that this juror was planning on voting not guilty. We also learn that when deliberations began, seven jurors believed in Avery's innocence, two believed in his guilt, and three were undecided.

The excused juror explains that some of those who believed Avery was guilty were vehement and were able to sway those who were less sure. He claims that they wore everyone down. He also claims that he thought a couple of jurors were biased against Avery from the beginning and had made up their minds before the trial had even started. Similarly, one juror, discussing her role on the jury against Tommy Ward and Karl Fontenot, explains to Tweel that she felt pressure to convict. She says that the majority thought he was guilty and that although she had doubts about the evidence and circumstances, she was afraid if she did not go with the majority, the defendants would be released and another tragedy could happen again.

Wrongful Conviction and the New True

The documentarians do not argue that the jury simply made a mistake. Instead, they probe elements of the state's cases that influenced outcomes. They expose routine practices in law enforcement and prosecutors' offices that stack the deck against vulnerable defendants and contribute to convicting the innocent. In this way, like American conspiracy films, these series can be seen as "a form of populist discourse."[12]

Exact numbers on the extent of wrongful convictions are by their nature impossible to produce, an unknowable "dark figure."[13] As of 2022, the National Registry of Exonerations includes 3,172 exonerations since 1989.[14] It is tempting to see wrongful convictions as tragic and anomalous instances of mistakes in the system, "private calamities," rather than "public matters," but many of the isolated errors in these cases are part of the fabric of a system wherein the presumption of innocence has become an irrelevant abstraction or even a "myth."[15] The New True present case studies in which this seems to be the case. Once the state casts the defendants as guilty, it sets in motion a course of events that preclude the subjects' innocence.

Innocence researchers have identified six independent factors that contribute to wrongful conviction cases: (1) eyewitness misidentification, (2) misapplication of forensic science, (3) false confessions, (4) incentivized witnesses, (5) government misconduct, and (6) inadequate defense. In addition, "tunnel vision" facilitates the intersections of these factors and amplifies their impacts.[16] These factors, also known as the "catalogue of errors," have been well documented and are "canonical" in wrongful-conviction research.[17] Although they can be seen as "isolated and fixable" problems, they in fact occur within a larger culture of popular punitiveness that deeply influences the criminal justice system.[18]

The country's emphasis on the crime-control model and community protection tends to cast due process as an obstacle course and barrier to justice, fortifying a system that is hostile to the rights of defendants.[19] Cultural and political shifts that emerged fifty years ago led to the policy implementations responsible for mass incarceration. They have empowered the criminal justice system in such a way that public demands for punishment powerfully influence routine law enforcement and prosecutorial processes and supersede concerns about collateral damages.

A system of norms prevails in law enforcement, district attorneys' offices, and the courthouse, including "the presumptions that most clients are in fact guilty" and emphasizing "processing, labeling, and sanctioning offenders" as the legitimate outcome of justice.[20] The former prosecutor Mark Godsey argues that elected district attorneys and judges have no choice but to appear tough on crime, which makes for a system that as a whole is "structurally imbalanced in favor of convictions."[21]

Social and political pressures contribute to confirmation bias and tunnel vision: state actors at every stage of the process start with a presumption of guilt and tend to gravitate only to information that supports their view of the suspect.[22] Confirmation bias and tunnel vision enhance the likelihood of official misconduct, including *Brady* violations and some aggressive interrogation techniques that can elicit false confessions. They also increase the likelihood that police and prosecutors will give credence to problematic or inconclusive forensic evidence and can motivate them to unethically incentivize witnesses such as incarcerated informants ("jailhouse snitches").

The New True narrate and dramatize the practices that contribute to wrongful conviction and are didactic in providing in-depth and nuanced illustrations of processes that lead to human tragedies. Each inform and educate audiences—the general public—with vocabulary, legal concepts, cases, and case law on innocence issues. In *Serial*, Koenig presents an argument that Syed's attorney failed in her responsibility to him and was incompetent, and by emphasizing gaps in the recording of Wilds's confession, she suggests it might have been coerced; the prosecution attacked Peterson with the unethical testimony of their forensic expert. But the state's most dramatic abuses of power are narrated in the cases of the poor defendants in *Paradise Lost, Making a Murderer,* and *The Innocent Man.* Additionally, both *Atlanta Monster* and *Atlanta's Missing and Murdered* present stories about the troubling behavior of the FBI agents and officials from the city of Atlanta and state of Georgia. We also see examples of bad eyewitness identification procedures and incentivized witness testimony in *The Innocent Man,* which I will discuss in the overall context of state misconduct. The series' strength lies in their ability to garner sympathy for the defendants, to cast them as victims, and to demonize the state. They are able to frame wrongful-conviction issues through emotionally charged scenes, constructions of villains, and complex plotlines, narrative techniques that are linked to influencing public opinion on issues.[23]

False Confessions

False confessions are an integral part of innocence work because of their prevalence and their undisputed contribution to wrongful convictions. Coerced false confession is among the leading causes of wrongful convictions, with some studies showing that it contributed to more than 25 percent of exonerations made through postconviction DNA testing.[24] False confessions are usually elicited from suspects under intense interrogation, and when these cases go to trial, the usually recanted confessions are nonetheless still known to result in a wrongful conviction.[25]

Interrogation strategies that have been shown to produce false statements have been well documented. Most suspects who make false confessions have been aggressively interrogated for many hours, often through the night, without a break.[26] They are sleep deprived and hungry and thirsty. Interrogators refuse to consider their denials and are allowed to lie to suspects, saying, for example, that they have failed poly-graph tests and that eyewitnesses saw them at the scene. This can cre-ate an overwhelming feeling of hopelessness.[27] Interrogators also often position themselves as vehicles for more lenient sentencing, potential saviors of the defendants, who they say are facing dire outcomes, and they attempt to convince suspects that a confession is in their best in-terests. If this takes place in a state with the death penalty, interrogators often portray that sentence as the inevitable trial outcome if the suspects do not confess. Interrogators then engage in processes of minimization, offering an account of events that seemingly makes the alleged perpe-trators appear less culpable and more sympathetic and provides plau-sible justifications for the crimes, or "a face-saving alternative."[28] Finally, interrogators provide opportunities for "coerced revisions," supplying information about the crimes that only the perpetrator would have ac-cess to and supplying language more in line with the facts. All this can lead a suspect to say anything they think interrogators want to hear "to get the interrogation to end and minimize the punishment," which they begin to see as "the lesser of two evils."[29] They just want to go home.[30] Very young people and those with developmental disabilities and mental illness are far more vulnerable to coercive techniques and more likely to make a false confession.[31]

Interrogators' aggressive questioning techniques are animated by their belief in the suspect's guilt. Training techniques can reinforce "gut hunches" that are often based on mistaken assumptions.[32] Many offi-cers are trained to detect signs of lying, which they believe are indicated when the suspect appears anxious or engages in certain nonverbal sig-nals, although most people would have some degree of anxiety under an interrogation. Studies in fact indicate that police are no better at detect-ing deception than others are and perform the same as chance.[33] Belief in the certainty of the suspect's guilt contributes to a confirmation bias, in which behavior and information supporting one view is focused on while contradictory information is ignored, further strengthening the state's confidence.

A confession, more than anything else, powerfully and irrevocably destroys any vestige of the presumption of innocence, which law enforcement now see as irrefutable.[34] Studies with mock jurors show that they view confessional evidence as more incriminating than any other type.[35] Indeed, "there is no piece of evidence that *if put before a jury* is more likely to lead to a wrongful conviction."[36] Mock juries are far more likely to convict when there is a confession, even one supplied by an accomplice or informant.[37] This is largely because people find it impossible to believe that an innocent person would confess to something they did not do.[38] Studies have additionally shown that even when jurors understand that a confession was elicited in unethical and coercive conditions, they still make a fundamental attribution error, seeing it as indicative of the defendant's actual guilt, rather than the situation.[39]

The average person's inability to accept that an innocent person would falsely confess may be an underlying cause of our fascination with watching them. In the New True, the videotaped confessions are returned to again and again, a twist on Marc Seltzer's view of the wound. Here the crime is the interrogation; we see the force of the state badgering an undereducated, confused, frightened, cognitively ill-equipped, and bewildered innocent young person right in front of our eyes. The state plays these coerced confessions for the jurors, convinced that they prove guilt, but the filmmakers play them to indicate the opposite. For all three storytellers—the prosecution, the defense, and the documentarians—the confessions have highly persuasive emotional power, representing battles of good and evil. For the state, the interrogators are truth and justice seekers, but for defense (and the filmmakers), the defendants are innocent victims of unethical, overwhelming domination tactics.

The convictions in *Paradise Lost* (Jessie Misskelley), *Making a Murderer* (Brendan Dassey), and *The Innocent Man* (focusing on Tommy Ward and Karl Fontenot) all involved false confessions. Misskelley and Dassey were both teenagers with low IQs; Fontenot similarly is alleged to have had a low IQ; and Ward was a young man who had dropped out of high school. In all four cases, the confession was the only evidence against the defendant. They are textbook examples of the power of confessions in convictions despite a lack of corroborating evidence. Dassey's confession is even taught in law school as an example of coercive tactics because, like the others, it bears all the hallmarks of the phenomenon. In *The Innocent Man* and *Paradise Lost*, the confessions trumped the defendants' solid alibis.

The confessions in *The Innocent Man* seem bizarre and surreal for a couple of reasons. Ward, like Williamson before him, confessed through a dream he recounted, which Tweel reenacts in ominous, shadowy scenes with foreboding music. The two confessions bear eerie similarities and raise unsettling questions: Were the defendants drugged while in jail? Were they hypnotized? Tweel frames them as too unusual to be coincidences and embeds the confessions within his overall narrative of state misconduct, suggesting that the dreams were products of an illicit ploy on the part of Ada law enforcement. When Ward had originally been brought in for questioning, after a caller identified him as resembling the composite drawing, he was let go because his alibi checked out. Months later, he was brought in again, and after nine hours of interrogation, he finally relayed the dream. He describes being at the town's cement plant with three other people and a truck; then he is at his kitchen sink washing dark liquid off his hands. The police told him that this matched the facts of the case, as someone had seen a pickup truck at Harraway's store. They then threatened him with the likelihood of the death penalty if he did not confess and followed this with more information, including the identity of two men with him. Ward's dream now includes Karl Fontenot and another man (who was quickly cleared as a suspect because of an indisputable alibi) and a rape and stabbing. The interrogators insisted the dream was in fact real, primed Ward to express the details that way, and brought in the camera to tape his story as a confession. This was the only evidence against him, corroborated by "facts" recounted in Fontenot's coerced confession, which later proved to be wrong (such as the blouse described in Exhibit A). Ward's case and his confession are the subject of two episodes of the podcast *Wrongful Conviction: The Confessions.*

The case against sixteen-year-old Brendan Dassey in *Making a Murderer* was also based entirely on his confession, which has been analyzed multiple times by a variety of wrongful-conviction experts. Brendan was reading at a fourth-grade level and was described by a psychologist as socially immature. The filmmakers show many excerpts of his confession, three hours of which were played for the jury. Significantly, the prosecution omitted the last hour and thirty-eight minutes, wherein Dassey explains to his mother that they "got to [his] head." I found these scenes painful to watch—Dassey seems so passive and dumfounded and miserable, utterly helpless. His responses to questioning are shocking in their naivety. When asked, "What did [Avery] do to her head?" he struggles and finally offers, "cut off her hair," showing his inability to understand the gravity of the situation or what they are investigating.[40]

Elements of these scenes function like another *punctum* (a "detail" whose "mere presence changes [the] reading"), disrupting the generally accepted and expected flow of events with the unintended prick of Dassey's elemental and essential lack of comprehension.[41] When "cut off her hair," fails to satisfy interrogators, they repeat the question, and this time Dassey says, "punched her." The next time they ask, he says, "cut her." Exasperated, police finally ask, "Who shot her in the head?!"[42] Here it seems clear they have fed him information they already had and have coaxed his statement.

The hopelessness of the situation, in which Dassey is outmatched by trained professionals, is captured in a phone conversation with his mother, who is terrified by the unfolding events. Trying to explain to her what happened in the interrogation he asks, "What does 'inconsistent' mean?" and she responds, simply, "I don't know exactly," exemplifying the family's powerlessness and lack of resources. Without access to the vernacular of the law, they become its victims.[43]

Dassey's mother is shocked that he would confess to something so awful if he did not do it, and he tries to explain that it was because they told him they already knew he did it. When she asks him how he came up with the gory details, he says he guessed. He was trying to find the answer they wanted. He appears completely lacking in guile when he then admits, dejectedly, "That's how I do my homework too." In a later conversation, Dassey's mother becomes frustrated with him and tells him he better "start thinking." He asks, helplessly, "How can I do that? I'm really stupid, Mom. I can't help it."[44] These scenes cast the Averys as sympathetic, even pathetic, and in this light, the state's actions seem incomprehensibly cruel.

The power of confessions over other forms of evidence can be persuasive to defense attorneys, who in some cases will treat their clients more harshly and expend their efforts trying to minimize punishment rather than prove innocence.[45] Dassey's second round of attorneys claim that his original lawyer and his investigator "failed in their loyalty to their client" because they chose to believe the confession and wanted Dassey to plead guilty.[46] These men are portrayed as villains and are often filmed basking in media attention. We see them speak to Dassey aggressively, as if they are interrogating him. They want him to provide details of the crime, and when Dassey tries to explain that he did not do it, the investigator insists, "That's not true."[47]

Dassey's attorney offers the police another interview with him without the attorney or his mother present. This time the police intimidate him but do not get another confession. They tell him to call his mother and tell her what happened. Passive and docile, he calls her, and in this recorded exchange, he tells her did it. He again quickly recants, and this appears to be a momentarily "coerced internalized" confession in which an "innocent but malleable" suspect is repeatedly told there is "incontrovertible evidence of their involvement" and comes to believe that he did it.[48] Rather than cement Dassey's guilt in the minds of the documentarians and many viewers, this further paints him as confused and ill equipped. When the judge learns that Dassey's attorney allowed him to be interviewed alone, the attorney is dismissed. His new attorney is an innocence lawyer with expertise in false confessions who was responsible for passing the law that made it mandatory for law enforcement in Wisconsin to video interviews.

Official Misconduct

Whereas the state attempts to cast the defendants as deviant, the New True cast the state as villainous. In the confessions, we see experienced adult interrogators callously overwhelm helpless youths using badgering tactics and deceptive techniques. They emerge as bullies willfully unaware of or unconcerned with the harms they are inflicting. This characterization becomes part of an overarching narrative about state misconduct and state harm. The defense positions in *Making a Murderer, The Innocent Man*, and *Atlanta Monster* and *Atlanta's Missing and Murdered* make the state's violations the centerpiece of their arguments.[49]

The tension in this arc is not about detecting the unseen sociopath in our midst; it veers from identifying the perpetrator of the murders toward the perpetrators of injustice instead. It is an altogether different thrill: detecting the hidden, coordinated, malign activities of the powerful other. This suggests another kind of ontological insecurity and lack of trust in appearances. As previously mentioned, the political thrillers that proliferated in the 1970s are in some ways antecedents of the new crime documentaries, playing to and creating a kind of agitated/pleasurable paranoia about authority. Unlike the corporate executives and political agents in those earlier films, however, law enforcement in *Making a Murderer* and *The Innocent Man* are not sleek, upper-crust, power brokers with access to high-tech surveillance they can use to protect their wealth and dominance. They do not wield the cultural authority of the actual American elite running companies and governments and are only slightly less excluded from such powerful arenas as the impoverished men they arrest and put behind bars. I see these docuseries as offering a form of "conspiracy low" that examines far less glamorous and much more mundane instances of coordinated criminal corruption.

Official or state misconduct generally accounts for over half of all exonerations.[50] The term refers to the violation of duty in the course of an investigation or prosecution of a criminal case. In an analysis of exonerations in 2021, the National Registry of Exonerations reported that 77 percent were attributed to official misconduct, including misconduct by prosecutors and by police.[51] Misconduct is understood in terms of discrete behaviors that include concealing exculpatory evidence, misconduct at trial, witness tampering, fabricating evidence, and misconduct in interrogations. Misconduct can occur at any stage of the criminal justice process, from the earliest parts of the investigation to charging decisions and discovery.[52]

Law enforcement and prosecutors face community and political pressure to convict, and prosecutors in particular fear being lenient on a defendant who may then be released only to do something truly horrible.[53] Usually elected to office, they are reluctant to be seen as taking the side of the accused.[54] The pressure to convict comes from the belief that "voters use convictions as a quantifiable measure of success."[55] This pressure has been enhanced over decades of popular punitiveness, and wrongful convictions can be seen as the "result of the expansive criminalization of problem behavior" as well as "collateral damage in the war on crime."[56] The punitive culture primes police and prosecutors to pursue convictions at all costs.[57]

Some of the literature on official misconduct emphasizes that law enforcement and prosecutors genuinely believe in the guilt of the defendant when they engage in behaviors that cross the line. They are not generally acting out of malice but instead act out of a sense of the greater good, and "for most prosecutors, cheating is unthinkable."[58] Like cops, they believe they are "the good guys."[59] Yet offices' culture tends to reward behaviors that fall outside the bounds of ethical and legal practice when they are in service of the goal of conviction. In district attorneys' offices, aggression and trial victories are highly prized, reinforcing "the drive to win at all costs."[60] The prevalent belief among law enforcement and prosecutors that most defendants are guilty reinforces and is reinforced by the goals of punishment rather than truth-seeking.[61] Such cultural norms and practices are antithetical to transparency, and police and other state actors distrust review practices and community oversight.

These self-perpetuating pressures and beliefs result in a tendency toward tunnel vision, which contributes to wrongful convictions, amplifying the effects of questionable forensics, coerced confessions, and the other factors.[62] Tunnel vision refers to

> the social, organizational, and psychological tendencies that "lead actors" in the criminal justice system to "focus on a suspect, select and filter the evidence that will 'build a case' for convictions while ignoring or suppressing evidence that points away from guilt" (Findley & Scott, 2006, p. 292). As more resources—money, time, and emotions—are placed into a narrative involving a suspect, criminal justice professionals are less willing or able to process negative feedback that refutes their conclusions. Instead, they may devote additional resources in order to "recoup" their original investment. As a result, evidence that points away from a suspect is ignored or devalued, and latent errors are overlooked.[63]

In the process of investigation, detectives develop a theory of the crime and, convinced of that theory, seek out evidence that proves it. Evidence to the contrary is seen as a hindrance to a righteous goal, not an indication that their theory might be flawed. Toward the end of the "real" goal of convicting the offenders effectively, they may conceal evidence that could subvert that goal, such as the alibis in the cases of Ward and Misskelley.[64] Prosecutors may adopt "a covert work system" that "nourishes a police culture of 'don't write it down' in anticipation of required disclosures," while "lies, cheating, distortions at the lower levels of the system are excused at higher one."[65] There is little accountability for misconduct at any level.[66] At the top, prosecutors are working "within an organizational context" generally "characterized by a presumption of guilt, tunnel vision, and public pressure."[67]

It is important to note, however, that confirmation bias is pervasive, and state actors are not the only ones who engage in it. Defense attorneys must also do a degree of it in constructing a narrative of innocence. And there is no reason to think this tendency does not exist among jurors, who may quickly develop a theory of the case or even come to the jury with one already formed. "Like all decision makers [they] tend to seek out and remember information that is consistent with their verdict preference and scrutinize and reject information that is inconsistent with their preference."[68] Additionally, confirmation bias affects filmmakers and documentarians, not to mention general audiences and cultural critics.

The ruling in *Brady v. Maryland* states that "suppression by the prosecution of evidence favorable to the accused . . . violates due process where the evidence is material either to guilt or to punishment."[69] That is, failing to turn over exculpatory evidence (a *Brady* violation) is not on its own grounds for an appeal, as it also has to be proven that that evidence would have led to a different verdict.[70] And the burden for doing so is on the defense.[71] Sometimes prosecutors omit evidence, and sometimes it has not been provided to them by the police.[72]

Brady violations include not turning over evidence that would impeach the credibility of state witnesses, evidence that implicates another offender or points to an alternative theory of the crime, evidence that could support the defendant's alibi, or evidence of some form of official misconduct at any stage of the investigation. Concealing evidence about alternative suspects has been identified as the most common type of exculpatory evidence not turned over.[73] Falsifying evidence includes planting evidence, providing false evidence for forensic analysis, or falsifying forensic results.[74] Witness tampering includes any form of coercion or threat or manipulation of potential witnesses.[75]

Official misconduct plays a significant role in the narratives told in *Making a Murderer* and *The Innocent Man*, as well as to a lesser degree in the two accounts of the Atlanta murders.[76] The filmmakers present an argument that official misconduct was intended to cement cases against men whom law enforcement presumed guilty in *Making a Murderer* and *Atlanta's Missing and Murdered* (and *Atlanta Monster*), while the story that Tweel relates in *The Innocent Man* suggests the deliberate framing of an innocent man to cover up widespread state corruption. Depicting people as intending to do harm is key to constructing villains, both fictional and real, and law enforcement and prosecutors in these series are portrayed as villains, that is, those who "intend and desire bad outcomes (intentionality), bring about bad outcomes (consequential actions) and are causally responsible for bringing about those outcomes (causal responsibility)."[77]

In *Making a Murderer*, Ricciardi and Demos build plot around elements of Avery's defense as put forth by his trial attorneys (season 1) and his appeals work (season 2). The crux of the argument is that Manitowac County police officers conspired to plant evidence against him. Their motive was resentment and anger over the civil suit that Avery had brought against the county following his highly publicized exoneration for his 1985 conviction. The suit named individual officers as well as the county. Avery's trial attorneys, Dean Strang and Jerome Buting, explain that after a 2005 deposition, the officers all knew they were in serious trouble and that a verdict favorable to Avery was likely. Furthermore, state insurers said their policies did not cover the officers' behaviors, so the county and named individuals (particularly officers James Lenk and Andy Colburn) would be on the hook. As a cousin of Avery explains to the filmmakers, there was no way Manitowac was going to hand over all that money without trouble. Because of the obvious conflict of interest, when Avery became a murder suspect, the nearby Calumet County was put in charge of the investigation, yet in spite of this, Manitowac officers, including Colburn and Lenk, were often on the scene and were the ones who discovered crucial evidence.

Neither Strang and Buting nor Avery's appellate attorney, Zellner, allege that the officers were responsible for the murder of Teresa Halbach. His trial attorneys state they do not believe the cops thought they were framing an innocent man but rather thought he was guilty and planted evidence to prove it. One of his attorneys argues, "They probably had no fear of ever getting caught. . . . Who better than a police officer would know how to frame somebody?"[78] Yet at trial they directly asked Colburn if he was so angry and embarrassed by the lawsuit that he framed Avery, raising the issue of motive for the jury. Zellner also does not claim that the officers actually committed the murder but argues that "the killers benefited from the cops' cover-up."[79] Throughout both seasons, the filmmakers work to paint unsavory portraits of Lenk and Colburn and the district attorney's office that support these theories, casting them as uninterested in ethics, uncurious about facts, and arrogant in their sense of righteousness. Different shots of them suggest villainy, and their expressions range from smug grimaces to hard defiance and blinking worry.

The specific allegations are numerous and include Colburn not reporting a sighting of the RAV4 off the side of a road two days before it was discovered on the Avery property; not writing up the report of the first conversation with Avery (before the RAV4 was found) until eight months later, after he was arrested; Lenk on the scene for several hours after the RAV4 was found but before Calumet County established an official log; planting Avery's DNA from a groin swab (collected after his 1985 arrest) on Halbach's hood latch; planting a key to the RAV4 in Avery's trailer; planting Avery's DNA from a saliva swab (also collected after his first arrest) onto the key; planting DNA from a tube of Halbach's Chapstick onto a bullet fragment; moving bones from the adjacent county gravel pit to the Averys' property; tampering with a vial of Avery's blood to plant in the RAV4 (argued by Strang and Buting) or planting blood collected from Avery's sink during an initial search in the RAV4 (Zellner's theory); and concealing "death porn" from the computer of Bobby Tadych (Avery's other nephew), which would have discredited his witness testimony and would have provided evidence of him as an alternative suspect.[80] The prosecutor is also accused of withholding this same evidence, as well as relying on testimony he knew to be false.

Colburn played a role in many key events in Avery's case. He had received a phone call in the 1990s with a lead on the real rapist in the 1985 case, and he did not report it. Had he done so, Avery could possibly have been released a decade earlier. He was the officer who was told about a sighting of the RAV4 on the side of the road but who failed to call it in. Zellner believes that if Colburn had called it in and gone to find it, Avery would not have been convicted or even arrested.

Ricciardi and Demos devote much of the second season of *Making a Murderer* to details of Zellner's theory and the compelling evidence she produces in building her case. She maintains that Avery's nephew Bobby followed Halbach off the property and murdered her, leaving the vehicle on the side of the road. Zellner's investigation of bone evidence leads her to conclude that he and his stepfather later returned and cut and burned her body at a nearby gravel pit. Then Halbach's ex-boyfriend found the RAV4 when looking for her and decided to move it to Avery's property, presumably out of fear that their relationship conflict would surface and he might emerge as a suspect. He then led the search of the property and gave a camera and general directions to the woman who discovered the RAV4. Manitowac officers on the scene at the Averys tampered with the vehicle, leaving Avery's DNA in several spots, and failed to properly log their comings and goings in order to obscure their tampering. After several searches, they planted the key in Avery's trailer and moved bones to his burn pit. After Dassey's confession and four months after their initial searches, officers returned to the property, where they found a flattened bullet fragment, on which they planted Halbach's DNA.

Zellner crafts an exciting story by presenting compelling evidence to support this version of events and leads viewers through reenactments of each stage. The different instances of official misconduct coalesce into an orchestrated cover-up facilitated by confirmation bias and tunnel vision: once the RAV4 was found, no further leads were explored, and evidence of alternative suspects was dismissed. Dassey's confession strengthened and reinforced law enforcement's commitment to Avery's guilt. Zellner's theory reframes our notion of the evildoer and lawbreaker, ascribing these qualities to the state as embodied in Lenk and Colburn (and District Attorney Kratz, as well as Dassey's first attorney), who all show contempt for the Averys and exude a sense of impunity regarding their own conduct.

In both *Atlanta Monster* and *Atlanta's Missing and Murdered*, we learn that from the earliest disappearances, the Black community in Atlanta believed the investigation into the children's murders involved a cover-up and felt that their concerns and pain were being neglected by the people in power. The community saw the murders as a civil rights issue and held that city officials were more concerned with political consequences than finding the perpetrators and preventing more Black suffering. Well before Williams was a suspect, community members, led by mothers of the murdered children, organized a march on the police commissioner's office, singing civil rights songs and accusing him of willful negligence. While most officials at the time, including the mayor, were Black, Williams's appeals attorneys, including the high-profile civil rights attorney William Kuntsler, believed they had a political need for the killer to be Black. Kunstler claimed that Georgia's governor wanted a Black man found guilty "to prevent a race war," and the mayor was worried that racial violence would destroy the economic progress being made in Atlanta. The HBO series shapes a tragic narrative about the state looking for a scapegoat at the expense of the community.

Officials' desire for a Black suspect might have contributed to the tunnel vision that characterized the Williams case after he was stopped on the bridge. From that moment on, no other leads were followed, even though there were multiple "strands of killings" that investigators came across.[81] The twenty-eight murders suggested a number of possible, and not mutually exclusive, explanations. The two most significant of these was the possible involvement of the Ku Klux Klan and the activities of a known "pedophile ring."[82] The Black community feared that the Klan was responsible for the murders, and investigators had a quite a bit of evidence supporting this theory. A large file of evidence on KKK involvement had never been turned over to the defense, which Wil-

liams's attorneys argued was a clear *Brady* violation. The state had tapes
of interviews with an informant who had infiltrated the Klan and who
described the activities of a group of brothers known as "the Sanders
clan," who broke off with the KKK because it was not "radical enough."[83]
They were notorious drug dealers, and when the informant went to their
house, he observed a collection of several official uniforms. As I noted
earlier, these included those for police, sanitation, and postal workers.
The FBI and GBI (Georgia Bureau of Investigation) theorized that the
killer must have been Black to have been unnoticed, but Williams's attorneys believe a white person in these uniforms would not have attracted attention. Even more troubling, the informant reported that one
of the brothers had bragged about killing Black people. The informant
thought that one of these brothers had killed at least one of the children
who was used in the pattern evidence against Williams. When this man
was interviewed by investigators, he claimed he had been joking. Law
enforcement claimed that further investigations cleared him as a suspect.
Unfortunately for Williams, the tapes of these interviews were destroyed
by the time of his postconviction hearings in 1991. His attorneys argued
that there was enough evidence against the Sanders clan to have produced a different verdict had the state turned it over and claimed that
this was a significant *Brady* violation.

There were also a number of convicted sex offenders in the neighborhood, and some of the victims had been known to go some of their
houses in exchange for money. Some of these men were under investigation for the murders, and one was observed in the laundromat where
one of the victims was last seen. Although this victim had also had the
notorious green fiber on him, the prosecution did not use this victim as
part of the pattern evidence. This case was not included because one of
the sex offenders had been named as a suspect in that murder. As with
"the Sanders clan" evidence, documentation of this investigation was also
never turned over to the defense.

Soon after Williams was imprisoned, some of these men were arrested and convicted of other charges. If they had been involved in some

of the child murders, this would explain the crimes stopping around that time. Because the state did not pursue other theories once it had Williams, it closed all the cases on the children. Both series implicate the state in suppressing evidence for political expediency. If these alternative theories were publicized, Atlanta would appear to be riven by racial conflict and home to a dangerous criminal underworld. These facts would damage the city's emerging reputation as a thriving postracial city and desirable business hub. The documentarians suggest that state actors, worried about optics, had sacrificed the truth in order to close the cases and attribute them all to a lone serial killer.

When an attorney in *The Innocent Man* tells us that Ada is "*Deliverance* country, and a small group of people have controlled the power structure there forever," she alerts us to an impenetrable boundary guarded with hostility to outsiders.[84] Tweel argues that Tommy Ward and Karl Fontenot were wrongly convicted for the same reason that Dennis Fritz and Ron Williamson had been: law enforcement officers and the prosecutor were covering up widespread corruption that included active participation in the Ada drug world, coercive sexual activities in the county jail, and blackmail. We learn of five alternative suspects with records of violence who were not pursued, including the man who actually murdered Carter. *The Innocent Man* posits that these credible suspects could have exposed law enforcement's own criminal conduct. Tweel repeatedly displays photos of lead investigator Dennis Smith, Oklahoma State Bureau of Investigations agent Gary Rogers, Assistant District Attorney Chris Ross, and District Attorney Bill Peterson, along a timeline of parallel events in the two cases, creating a graphic representation of the colluding villains. The black-and-white photos are presumably from the 1980s, but the officers' style and the texture of the images hark back to the pre-civil-rights, Jim Crow South, a time when violence and police authority were infamously intertwined.

In both murder cases, witness reports were undated and statements "sanitized";[85] witnesses were pressured by District Attorney Peterson; the same jailhouse informant was threatened and blackmailed by local authorities and by Peterson; false confessions included descriptions of dreams; and evidence was suppressed against other suspects who were drug dealers. There were 800 pages in the Ada files for the Ward and Fontenot investigation, but the defense received only 150. The defense attorneys believe not only that a *Brady* violation was committed in withholding this from the defense but that law enforcement withheld it from Peterson in an unofficial practice that created a controlled flow of information and gave the district attorney "plausible deniability." While they believe Peterson was responsible for uncovering all exculpatory material, he was able to argue that he only had what the investigators provided him. John Grisham points in his interviews to a general willingness to trust authorities, explaining that juries want to believe the police, they do not want to think police might conceal or distort things, and they tend to think that if someone was arrested, there must be a reason—all of which contributes to the state's ability to act with impunity.

Framing Ward and Fontenot was a multipronged effort. The interrogators at the recording of their confessions included Smith and Rogers. Ward maintains that they told him about the flowered blouse Denice Haraway was believed to be wearing, but the jury was told that only Ward and Fontenot knew what she was wearing and that this detail came from them, not the police. However, a statement about Haraway having a blouse that matched that description was later found in their files. The statement was dated well before Ward and Fontenot had been brought in.

The eyewitness who identified Ward was later said to have claimed that the police had the wrong guy. This witness claims that he had been shown a picture of Ward that was not part of an array and that when he said it could be the same person, police then brought Ward out for him to observe while they transferred him to the lineup room. A local journalist was at the keg party that Ward said he attended the night of Haraway's disappearance, and she relayed this to the lead investigator, Smith, to corroborate Ward's alibi. But she says that he did not want to hear it and walked away from her without writing a report. She was able to testify for the defense at trial, during which she was called into Peterson's office, where she claims she was threatened. Debbie Carter's actual murderer, Glen Gore, also claimed that Peterson threatened him.

The district attorney's threats were a factor in another witness's testimony. Terri Holland was the jailhouse informant who testified against the defendants in both murders, claiming that they each spontaneously confessed to her. Even when juries are aware of a positive incentive offered to jailhouse informants (such as a sentencing recommendation), they are still highly likely to convict when such "secondary" confessions are heard at trial, and incentivized witnesses contribute to 17–45 percent of wrongful convictions.[86]

Several years after the guilty verdicts, Holland signed an affidavit stating that while she was in the Ada jail for drug charges, she was videotaped having sex, sometimes with officers. She claimed that these tapes were then used to blackmail her into testifying against Williamson and Fritz, and Ward and Fontenot. She said that Peterson told her that he had the tapes in a file cabinet and then showed them to her. Assistant District Attorney Ross reportedly joked that she had a "c-spot"—meaning she was able to get full confessions from other inmates. Her husband later said that her testimony saved him from a forty-year prison sentence, and her son claimed that his parents sold drugs with Ada law enforcement, suggesting that Ada officials needed leverage to prevent her from exposing their own drug involvement.[87] We see her life, like others we glimpse in *The Innocent Man*, as ravaged by addiction, which made her additionally vulnerable to the district attorney's office and investigators. Addiction, poverty, and violence form the context for the state's crimes against Ada residents, a milieu in which residents are easily victimized by law enforcement and powerless against the bad acts of the prosecutor.

The New True and Innocence Issues

Some scholars, such as Saundra Westervelt and Kimberly Cook, look at wrongful convictions as instances of state harm, arguing that many of the wrongfully convicted have been incarcerated "as a result of explicit illegal state action or the misapplication of state power. Whether the result of willful, illegal conduct by state officials, implicit public pressure on and tunnel vision by police, an imbalance of resources in favor of the state, or sheer carelessness by investigators and prosecutors, wrongful convictions cause harm and produce victims."[88] Shifting the criminological gaze from the defendant to the state, the New True offer case studies of this type of victimization. Like other victims of state crime, the defendants here are "among the least socially powerful actors," in contrast to the well-funded prosecutors with broad discretionary authority.[89] Their stories provide examples useful for fleshing out a state-harm theory of wrongful conviction.

Westervelt and Cook describe the revictimization that some exonerees have faced, including increased police surveillance and possible "attempts by officials to bait them into activities that could land them back in prison."[90] These experiences are similar to the theory that Manitowac County officials went out of their way to implicate Avery in Halbach's murder following his exoneration for the 1985 rape. The broad authority of the state allows bad-faith actors like those in Ada to victimize innocent residents to protect their own criminal conduct. It also facilitates the state's ability to achieve political goals at the expense of truth, as Williams's defense posits.

Various innocence groups, such as the Innocence Project, the Center for Wrongful Conviction, and the National Registry of Exonerations, have brought numerous cases into public view, and "high-profile cases of innocence have garnered great sympathy . . . toward the wrongfully imprisoned and anger towards the system that caused them."[91] The New True dramatize these injuries by framing state actors as the heroes' antagonists and highlighting the powerlessness of their victims. They further implicate the state in that these narratives suggest the inability of the state to protect citizens from the actual murderers.

Narrative frames of wrongful conviction—the storytelling around this type of injustice—are effective in shifting public attitudes and increasing support for policy reform.[92] The advocacy movements that have formed around individual New True cases attests to the series' capacity to inspire action. Some of their cultural impact is captured in critical reviews, but activists and media writers are a small part of the New True's audiences. Do people believe the theories in the docuseries, or do they see them as biased and manipulative?

Judging the Jury

Redditors came out in support of *Serial* as a catalyst for justice, exposing wrongdoing and error in the criminal justice
process . . . [they] saw themselves as citizens with a stake in
the case—all emphasizing their quest for justice.
—Elizabeth Yardley, David Wilson, and Morag Kennedy,
"'To Me Its [*sic*] Real Life': Secondary Victims of Homicide
in Newer Media" (2017)

OCIAL media transformed our relationship with crime stories
into an interaction. A notable instance of this phenomenon is
the case of Elisa Lam, a young woman who disappeared while
visiting Los Angeles and whose body was later found in the water tank
on the roof of her hotel. Lam had developed a large following on her
Tumblr site, where she kept a daily record of her thoughts. When she
had not posted in a few days, her followers became concerned. When
they learned of her death and saw a surveillance video of her strange
behavior in the hotel elevator, they began investigating on their own,
distrusting law enforcement and official reports. They developed their
own theories of the case and pointed to suspects. When it was determined that Lam's death was an accident related to her mental illness, her
followers refused to accept the conclusion. To this day, the cause of her
death is debated on social media sites such as Reddit.

Thus far, I have closely examined several entwined aspects of the New
True, looking at the roles of evidence and character in the narratives and
how wrongful-conviction issues are presented. From media reviews, we
have a sense of how these series have been received and what parts stand
out, but we do not know the extent to which audiences are agreeing with

the New True. Whose arguments do they believe and why? Audiences often have strong opinions about the cases and seek out a variety of forums to discuss them, as is evident on Twitter, Facebook, and Reddit. Looking beyond reviews to get a better understanding of how audiences responded (particularly their opinion of the jury verdicts and their engagement with innocence issues), I investigated these sites, following lengthy threads and sometimes heated debates. I spent most of my time reviewing Reddit discussions, but I also considered Facebook groups and looked at user reviews on Rotten Tomatoes. I chose to spend most of my time studying subReddits because there is a wider range of these and more detailed discussions. But each platform provides a glimpse into different segments of series' audiences.

Facebook hosts a number of pages and private and public discussion groups devoted to these series. There is a great range in the number of group members and page "likes" among these accounts. The series with the most Facebook followers is by far *Making a Murderer*. One page devoted to it has 517,000 likes, and the group "Theories and Discussion" has 20,000 members. The private discussion group "Justice for Adnan Syed and Hae Min Lee" has 14,800 members. This is mainly for supporters of Syed's innocence (unlike Reddit forums on his case) and features photos of members wearing #freeadnan merchandise.

The private discussion group for *The Staircase* has 3,300 members, and posts here are less unified about Peterson; many believe him to be guilty and use this group to debate the import of evidence and observations about his character. Some posts have little commentary, and some have over eighty comments. A page devoted to the WM3 has 9,300 likes. Damien Echols's own page has 156,000 followers. The page for the *Atlanta Monster* podcast has 7,000 likes, while the page for the HBO series has only 547. I was not able to find a Facebook page devoted to *The Innocent Man*, but a news story on Facebook about vacating Ward's sentence had 713 views.

Reddit is an online discussion forum that began in 2005 and is now the fourth most visited site in the US, behind Facebook, Google, and

YouTube.[1] Writing in the *New Yorker* about the persistent and alarming problem of hate speech on the platform, Andrew Marantz states that its "astronomical popularity seems at odds with the fact that many Americans have only vaguely heard of the site and have no real understanding of what it is. A link aggregator? A microblogging platform? A social network?" It is made up of discussion forums (subReddits) that can have as few as zero or as many as twenty million subscribers.[2] Topics range from current events and news items to baking disasters, hobbies, and popular culture. While many people (including me) find Reddit confusing and do not stay long, "people who do use it . . . often use it all day long, to the near-exclusion of anything else."[3] For this reason, those who discuss the New True on Reddit are probably not typical audience members but rather represent people who are particularly committed to social media and passionate about these series.

Neilson reports that the audiences of subscription streaming services like Netflix skew younger. While Reddit does not collect user data or provide demographic information, one study of the responses of users (known as "Redditors") to *Making a Murderer* includes a survey that indicated that 69 percent were male and 91 percent white.[4] This, of course, cannot be generalized to apply to all Redditors and not necessarily to all viewers of *Making a Murderer* either, but it does provide some insight into the characteristics of New True audiences who are motivated to discuss the series online and who might be disproportionately young, white, and male.

I reviewed the three sites with the intention of understanding how the docuseries impacted audiences' views of the defendant's guilt or innocence, what types of evidence was most convincing, and how audiences engaged larger issues in criminal justice. For each series, I looked on Reddit at subReddits that had the most posts and studied those posts that had over thirty-five comments. There were many for each series, and often they had no comments at all. However, for all these series, there were also many with prolific comments (as many as eighteen hundred). I read over one hundred posts or comments each for *The Stair-*

case, *Making a Murderer*, *Serial* and *The Case against Adnan Syed*, and *Atlanta Monster* and *Atlanta's Missing and Murdered: The Lost Children*. I reviewed slightly less than one hundred for the *Paradise Lost* trilogy (which was released before Reddit became popular) and for *The Innocent Man*, which has not had the same cultural impact as some of the other series.

After my first review of posts, I identified prominent themes pertaining to innocence, evidence, character, juries, and wrongful conviction. From there, I looked at the most substantive responses, reading through them again for more nuance. In the rest of this chapter, I look at how Reddit audiences assessed the guilt or innocence of the defendants with regard to physical evidence and deviance and the extent to which discussions led to a greater awareness of flaws in the criminal justice system and engagement with reform efforts. Many posts addressed the issue of reasonable doubt, which is the subject of chapter 7 and not discussed here.

I did not consider posts about ongoing news stories pertaining to the cases, of which there were many, because I was specifically looking at the impact of what is presented in the documentaries. This proved challenging because even on posts that were devoted to the series, many commenters relied on additional sources of information, such as other podcasts and documentaries, books, news stories, websites, and transcripts, with many Redditors looking for as much information on a case as possible. In fact, on both Reddit and Facebook, users seemed to be more interested in the cases themselves than in the docuseries per se. The docuseries often seemed to function as an introduction to the material, which users then followed up with on their own.

For all of these series, it became clear how much thought Redditors put into their posts, reflecting the amount of time and energy they devoted to understanding the series and the cases. For instance, one individual post on *Serial* was fourteen hundred words. Each series had a number of lengthy posts similar to this. Even though there were some hostile exchanges, for the most part posters were respectful of each other and appreciative of the work others did in articulating issues point by point. Comments such as "Wow, this is great" were common. In some regards, my findings were unsurprising: many Redditors found one piece of evidence against a defendant irrefutable, while many formed opinions about the character and behavior of subjects, usually the defendants, but also of lawyers and members of victims' families. Overall, more people viewed the defendant as guilty than I would have expected.

The first time I watched or listened to each of these docuseries, I too was a wide-eyed audience member, accepting unquestioningly the series makers' narratives of injustice. In contrast, many others felt the juries got it right. Often, they disliked the subjects more than I did. This was particularly true of the middle-class defendants (Peterson, Syed, and Williams), who were each described as narcissists who thought they were smarter than everyone else. Avery and Ward received the most sympathy, with mixed responses to Damien Echols and his codefendants.

Reviewing Reddit, I was disappointed to find that even though many commentators felt cynical and were angry at the criminal justice system and demonstrated sophisticated knowledge of its workings, few engaged problems of wrongful conviction beyond the docuseries. However, the two wrongful-conviction issues discussed the most were false confessions and state misconduct, which reflects the narratives put forth by documentarians. Here I present an overview of how these series were received by audiences and what elements of the narratives were most resonant. All the quotes I have selected are emblematic of sentiments expressed by many others on the forums. All quotes from social media are presented verbatim, with original spelling and grammar.

"If I Shake My Head Anymore, I'll Need Neck Surgery": Brendan Dassey and Steven Avery, *Making a Murderer*

The first season of *Making a Murderer* received an audience score of 96 percent fresh on Rotten Tomatoes, based on 1,975 user ratings. The second season scored 99 percent, based on more than 2,714 user ratings. Most of the user reviews I looked at gave the series four and five stars, and the majority of reviews expressed outrage and dismay and highly praised the series. Here is an example of a common sentiment: "Truly shocking! I'm more disgusted about my government than ever. You couldn't write this because it's so outlandish, you would think it's unbelievable . . . and it's real!!! Wow! One of the best, if not THE best documentary ever."[5] I came across a handful of one- and two-star reviews that complained about *Making a Murderer* being boring, but by far most people found both seasons gripping.

SubReddits for all of these series included long, detailed comments, passionate opinions, and lively back-and-forth. This was most true for both seasons of *Making a Murderer*. These commenters expressed the most emotion about the cases and the way the series presented them. One comment was twelve hundred words. By far most of the Redditors believed Dassey and Avery to be innocent, and they were outraged at what they believed to be an injustice. Those who were not fully confident Avery was innocent believed there was reasonable doubt.

Viewers' emotions about this series have already been analyzed in Liam Kennedy's article "Man I'm All Torn Up Inside: Analyzing Audience Responses to *Making a Murderer*," which looks at 6,005 Reddit comments about the series and which finds that powerful emotional responses include experiences of heartbreak, anger, frustration, and helplessness, which are linked to outrage and criticism of the criminal justice system. Responses included expressions of disgust for individual state actors and beliefs about those who are deserving (Dassey and Avery) and undeserving (law enforcement and prosecutors) of viewers' sympathy.

My own review of two hundred posts and comments on r/MakingaMurderer, including a post that had eighteen hundred comments, also found strong emotional reactions to the series, for example, "God fucking dammit the more I watch this the more enraged I am. This is such horseshit."; "What the actual fuck! It's disgusting."; "I just wish there was something I could do to help, it really hit me hard this series."; "It's been a long time since I ever watched something that made me jump off my couch and say 'Are you fucking kidding me?!'"; and "My GF threatened to turn it off if I couldn't control my outbursts!"[6]

Audience members discussed numerous forms of physical evidence that convinced them of Avery's and Dassey's innocence, as well as of the misconduct on the part of the state. These include the coroner's exclusion from the crime scene, ballistics, the key to Halbach's RAV4, blood, and Halbach's day planner. Many found the prosecution's theory absurd on its face: "I don't get it?! He chained her up in his room, he and Brendan raped her then Brendan cut her throat. They then dragged her out of the trailer and put her in the rav4 trunk and drove to the garage, threw her on the ground and shot her. Then carried her to the burn pit and burned her, then took the bones and put them all over the property and the quarry? There should be blood everywhere!" Redditors engaged in detailed, technical discussions about ballistics, bullet fragments, and the tests that Zellner conducted, including sophisticated analysis such as this:

> Now MAYBE at the distance they were shooting from, the muzzle energy and velocities are similar from both types of guns? Regardless of that, the bullet they used as evidence was lacking trace of bone. . . . Phosphorus was not present at all and there was an abundance of calcium. . . . Calcium is found in concrete. There was wood particles on the evidence bullet that were typical of plywood. Imo, they found a random bullet on the floor that had been fired through a plywood target, exited and hit the concrete floor. I'm not an expert and certainly no investigator, but that should have eliminated that bullet as evidence.

The key to Halbach's vehicle, discovered after numerous searches of Avery's trailer, was also often cited, with Redditors simply pointing out what they believed to be absurd on the face of it: "the fact they found the key after months of searching that room and it only pops up when Colburn was searching the room unattended does create a great deal of suspicion to me." Since they believe the key was planted, their discussions of this issue implicate law enforcement and point to state misconduct, which I address later in this section.

Redditors frequently discussed the lack of Halbach's blood on the Avery property, often expressing incredulity at what they believed was a preposterous theory of the crime, such as the following quotes: "The most important part of the whole case is the total lack of blood evidence. This case should NEVER have gotten this far considering the testimony that her throat was cut in the bed while handcuffed and nobody found any blood to suggest that a throat cutting ever took place!" Another piece of evidence frequently discussed was the handwritten entry in Halbach's day planner, which her ex-boyfriend (Ryan Hillegas) provided to the police. Zellner argues, based on cell phone records, that the entry had to have been written after she left the Avery property. And yet it was not discovered in the RAV4. Instead, Hillegas had it. For Zellner and many Redditors, this means that (a) she left the property alive and the crime did not happen the way the state argued, and (b) Hillegas was somehow involved. Audiences of *Making a Murderer* are not presented with any counterargument for how the entry got there, and many people (including me) found this alone (absent a plausible explanation) very convincing. In response to someone's assessment, "The day planner is so damning," someone else wrote, "Yea, that completely blew my mind. How is that not of interest? That something proven to be on her 20 minutes before her disappearance materialises in the hands of her ex-boyfriend!"

Redditors who discussed Dassey's confession were united in their outrage and their conviction that he was manipulated and coerced. A number of comments revealed that even the few who had some doubts about Avery's innocence firmly believed in Dassey's. They found the video footage of his confession and audio of his conversations with his mother to be the most painful part of the whole painful series, for example, "Listen to the part where his mother asks him why he said the things he said: 'I guessed', 'Like I do on my homework'. He has *no idea* what's going on around him, *no idea* of the gravity of the situation, and they're shoving plea deals in his face, that are effectively holding a gun to his head." Law enforcement's behavior during Dassey's interrogation and his first lawyer's (Kachinsky's) complicity figured high in people's theories about state misconduct, which also included the officers on the scene at the Averys, particularly Lenk and Colburn, as well as the district attorney, Kratz. Viewers expressed horror and disgust about their conduct. As one Redditor put it, "Never were there so many punchable faces in one documentary." This comment continued to specify the behavior of Dassey's attorney: "And OMG, that shitty little grin on that Len dude whenever the media came around . . . and then to see what he did to Brendan . . . argh!" Another commented on this attorney in the larger context of the entire first season:

> First thing I thought when he started showing his true colors was "look at this fucking greasy salamander" That little twerp was IN LOVE WITH THE CAMERA. Sheeesh. I've cried about three times watching this mess. There's just too many fucking ridiculous things to begin to point out. If this was a movie, about half way through I'd be thinking that how I wish the director would've at least tried to keep the story and the characters a little realistic. Can't believe that sheriff saying on fucking TV that if they wanted to eliminate Avery they would've just killed him. Okay so if they wanted to frame him for murder then what would they have done? Fucking hell. I need a drink

Many commenters similarly pointed to what they believed to be a conspiracy within Manitowac County law enforcement to convict Avery: "[Colburn] and Lenk were the worst two people in the whole doc in my opinion. When they played the tape of Colburn calling in the vehicle's plates I thought SURELY that's enough to show corruption. BUT instead he just stammered along and played dumb and no one questioned it for even a second. My neck hurts today from shaking my head so much after that." Many others expressed disgust with the prosecutor (who was later accused of sex crimes): "Just hearing the prosecutor Ken Kratz' high lilting voice slither out of that balloon of a face made me viscerally sick. I knew at about Ep. 4 or 5 that he was sexual pervert. He deserves vigilante justice for what he did in this case, and likely many others." The subReddits included animated discussions of the jury pool and dynamics among jurors. One described them as "absolute knuckle-dragging morons," and many vehemently expressed how they never would have convicted.

Echoing some of the findings in Lourdes Rodriguez et al.'s study of Wisconsin residents' prior knowledge of the case, some Redditors believed that jurors had made up their minds before the case: "They tried the case in Manitowoc county, and I believe a lot of people felt he was guilty before the case was even tried."[7] A number of Redditors commented on the role of the media in influencing jurors: "They held a press conference using the nephew's version of the murder and advertised that as how the murder took place, with no physical evidence to support it." The filmmakers brought attention to how problematic these statements were, and the move seems to have worked: Redditors echoed this critique.

Still others speculated about the jury's decision-making process, citing the filmmakers' suggestion that a few biased jurors had undue influence on the rest: "[One juror] also testified that he was . . . disturbed by the comments of another juror on March 15. He testified that juror . . . made the comment when deliberations began that Mr. Avery was 'f***ing guilty.' . . . In his opinion [those jurors] apparently had made up their minds and were not willing to thoroughly evaluate the evidence." A number used the word "corrupted" to describe what happened in the jury room, and many expressed contempt, such as, "What low-lifes." Judging the jury in this way was a common feature in discussions of some of the other New True as well.

"I Learned a Lot about Law and Murder Cases": Adnan Syed, *Serial* and *The Case against Adnan Syed*

Because *Serial* is a podcast and not a movie or television show, it has no review page on Rotten Tomatoes. I looked for one for the HBO series and kept getting an error message. On Reddit, I reviewed 200 posts and comments about Adnan Syed, regarding *Serial* and the HBO series *The Case against Adnan Syed*, all on the subReddit r/serialpodcast. One post devoted to the HBO series had 79 comments, while the other had 188; two posts on *Serial* had a combined total of over 400 comments.

There were more hostile exchanges in the posts about Syed than in those about any of the other series I reviewed, with people on both sides becoming frustrated with those who held opposing views. The majority of Redditors thought Syed was guilty, but many pushed back on this and argued his innocence. The latter tended to focus on holes in the prosecution's case and the concept of reasonable doubt, rather than a firm view of his innocence. Many listeners of *Serial* enjoyed Koenig's storytelling, regardless of whether they thought Syed was innocent, for example, "But it was such an awesome podcast and it's still a great case to go through all the details. I learned a lot about the law and murder cases."[8]

As with other series, Redditors responding to this series relied on information from other sources. They read complete trial transcripts available online and listened to the *Undisclosed* podcast season devoted to the case. A lot of these posters expressed that the transcripts convinced them of Syed's guilt, making it challenging to gauge the impact of *Serial* and *The Case against Adnan Syed* on their own.

Several Redditors expressed the idea that the opposing argument was not compelling enough. One wrote, "I'm completely open-minded and look forward to factually based reasoning to dispute my belief but, so far, no theory of Adnan's *guilt* that I've seen, ever, has held up to scrutiny" (emphasis added). In response, another wrote, "There's no theory of Adnan's *innocence* that I've seen, ever, that holds up to scrutiny" (emphasis added). These comments indicate that it is less the strength of a single piece of evidence that proves the case against him and more a sense that there is not enough to refute it—or vice versa: that there is too much indicating that he is innocent and not enough to refute that. They also reflect a careful reading of the totality of evidence on the part of these audience members and an ability to weigh the value of each piece.

In response to one Redditor's presentation of evidence in favor of Syed, another wrote, "They are both things that if true, look good for Adnan, but if not true really have no bearing on his guilt or innocence." We also see the ambiguity of evidence, as people applying similar degrees of time, care, and reasoning can come away with polar-opposite conclusions. Sometimes Redditors argued that holes in one side of the argument did not necessarily have that much meaning. In response to questions raised in one comment, a Redditor who thought Syed is guilty said, "all that does is show there [their] investigation may have had holes."

The evidence most often cited as indicating Syed's guilt was the fact that Wilds knew where Lee's car was. This was seen as irrefutable, even as many commenters acknowledged the inconsistencies in Wilds's statements and his possible conflicts of interest. There was much discussion and speculation about Wilds's motives and possible legal predicaments as well as his possible involvement in the murder. People who believed Syed was innocent argued that Wilds was "scripted," yet people who believed Syed was guilty often conceded this as well. They believed enough of what he said. As one wrote, even though Wilds was "doing as the police directed . . . it's hard to refute the basics." Another said, "yeah, Jay's scripted and accomplice but still." These comments reflect an important ability to recognize two things as true and assess their relationship. For this reason, discrediting Wilds (as the defense tried to do) may in some instances only go so far, because people are able to critically assess information in the context of the totality of factors.

Fewer people responded to the posts about the HBO series, and those who did were frustrated that it was "biased" or did not show anything new ("It's definitely biased in favor of Adnan"). The new evidence the producers presented—the condition of the grass under Lee's car, the shoe print that seemed related to work in concrete, more information about Don, Lee's boyfriend at the time of her murder, and a copy of the class schedule of one of the teens—was largely not seen as convincing, although I reviewed much discussion of the class schedule and at least one debate about whether this was actually shown in the documentary (it was). Audience members did appreciate being able to see the "characters" and video footage of the trials (which a number of posters felt "solidified Adnan's guilt"). The series importantly gave dimension to the people whom podcast listeners had come to know through their voices and Koenig's description.

Syed's case had initially been brought to Koenig by his family friend Rabia, whose efforts on his behalf are featured in the HBO series. Many commenters thought the makers of *The Case against Adnan Syed* were championing his cause, rather than presenting an objective inquiry— that it was "really Rabia's cause," "it's really the Rabia show, all in all," "propaganda" for her "agenda," and "another move by Rabia and Co." Rather than sympathizing with her, many people strongly disliked her. A few mentioned that the series inadvertently changed their opinion from innocent to guilty, for example, "To be honest from listening to the podcast I harbored some serious doubts about Adnan's guilt. Watching that show basically erased those doubts and made me believe: 1. Adnan is definitely guilty. 2. Rabia is a self-serving slime bag operating in bad faith." In general, many people characterized Syed as "a narcissist" and also disparaged Wilds. However, the posts specifically about the HBO series focused more on characterizing secondary characters; they negatively assessed Rabia and Syed's family members while praising the former friends of Syed, Lee, and Wilds. While the majority of all posters saw Syed as guilty, in the posts I looked at, this was even more so on those that focused on the HBO series.

"Spatter Is Not Just a Blood Stain": Michael Peterson, *The Staircase*

Users on Rotten Tomatoes gave *The Staircase* an 83 percent audience score, based on 318 ratings, with scores ranging widely from one star to five. While many users found Peterson guilty, a number believed in his innocence. One reviewer called it "one of the great documentaries of our time" and praised it for its footage and allowing "the viewer to learn new information and to sit with it and be a part of this family," while others complained that it dragged and did not go anywhere.[9]

I reviewed nearly 150 posts and comments on the subreddit r/TheStaircase, including one with 156 comments and one, titled "Reasons I think MP is guilty," with 354 comments. One Redditor posted a fourteen-hundred-word comment that dissected many details of the case, point by point, as others have done on subReddits for other series. The majority of respondents believed that Petersons was guilty. Those that did not usually pointed to reasonable doubt and, while outraged at an injustice, did not feel confident in his innocence. A number of Redditors posted links to other sources. Many watched YouTube videos on the case and read the autopsy report, and more than one researched the local weather on the night of Kathleen's death, when Peterson claimed they were sitting by the pool and he was wearing shorts when the police arrived. One poster claimed that "a forensic meteorologist was consulted (no kidding)."[10] Another, who had read the autopsy report, wrote with an air of medical expertise, "she had lacerations only in the portion/dorsum of the hands and arms." This poster believed Peterson guilty, but another responded, with a similar air of expertise, "Blunt force trauma to the head does not always cause fracture," and then mentioned "the occipitial [*sic*] region" and provided a link to the National Institute of Health website.

In *The Staircase*, we hear Peterson's defense team discussing how incriminating and problematic the blood at the scene is to their case. The defense believed that this, more than anything else, needed to be explained. It is also what Redditors most pointed to in arguing his guilt. They referred to the fact that the blood had dried by the time the police arrived, that there were tiny spots of blood on Peterson's shorts, that luminol showed evidence that blood had been cleaned up, and that blood was on the door frame to the pool area, as well as referring to the direction of the spatters and "the sheer amount of blood." Debates on the nuances of this evidence included Redditors asserting their knowledge in phrases such as, "Spatter is not just a blood stain. By definition, it's a blood stain that is a result of splatter from force." Although blood evidence was cited repeatedly as evidence of guilt, some Redditors questioned its salience, echoing arguments made by Peterson's defense.

Lestrade made much of the missing and later somewhat mysteriously found blow poke. As we have seen, the filmmaker devotes considerable footage to it. Few Redditors found this compelling one way or the other. I did not come across any poster who cited it as evidence of guilt, and one person, who believed Peterson was guilty, said, "it was stupid for the prosecution to assume and talk about that shit during trial."

Although Lestrade has maintained that he does not know if Peterson is innocent, he also presents a documentary that some viewers, including Reddit users, have seen as championing him.[11] *The Staircase* comes across as supporting Peterson's defense, and presumably the filmmakers found him sympathetic. One of the producers even began a romantic relationship with him while they were filming.

Yet many of the posters on Reddit found Peterson extremely distasteful. Many believed that the way he acted, both at trial and, more often, on camera for the series, indicated that he was guilty and not deserving of sympathy. They cited his "over-the-top attempts to sound romantic," his "smoking a cigar and speaking about Kathleen's death . . . as if he's remembering it fondly," and his "romantic life of leisure. Wine by the pool" as reasons they disliked and distrusted him and thought he seemed guilty. One said, "He's a bit of a strange man. . . . Difficult to relate to. Difficult to read or perceive. . . . He's always smoking his pipe, talks to[o] analytical of the situation he is in." A few argued that his 911 call seemed "staged" and "phoney." His demeanor and behavior were cited as often as physical evidence against him, and a number argued that he was a "narcissist" or "sociopath."

On the other hand, sometimes Redditors pushed back against these assessments, with one stating, "I don't care about a suspect's aloof behavior. People respond to the extrema of human experience in wildly differing ways." Another wrote, "Man, you are way too confident in your assessment of human behavior." Some took issue with diagnosing someone on the basis of how they are presented in the series, and others questioned the concept of a sociopath: "I would love if any of you people accusing MP of being a sociopath could perhaps prove your ability to diagnose somebody as one?" Echoing Janet Malcolm's description of the paradox inherent in the term, one wrote, "It's also very convenient for your argument that sociopaths are able to replicate emotions for certain situations when needed. Because it means that literally any emotion shown by MP can be explained away."

While most posters found Peterson guilty, often the same behavior was read by some as incriminating and by others as exculpatory. One poster found him "somewhat endearing, like when they show him playing with his grandsons." But another used the same behavior to express their disgust: "I was sick to the stomach of looking/listening to Michael Peterson. His pathetic attempt of acting deep and tortured. . . . His weird fuck up dynamic with his creepy step daughters and arrogant prick of a son. The way he plays 'granpappy' to whoever kids they were." It is worth noting that even his relationship with his daughters was interpreted differently. The preceding poster called it "fuck up," while another said, "I think they have a wonderful relationship with their adoptive father." Still another described it as "codependent" and "a cult of the parent." Whether they interpreted Peterson's character and behavior in a negative or positive light, Redditors engaged in discourses around his deviance and linked it to their assessment of his guilt or innocence.

"You're Just Filled with Racist Bullshit, Aren't You?": Wayne Williams, *Atlanta Monster* and *Atlanta's Missing and Murdered: The Lost Children*

Because *Atlanta Monster* is a podcast, it did not have a Rotten Tomatoes score, and the fresh score of 67 percent for the HBO series was based on only fifteen ratings. The reviews for it were mixed, with some praising it for being informative and others noting that it contained little new information.

More so than for the other series, comments about the Atlanta murders on Reddit relied on other sources, and the subReddits on which people posted about them were not devoted specifically to the series. Many Redditors were familiar with the case prior to the podcast and HBO docuseries. They had read books about it and watched other documentaries, in addition to finding documentation, testimony, and other information online. A number of people claimed that they had watched, read, or listened to everything they could find on the case. One person described themselves as "obsessed" since listening to *Atlanta Monster*.[12] I looked at five posts devoted to the series that each had between 46 and 128 comments. There was more discussion of the HBO series than of the podcast, and many Redditors disliked the latter and praised the former (although some critiqued the HBO Max series for being biased in favor of Williams). Almost everyone who posted thought Wayne Williams committed *some* of the murders, but hardly anyone thought he committed *all* of them. Only three thought he was not responsible for any of them. The racial issues raised in the series and the podcast were often discussed, and those who thought he committed some of the murders still recognized racist elements at work in the investigation and articulated an understanding of the racial dynamics in Atlanta at the time.

Unlike discussions of the other series, which concern a single murder, opinions on the Atlanta murders covered a range of views beyond the binary of guilty/innocent. Many felt definitively that Williams did not kill the two female children. Others believed that he killed only one of the adult victims. As mentioned, very few thought he committed either none or all of the murders, and there were Reddit comments expressing everything in between, from "I definitely believe WW is guilty and killed *most* of them" (emphasis added) and "He probably didn't commit all the murders" to "I feel that there were tow [two] or maybe even more perpetrators responsible but Wayne killed some of those children, at least more than what he was convicted for," "at least one killer was never caught," and "I don't think there is 1 Atlanta Child Murderer." Some were "on the fence" about "whether he was innocent, guilty of some murders, or guilty of all" but still thought there was "no way he could have dropped all of them, like mathematicly, surely?"

There was some degree of discussion of the fiber evidence, but this was not what animated most of the posters. Many posters pointed to the unlikely explanation that Williams gave for being on the bridge that night. A number of Redditors pointed to its seeming absurdity: "WW claims that he was checking on a house the night on the bridge is just bonkers, was he going to knock on the door at 2 in the morning just to check that the right person lived there, it's making an extra trip out in order to try to save yourself a trip."

Yet other Redditors brought up the fact that had Williams not been on the bridge that night, there would be no case against him. In addition to the fibers and bridge incident, other posters thought the fact that the murders stopped after Williams was arrested was particularly compelling ("It is amazing how the murders stopped after he was caught"). Although both the podcast and HBO series offer the counterargument that some possible perpetrators were soon incarcerated on other charges and that others might have stopped when they realized Williams's arrest was opportune for them, many Redditors still brought up this point. Still others were impressed by the brother of a victim who was interviewed in both the podcast and the series and who claimed that he distinctly remembered being taken by a man he was certain was Williams.

In one way or another, many Redditors expressed that Williams was "his own worst enemy" and that he "trips himself up in lies almost every time he is interviewed." A number of Redditors were frustrated by the conflicting accounts of the Post-It note containing the phone number of the woman whom Williams claimed he had an appointment with. Many discussed how at one point, he says his mother wrote the note, and at another, he says that he did: "I am not sure whether his final story was that he, or his mother, was the one who talked to the mystery Cheryl. This whole story was very suspicious."

A number of commenters took issue with Williams's personality and demeanor, believing that he was "smug" at trial and that he was "a narcissist who . . . thought he was smarter than everybody else." Even those who did not think his personality should have played a role in the jury decision made statements like, "his smart-assed attitude and losing his temper on the witness stand definitely di[d] not help him in court." And those who gave him the benefit of the doubt conceded that "Wayne is sketchy for sure."

Usually, when Williams's character and behavior were mentioned, it was to argue his guilt, but a number of interesting comments echo James Baldwin's assessment of Williams as overprotected and lacking the will or follow-through to pull off any murder. A few times Redditors described him as too "nerdy" to have committed the crimes. One poster who claimed to have grown up in the community said, "I'm still not buying that a little 5'5 nerdy, pampered and sheltered grown man from a good home was able to hang out in the worst areas of Atlanta and overpower a bunch of street kids. . . . Doesn't make any sense. . . . Bro, I grew up in that same part of Atlan[ta] a lot of those kids where from." This poster went on to argue, "he would've become a Vic to a robbery long before he ran his tally up to 20+ kids."

Even among those Redditors who thought Williams was guilty of some of the murders, many thought it was unjust that he was held responsible for all of them. Audiences of the podcast and HBO series engaged a number of theories about Williams's possible wrongful conviction, and there were animated discussions of law enforcement practices and racism. Both series highlighted the possibility that members of the KKK were involved and suggested that federal and state investigators did not sufficiently follow up on this theory. Overall, there was a willingness to believe that the "Sanders brothers" might have murdered some of the children or at least that this either needed further exploration or more presentation to the jury. The poster I quoted earlier who claimed to be from the neighborhood wrote, "after watching the HBO doc and hearing them mention the part about the KKK brothers having a shit load of official uniforms brought everything home for me. That makes sense. White men in an official looking uniform posted in the hood all day and no one bats an eye." Overall, Redditors were receptive to the idea that white men had committed some of the murders, that racial hatred was the motivating factor, and that Atlanta officials were worried about exacerbating racial tensions in the city.

A number of comments expressed sympathy for the families of the children and the Black residents of Atlanta who distrusted law enforcement and believed that their interests were not served by officials at the time. Their distrust was described as "justified," and many, including those who believed that Williams committed some of the murders, expressed a belief that justice was not fully served. One Redditor (who relied on numerous sources in addition to the HBO series) stated that they "came away with 'huge miscarriage of justice for all of these victims & their families' (still undecided on WW)." Many of these Redditors, regardless of how many murders they attributed to Williams, understood race to be at the heart of the case—even if it was not a factor behind the murders, it was a significant factor in the investigation, trial, and aftermath. On the other hand, many Redditors felt that race was overemphasized and an "excuse." They claimed that people wanted to point to race "no matter what" and that arguing that the Williams case was mishandled because of it was "racist bullshit." One person expressed a view held by a number of posters: "Many members of the black community don't want to accept that a black man murdered these children. As one of the police officers said, 'If Williams stood up and confessed to every one of the murders, there would still be those who would say a white man murdered the children.'"

"I Enjoy Having Discussions with People Who Have Done their Homework": The West Memphis Three, *Paradise Lost* trilogy

On Rotten Tomatoes, each of the films in the trilogy is rated separately. The first, *Paradise Lost*, received an 84 percent audience score, based on more than five thousand ratings. *Revelations* received 84 percent, based on more than twenty-five hundred ratings, and *Purgatory* received 93 percent, with more than one thousand ratings. Many reviewers found it compelling and expressed that it offered insight into the criminal justice system.

There are far fewer posts on subReddits about the *Paradise Lost* trilogy than about the other series, perhaps because the last episode of the trilogy aired in 2011, and the series is in some ways a precursor to the New True. I reviewed just under one hundred comments from four posts on r/WestMemphisThree with as few as fifteen comments and no more than forty-seven, and every post I read relied on sources in addition to the trilogy. These included another documentary (*West of Memphis*), the book *Devil's Knot*, transcripts of Misskelley's confessions, the autopsy reports on the victims, and other online sources, some of which were directly linked to. In fact, having done research was a point of pride for many Redditors ("I enjoy having discussions with people who have done their homework").[13] A couple of Redditors mocked their own air of expertise, for example, "Source: too many forensic files type shows, true-crime books, and pulled from my own ass." Often Redditors complained about how much evidence they believed *Paradise Lost* left out. Many expressed that at first, after only seeing the film, they "leaned towards innocence": "but when I researched the case I became more & more convinced of their guilt." One Redditor echoed others' sense of confusion about conflicting information: "I believed they were innocent after watching the documentaries but after reading a bit into the evidence I'm a lot more skeptical of that, but it's way too much of a rabbit hole so I just like reading Reddit comments about it and remaining neutral haha."

As with the other series, often the comments were lengthy (such as a fourteen-hundred-word one that presented evidence in a point/counterpoint style), and Redditors expressed appreciation for the work others had done in laying out their arguments: "I actually had to do a lot of online research to come up with what I did. I just looked at the evidence logically. I just wanted to see what other people thought and I got that. Thank you again for a great discussion." The evidence from the series they discussed includes the confession, the possible bite marks, the knife found in the lake behind one of the teens' homes, and the two alternative suspects whom the series explores.

Similar to the discussions about *Serial*, Redditors discussing the West Memphis Three felt that people made up their minds one way or the other early on and were not willing to change it: "people in the innocent camp seem to have already made their minds up and won't accept glaring evidence." Another similarity with other New True is that Redditors pointed out a few times that the same piece of evidence can have different interpretations and lead to different conclusions: "Guess what? I've seen the same evidence. I came to a different conclusion. It's extremely condescending to assume that people who think they're innocent only believe so because they watched a movie."

Deviance was often raised in relation to the teens, whom, to my surprise, the majority of Redditors believed were guilty, particularly Damien. While they often made clear that they were not judging him for his tastes in clothes and music and did not believe the satanic rumors, they characterized him as "troubled" and "violent" from their reading of other sources. A number of the posters took issue with the trilogy for making it look like the prosecution's case was only about his style and hobbies and, by so doing, painting Damien and his codefendants as sympathetic. One stated, "I'm literally disgusted at all the information the Paradise Lost series leaves out. Damien Echols ABSOLUTELY is a psychopath and horrible person." Another explained their theory of his character: "[They] present something that a lot of us could relate to in our high school days—the all black clothes, the emo haircut, the lone wolf rebellious attitude. Damian is just like us! But no, he's not. He bites people and tries to lick their blood. He hurts animals. He makes descriptive threats to his loved ones. He journals about satanism and obsesses over the sacrifice aspect of it. He wants. To. Hurt. People. Why won't people see this is a bad thing?" Among the few who thought the teens were innocent were some who believed the jury was biased. One lengthier comment implicated provincial thinking and West Memphis residents' willingness to believe the worst of a nonconformist:

> It seems to me that everybody had their mind made up on this case from the beginning. Nobody was going to convince them otherwise. . . . Was the jury wrong? No the prosecution, judge and pathologist were wrong this is a fact. Which convinced the jury to make the wrong decision. Again I am using common sense here if the original jury had heard all the evidence available today they would have never convicted these three. . . . These guys never had a chance. . . . The prosecution seized upon the hysteria and fear of satanic cults and used this to convict them. Just because Damien practiced Wicca doesn't make him a Satanist quite the opposite actually. You can't convict somebody just because they think differently then [than] the moral majority of people. It's just not right.

"Why Does American Justice Not Learn from Its Mistakes?": Tommy Ward, *The Innocent Man*

The Innocent Man received a 74 percent audience score, based on eighty-seven Rotten Tomato ratings, and many reviewers critiqued it for jumping around and utilizing convoluted narrative techniques. Yet they often still found the story engaging, and some were shocked by the injustice and flaws in the system.

There were many subReddits about Karl Fontenot's and Tommy Ward's sentences being vacated in 2019 and 2020, a year after *The Innocent Man* first aired on Netflix. Most of these posts linked to recent news stories and had few comments. Constraining myself only to posts focusing on the Netflix documentary, I reviewed only three, as few had more than a handful of comments. The posts I reviewed from r/TheInnocentMan had fourteen, thirty-five, and thirty-eight comments, and very few Redditors expressed a belief in the defendants' guilt, although a very small number remained unsure of their innocence ("we just will never really know").[14] Some Redditors highly praised the series: "Strap yourself in for a crazy story. . . . Just when you think you know what's going on the rug is pulled out from under you several times." Others were more lukewarm. Among those who relied on other sources were many who had read the Grisham book, and these Redditors consistently stated that the series was less thorough, glossing over crucial information and only telling a partial story.

Posters often expressed outrage and dismay about the injustice done to Tommy Ward and Karl Fontenot (as well as to Ron Williamson and Dennis Fritz), and some had emotional responses: "It angers me that life means so little to people that someone sent to prison, for life are no problem to them as long as their asses are covered & they can mark something as solved." Such outrage was often voiced in the context of discussions that raised issues relating to wrongful conviction. This is to be expected, since the series highlighted multiple examples. Redditors reflected on the unreliability of eyewitness identification and unethical interrogation techniques, often recognizing the danger for innocent defendants when the prosecution presents a weak case.[15] They recognized that problematic forms of evidence, such as tainted identifications and confessions that recount dreams, can lead to wrongful convictions. Several Redditors argued for the need for "empirical" evidence such as fibers or DNA for a serious case to go to trial. State misconduct was identified often, as the narrative of *The Innocent Man* suggested coordination between law enforcement and the prosecutor's office. One poster characterized the series as "a tale of local corruption," and others echoed this description: "we can see LE wanting to close a case and being willing to do so at all costs, even letting the real perpetrator go free. A Prosecutor who deliberately withholds and camouflages evidence from the defense because he wants to win. A conspiracy of silence about any of this wrongdoing that lasts a very long time." Responses to this narrative included expressions of helplessness similar to comments about *Making a Murderer*, as well as expressions of cynicism about the criminal justice system. A Redditor who seemed not to be from the US asked, "Why does American justice not learn from it's [its] mistakes? Why is it set up to perpetuate them? Why do you have such a high % of wrongful convictions there?"

From Production to Reception

The New True are long works of entertainment that offer an extremely detailed look into the evidence presented in criminal trials while simultaneously presenting their own investigation of the cases. Documentarians' attention to detail seems to have paid off, as audiences on Reddit and other sites dissected the facts from multiple perspectives and developed sophisticated arguments and analysis about them. Even as they researched the cases on their own, audience members generally focused on the same evidence that the series makers presented. Producers "got it right" when they decided to go deep and granular, as audiences were very responsive to these details and animated by their nuances.

In many of the New True, the documentarians cast a critical lens on the prosecutors' use of deviance in constructing guilt. The series often seem to attempt to portray their subject as sympathetic, while positing that deviance tropes are not rational, fair, or just but are rather reflections of small-mindedness and ugly stereotypes. Redditors discussed the defendants' characters along the same lines as the prosecution did, often affirming the equation of deviance with guilt and basing their opinions on their assessment of the defendant. The disparity between the documentarians' case and audience responses was most pronounced in *The*

Staircase and the HBO series *The Case against Adnan Syed,* about which Redditors articulated that their opinions were at odds with series makers' intentions.

For many of the series, Redditors judged the jury. Those who found the defendants to be innocent often expressed dismay at juries' decision-making. Reasonable doubt was brought up time and again by posters who did not see how juries arrived at their verdicts. In some cases, they pointed to corrupt processes and the role of the media; in others, they implied that the jurors were simply stupid; and in still others, they expressed that the jury's flawed verdict was due to a lack of proper information presented at trial.

The innocence issues that the New True raise include eyewitness misidentification, inadequate defense, faulty forensic science, false confessions, and state misconduct. The particular series that focus on false confessions and state misconduct were the most successful in impacting audience's thinking. These two issues were the most fully explored in these series, and audiences were receptive to these arguments, particularly regarding state misconduct. Redditors and Rotten Tomatoes reviewers responding to *The Innocent Man* and *Making a Murderer* were outraged by the portrayal of the government. These audiences were most unified in seeing the subject not only as innocent but as a vulnerable victim. This reaction can be seen as a reflection of the strength of narratives that present injustice as the result of human wrongdoing, even malice. In contrast, those who believe that Adnan Syed is innocent sometimes characterize him, as Koenig did, as "unlucky," the victim of a bewildering confluence of coincidences and his inability to account for twenty-one minutes after school. This is a less satisfying story than a conspiracy between powerful state actors controlling events from behind the scenes, against which the average person is helpless.

7

Where Truth Lies

Reasonable doubts are for innocent people.
—Ken Kratz, closing statement in Steven Avery's trial

FACTS are slippery in the New True. Truth is presented as in the eye of the beholder; one piece of evidence can be interpreted in two completely opposite, utterly contradictory ways, serving mutually exclusive realities. This tension is an electric current through all the series. Even as the documentarians more strenuously make the defense's case, they heighten drama by providing frameworks for both sides. Because they make room for two contradictory truths and because innocence is not definitively proven, through either a DNA exoneration or a confession or any overwhelming evidence pointing to the real perpetrator, the New True end without decisive resolution. Where does the truth of these murders actually lie? Its elusiveness is related to the presumption of innocence and the standard of proof beyond a reasonable doubt, which in some storytelling is shown as having the ability to legitimize uncertainty and destabilize the meaning of innocence.

Postmodernism and the Elusiveness of Truth in *Serial* and *Atlanta Monster*

Trials are ideally seen as truth-seeking and truth-establishing enterprises. Yet in the 1990s, when scholars were particularly concerned with postmodernism, media representations of actual trial came under scrutiny. In "Trials of the Postmodern," John Fiske and Kevin Glynn argue that crises of meaning and representation have impacted trials as they become increasingly saturated with the images of and around them on television news and tabloid television, "where modernist notions of reality and transcendent principles meet postmodern forces of destabilization, localization, and volatility."[1] Legal outcomes no longer necessarily have solid, absolute authority over truth but are merely products of competing truth claims. This effect is heightened by "the conversion of criminal cases into television images," which "rips the contestation between prosecution and defense truths out of the courtroom . . . and resituates it in a multitude of television viewing ones. Audiences become juries as images are placed on trial."[2]

Throughout the 1990s and into this century, as entertainment and media technology expanded its platforms and transformed audiences' experiences and consumption, courtrooms (both real and fictional) have further grown as sites of competing ideologies where justice and injustice are made visible and subject to further debate. Lynn Chancer's analysis of high-profile crimes brings into focus the way law and media intersect in the creation of highly charged, polarized debates. These cases "become vehicles for crystallizing, debating, and attempting to resolve contemporary social problems" such as "discrimination based on race or gender."[3] Trials thus have a life beyond the immediate cases and within the culture at large, and beyond the specific set of facts and within a landscape of representations and meanings. In an interview with Janet Malcolm, the civil attorney for the convicted murderer Jeffrey MacDonald, who was suing a journalist for how he covered the case, notes that our judicial process is not the search for truth people think it is, that it has a cathartic function of "allowing people to air their differences, to let them feel as if they had a forum."[4] Justice is another discourse in the public square, an opportunity for emotional release, and the expression of emotional truths. But journalists who cover murder cases, like the documentarians, see themselves as working to uncover the same truths sought in court.

The New True series makers have chosen high-profile cases, interjecting themselves into the formation of representations about crime and justice and contributing to the whorl of images surrounding Echols,

Baldwin, Misskelley, Syed, Peterson, Avery, Dassey, Williams, Ward, and Fontenot, as well as their communities and their local and state law enforcement. Questioning legal outcomes, the docuseries throw a spotlight on the creation of institutional truths, deconstructing "the logic, evidence, and context of the conviction of the accused" and "refusing to privilege institutional sources over the accused in the representation of the reality of a crime, thereby recovering the accused as a source of knowledge production."[5] They reinvest the defense with authority that was lost with the verdicts.

Even though the documentarians are creating media, they position themselves outside the media frenzies they critique. They see themselves as seeking actual truth where courtroom processes have possibly failed, and often the New True "make claims that their evidence is more truthful, more compelling, than the evidence that had been relied upon in court."[6] They attempt to persuade their audiences by replicating the relationship between lawyers and jurors, presenting their own "forensic rhetoric," "insisting that their own work is grounded in the evidentiary truth claims of mainstream journalism."[7] All the series present more detailed and thorough investigative efforts than what was produced for trial, furnishing considerable actual evidence in support of their alternative theories. They give weight and substance to the culture's sometimes inchoate, sometimes clearly articulated undercurrent of suspicion toward police, prosecutors, and courts; they produce new realities while contradicting the institutional ones.

But where, in the end, does that leave truth? Uncertainty runs through the New True like an electrical current, fueling dramatic tension. Does truth lie in one incontrovertible piece of evidence, like a blood-spatter pattern or a fiber? Can it be known by unveiling the authentic self of the defendant? Or does it lie in the legitimacy of our courts, in due process, voir dire, and judicial rulings? Are the New True simply longer, more researched representations in an ever-complex arena of images for fractured yet overlapping niche audiences? And if so, what does that mean for our punishment practices?

Serial and *Atlanta Monster,* as well as the HBO series devoted to the same cases, suggest that the truth may never be known. It is out there; it does exist; there is a real, actual truth. Someone killed the victims, without question. But who that person is may never be proven to the satisfaction of all fact finders and truth seekers. As narrators, Koenig and Lindsey place their questions, frustrations, and uncertainty center stage. As we have seen, Koenig is known for presenting "a sort of ago-nized pleasure in not being able to make up her mind."[8] She painstak-ingly grapples with the fact that there are many problems with the state's case but just as many with Syed's as well. She poses one possible sce-nario or explanation to one expert after another, and everything seems equally plausible yet also somehow equally unsatisfying. In addition, she presents *Serial* as an inquiry into the reliability of memory and the dif-ficulties inherent in the mental act of recounting the past, furthering the sense that truth may be irretrievable. When Lee's body was found six weeks after her disappearance, the teens were all asked to recount that day from their past. The police and subsequent fact finders, includ-ing Koenig and her listeners and Berg and her viewers, were all in the position of reconciling existing official records (class schedules, phone records, etc.) with conflicting accounts of the day in question. Koenig persuasively explains the difficulty of accounting for one's actions dur-ing the course of a random ordinary day a few weeks before. But she also persuasively argues that Lee's disappearance was quickly discovered that day and most of her friends were called about her. They would have, on that day, naturally reviewed their actions that would still be fresh in their minds. It would probably have made a mental impression.

At the same time, she also problematizes clear memories. During the airing of *Serial,* two people came forward who remembered seeing Syed and Lee that day. Koenig points out that McClain's memory of seeing Syed at the library is "remarkable" and is similarly impressed with a student's memory of Lee before a wrestling meet.[9] She suggests that their clarity should not be wholly trusted but also explains that if your classmate disappeared and was found murdered, your last conversations with her, and with the prime suspect, would have particular significance. Koenig reflects that all the witnesses' memories are colored by what happened later and that those who felt Syed was guilty after his arrest had a different recollection of the relationship with Lee than those who felt that he did not do it. The question for Koenig comes down to whose memory is trustworthy, but she does not make a case for one actor's claims over another. Rather, it is field of memories and a field of truths.

Of the case against Wayne Williams, James Baldwin says, "It is impossible to claim that his guilt has been proven any more than it can be proven that the murders have ceased. . . . It is absolutely meaningless to say that there have been no murders that 'fit the pattern.' What pattern? In Georgia?"[10] Over thirty years later, Lindsey and the HBO producers fail to offer any more certainty than this. The case is still, to them at least, laden with mystery. Like Baldwin, they are unable to argue that the prosecution proved its case for all the murders. They are also equally unable to provide enough information to prove that it was wrong.

Lindsey's podcast is dizzying in the variety of truth it considers: the murders fit a pattern or were all different—different ages, different methods, different areas, different modi operandi—and there was never any pattern; the murders stopped after Williams was arrested, or the murders did not really stop; or, contrary to popular beliefs, sometimes serial killers stop on their own, without being arrested; it might have been Williams, or it might have been someone else, or it might have been a bunch of different people.

The HBO series and the podcast juxtapose the anguished certainty of the victims' families that Williams was not the perpetrator and that their children's cases remain unsolved with the firm memory of a couple of former Atlanta residents who recall scary incidents from their childhood in the year before Williams was arrested and who feel certain that they were almost killed. A coworker of Williams's cries on the stand and has to admit that Williams could have done it, yet a man who was once in one of Williams's teen acts feels the other way. The question is not merely whom does one believe but whom do the producers want you to believe? Whom do they believe and why? Lindsey cannot make up his mind, and his podcast is ultimately a story about arriving at questions, not answering them.

Berlinger and Sinofsky in the *Paradise Lost* trilogy and Tweel in *The Innocent Man* leave less room for doubt than the other series makers do. Berlinger and Sinofsky were deeply connected to the cause of the WM3 and saw themselves unequivocally as advocates, rejoicing at their release, and Tweel made his series after reading Grisham's book and *The Dreams of Ada*, ready to tell the story of an outrageous injustice.[11] They give less credence to the prosecution's case than Koenig and Lindsey do or than Lestrade and Ricciardi and Demos do. They make a clearer argument for wrongful conviction.

In the following section, I look at some problems that arise in those efforts for all the series, but here I will say that they place philosophical questions about the knowability of the truth aside while they lay out their arguments on behalf of their subjects' innocence. Lestrade's and Ricciardi and Demos's work falls in the middle of this spectrum. Like Berlinger and Sinofsky and Tweel, they emphasize arguments on behalf of their subjects to the extent that they have been accused of bias and distortion, but the prosecutions' facts in evidence in these cases emerge as more compelling than in the *Paradise Lost* trilogy and *The Innocent Man*, where it appears the prosecution had no case at all. In *The Staircase* and *Making a Murderer*, the cases against the subjects have more foundation or substance and require more work to undo. These series dispense with "tidy resolutions" and present reality as "disquieting" and "dysfunctional" by giving a degree of weight to the state's evidence.[12] For this reason, opinions, like those we have seen in chapter 6, are as divided as they are for the more equivocal *Serial* and the treatments of the Atlanta murders. Just because they showcase their interpretation of events does not mean that in their case, "the interpretive function is . . . at the expense of independent thought"; they provide more fodder for the audience to chew over.[13]

Documentary, Objectivity, and the Problem of Truth Claims

Stella Bruzzi maintains that because documentaries are the product of individuals, they "will always display bias and be in some manner didactic."[14] She further asserts that documentarians do not believe they can represent events in some pure, unmediated form separate from their representations.[15] However, neither are they "simply an elaborate fiction."[16] Rather, documentaries are "a negotiation between two potentially conflicting factors: the real and it's representation."[17] Examining *The Staircase*, Kristen Fuhs argues that the "contradictions between documentary narrative and the courtroom narrative" call into question "the film's editorial choices and narrative structure" and reports that Lestrade amassed 650 hours of footage over twenty months of filming, of which only a fraction appears in the final product.[18] Like all documentarians, he only gives us a glimpse of what he has amassed, and the product is a representation of his editorial choices and point of view.

When a documentary about a trial challenges the outcomes of the trial, it is important to look at the mechanism by which documentarians create their argument. A number of scholars, critics, and audience members have brought attention to the ways filmmakers manipulate representation to bring about a desired response in viewers. My examination of Reddit and other social media forums shows that for all these series, there were audience members who did not accept the documentarians' overall contentions about innocence, and many of them argue that the series are biased and leave out crucial information.

All these series exhibit elements of the complex journalist-subject relationship, which Janet Malcolm documented in *The Journalist and the Murderer*, in which she points to a purportedly common phenomenon of subjects trusting the journalist to empathize with them and to report their side of the story as truth. Malcolm states, "Something seems to happen to people when they meet a journalist, and what happens is exactly the opposite of one would expect. One would think that extreme wariness and caution would be the order of the day, but in fact childish trust and impetuosity are far more common. The journalistic encounter seems to have the same regressive effect on a subject as the psychoanalytic encounter. The subject becomes a kind of child of the writer, regarding him as a permissive, all-accepting, all-forgiving mother, and expecting that the book will be written by her."[19] In addition, there is a way that the filmmakers present the WM3, Avery and Dassey, and Ward and Fontenot, who are all shown as vulnerable and in need of protection, that also indicates a complex journalist-subject relationship. Their portrayals elicit an emotional reaction in viewers that has similarities with maternal urges. Unlike the case that Malcolm was writing about (McGinnis's book on MacDonald) or Andrew Jarecki's *The Jinx*, in which subjects are betrayed and framed as guilty by the journalists they trust, in the visual documentaries of the New True, directors do justice to the trust their subjects put in them. Even Michael Peterson, who lacks the helpless expression of these others, is portrayed with respect, dignity, and empathy by Lestrade.

In fact, Lestrade was very much on Peterson's side from the outset, though his trust in Peterson was always tempered with skepticism. In an interview, Lestrade explained that when he first met Peterson, he "felt right away that he was a very good character": "You could feel that when he was talking about his love for Kathleen, it was very sincere. On the other hand, you could also feel maybe he was hiding something."[20] He said in several interviews that when he first encountered the case, he was convinced that Peterson was being prosecuted because of his bisexuality and the gay pornography on his computer, violating what Lestrade believed was the community's shared provincial morality. In an interview for *Vulture*, he told Josh Modell, "It was much more about who he was and where he was living than anything else."[21]

In response to accusations about the series's bias, Lestrade has claimed that it was not his objective to convince audiences of Peterson's innocence, but he concedes that there was an imbalance of sources that influenced the final project. He spent most of his time with Peterson and his defense team, particularly his lawyer, David Rudolf. Although the prosecutor's office initially granted him interviews, prosecutors soon declined to participate, perhaps, as Lestrade speculates, because they realized they were being cast as villains. Lestrade reflected on some of these criticisms in his interview with Modell:

> It's difficult to be an objective observer, especially when the other side doesn't want to participate. We kept trying to shoot with the prosecution and with Kathleen's family. I really wanted them to be in the film. But because they refused, we were much more close to Michael Peterson. It's more his point of view, yes, but I really tried to be objective. But it's the real world, it's impossible to be objective. I hope that I let people think what they want. If they think he is guilty, that's fine. The purpose of the series was never to let people think Michael Peterson wasn't guilty. It's the mystery of Michael Peterson that was really interesting.[22]

There is a scene in *The Staircase* that has been cited as an example of bias: after Peterson enters his *Alford* plea, Lestrade comes out from behind the camera and hugs him. Lestrade has said that he struggled with the decision to include this moment but that it was ultimately part of the story about a "victory for justice."[23] Phrasing it this way actually shows that Lestrade believes in Peterson's innocence and that justice is on his side, not Kathleen's family's. In the same interview with Modell, Rudolf explained that Lestrade did not do anything wrong and that "when you spend that much time around someone and observing them and watching them interact with their family and friends, an empathy is created": "They never went out for drinks or dinner or anything like that, that I'm aware of. He empathized with him as a human being." Yet these words are belied by the fact that one of Lestrade's producers began a romantic relationship with Peterson, a clear blurring of social and professional boundaries and a sign that the series makers viewed him sympathetically. One assumes that the producer did not think Peterson was the murderer. The truth of the Peterson case becomes slippery and unclear in part because Lestrade extends an exercise in doubt over thirteen episodes and sixteen years yet still cannot yield a definitive conclusion.

As mentioned earlier, the first season of *Making a Murderer* roused viewers to "near-universal outrage about the verdicts" and quickly led to more than 275,000 signatures on a petition to President Obama to pardon Avery.[24] It is difficult to read the series as a balanced, both-sides, analytic portrayal of a case. Ricciardi and Demos have expressed satisfaction in the support for Avery and the degree to which their series helped him and his family.[25] Following the first season, the cultural critic Kathryn Schulz questioned the ethics of their endeavor in the *New Yorker*, asking readers to consider "what it means when a private investigative project—bound by no rules of procedure, answerable to nothing but ratings, shaped only by the ethics and aptitude of its makers—comes to serve as our court of last resort."[26] She problematizes Ricciardi and Demos's concrete accomplishment: gaining enormous public support for the defendant. Are we sure we want to accept documentarians as extralegal agents in the justice system, when they are creating news-like pieces that function, at least in part, as entertainment? Schulz thinks we should not do so uncritically and points out that while documentarians position their work as "intellectually serious" and "morally worthy," these series may not be as distinct from the types of shows they suggest are "shallow and exploitative," such as *Dateline*, *48 Hours*, and *America's Most Wanted*. Echoing critiques of Berlinger and Sinofsky, who used their films to mount cases against alternative suspects who were not afforded due process in their films, Schulz argues that by stacking the deck for Avery, Ricciardi and Demos "wind up mirroring the entity that they are trying to discredit."[27]

Once the first season of *Making a Murderer* aired, Ken Kratz, the prosecutor, quickly released a statement and gave interviews proclaiming the film's bias and its selective presentation of the evidence, arguing that if the audience saw what jurors saw, there would be no doubt. Specifically, he pointed to the fact that Ricciardi and Demos neglected to include evidence about Avery's sweat on a latch under the hood of the

RAV4 and bullet casings that matched Avery's rifle. The directors further their advocacy of Avery and Dassey in the second season, in which they feature Zellner rebutting the evidence that Kratz referred to and focus exclusively on the postconviction work of Zellner and Dassey's attorney. Demos has said that their primary intention in the second series was not to respond to that criticism. They did, however, try "to confront the ways in which *Making a Murderer* changed the world that they were documenting."[28] The way it changed that world, of course, is that it created an enormous outcry against the state and an emotional identification with Avery's and Dassey's plight.

The response of victims' families to the New True is also of near-universal outrage. Most acutely feel that the series are biased and lack objectivity. At press conferences after the hearings covered in follow-up episodes of *The Staircase*, Kathleen's daughter and sisters were apoplectic at the sympathetic portrayal of Peterson in the series. Kathleen's sister Candace is particularly villainized, and her portrayal is hard to reconcile with the idea that Lestrade was unbiased. Because his picture of Peterson is so sympathetic, the sisters are, in contrast, shaded as mean and crazy antagonists. Candace's passion seems vengeful, and this is not tempered with any coverage of her grief or loss or any hardships she may have endured. We see her testifying vehemently against Peterson's being released on house arrest and proclaiming that the court should be there for the victims. She makes a forceful speech on the courthouse steps, advocating for victims' rights, saying the judge's sole responsibility is to make victims heard and to protect their rights, dead or alive. Peterson states that the only reason he is still in court is because of Candace and Kathleen's daughter. Also on the courthouse steps, Candace expresses her indignation at the first release of *The Staircase*, proclaiming that Lestrade made a "pseudo-documentary about [her] sister's murder without [her] family's cooperation or consent": "Michael Peterson had a movie made where he could pontificate and tell everyone how bad the criminal justice system is. *The Staircase* film was made, and twice episodes were used to threaten and scare Kathleen's daughter and myself.[29]

In a study of *Serial* on social media, Elizabeth Yardley et al. show how Hae Min Lee's family had a similarly intense emotional response to *Serial*, and some audience members likewise felt the Lees were not adequately represented.[30] Informed about the podcast by a cousin, Lee's brother took to Reddit right after listening, titling his post "I am Hae's brother" and using the moniker "brotherofhae." His post received 429 responses:[31] "But sorry I won't be answering questions because . . . TO ME ITS [*sic*] REAL LIFE. To you listeners, it's another murder mystery, another crime drama, another episode of CSI. You weren't there to see your mom crying every night, having a heart attack when she got the new[s] that the body was found, and going to court almost everyday for a year seeing your mom weeping, crying, and fainting. You don't know what we went through. Especially to those who are demanding our family response and having a meetup, . . . you guys are disgusting."[32] This post lays bare his family's suffering in a raw, heartfelt way that cuts through the intellectualizing of the case. "In addition, he appears to push back against his sister as public property, asserting ownership over her and his grief for her."[33] Her neglect of the victim's family is one reason why Koenig's otherwise exhaustive efforts can seem biased. Despite her elaborate consideration of the validity of each aspect of the prosecution's case, it is Syed's voice that she ultimately centers, and in spite of her inability to come to a conclusion, *Serial* is his story.

The Case against Adnan Syed addresses this problem, devoting more time to Lee's family life as well as to the Korean American community she lived in. We learn that Korean American businesses were often the targets of crime and that they felt their victimization never got its due attention. We see footage of the Lees advocating for previous crime victims and demanding rights. Hae's death was mourned by the whole community. Berg also shows us footage of Lee's family during the time she was still missing. They are sitting close to each other in their home, clearly frightened and bewildered in front of journalists and cameras. The situation feels overwhelming and invasive. Berg interposes the documentary with animated sequences of Lee's diary and a voice-over, making her voice a central character, which is enhanced by Polaroid photos of her taken by her friends.

The grief of Halbach's family and friends is not seriously touched on in *Making a Murderer*. In the first season, we see a vigil held for Halbach, as well as the home video she made of herself. At Avery's sentencing, we hear audio of her listing the things she loves, but there is not much more. Her family and friends emerge more visibly in the second season, but they are not shown in a sympathetic light. In fact, in most of the New True, the expressions of anger by victims' families often seem to work against them. Like Candace, when the Halbachs are shown in the second season, they seem vengeful and blind to reason. The Manitowac community is on the Halbachs' side and is seen participating in a fundraising drive in support of the family and at the courthouse awaiting a verdict in Dassey's habeas case. The residents of Manitowac, the county law enforcement, and the Halbachs are united in feeling unjustly villainized by the show. They are outraged that Avery and Dassey are depicted as innocent victims and that they received such an outpouring of support. Of the attention Dassey received, one community member says to a journalist, "He's not a rock star; he's a killer!"[34]

In stark contrast is the portrayal of Avery and Dassey's family. Anticipating Dassey's habeas release (which ended up being denied), his mother's hopeful face shows traces of fear. Scenes with her and with Avery's parents show love and loyalty to their imprisoned sons but also the ravages of time and the devastating impact these incarcerations have had on all involved. The filmmakers spend a lot of time with the family members, and we see how meaningful all the gifts and cards from supporters are. We also see signs of squalor and decline in their environment and in the way the health of Avery's parents is deteriorating. On his mother's seventy-ninth birthday, she goes to visit him in prison, and her slow hobble across the parking lot evokes the heavy toll that his conviction has had on the lives around him. Avery tears up in an interview with the filmmakers about the prospect of his mother dying while he is still in prison, and it is hard not to feel some compassion for him.

Halbach's ex-boyfriend Ryan Hillegas and her brother are shown as strong supporters of the prosecution and as Ricciardi and Demos's antagonists. This dynamic is heightened as Zellner's investigation focuses on Hillegas's potential involvement with the murder. Much of this narrative concerns evidence relating to him, to which Zellner attaches great significance. This includes Halbach's day planner, which Hillegas provided to police but which has a pencil note that Zellner argues had to have been written when she was in the RAV4. Hillegas also provides information about a broken taillight that is relevant to her theory. Given that Ricciardi and Demos center on Zellner, who points the finger at Hillegas and others close to Halbach, it is little wonder that they are not open to participating in the project.

With regard to bias and representations of victims' families versus defense theories, Tweel's work has an interesting dynamic surrounding the two cases. Debbie Carter's mother and family members were united in their support of the case against Williamson and Fritz and in their feeling that no punishment could be too harsh. They had no doubt as to the men's guilt. However, when DNA evidence of wrongful conviction was presented, they understood their error and had deep, complicated feelings about their role in the men's imprisonment. Carter's mother and Williamson, two clearly broken, fragile people, became friends on the basis of a shared bond rooted in the tragic death of her daughter. Carter's cousin became an innocence advocate. Both participated in the documentary and illustrate the extended emotional impact that wrongful conviction makes on everyone involved. In the Denice Haraway case, Ward and Fontenot had not been exonerated, and her family refused to participate in *The Innocent Man*. Like Candace in *The Staircase*, they expressed outrage that the series portrayed the defendants as victims.[35]

The depiction of the victims' families in the first installment of *Paradise Lost* is intense. Their screaming vengefully on news cameras is not portrayed with compassion and not framed as stemming from unfathomable grief but rather from some venomous religious ardor. Their on-camera passion is juxtaposed with footage of them seeming more composed off camera, as if their expressions of grief are not authentic. Because the WM3 are portrayed as vulnerable and clueless, the families are more easily villainized by their expressions of fury and desire for retribution. John Byers, the stepfather of one of the victims, comes across as particularly melodramatic in his passionate hatred and flamboyantly expressed desire for the defendants to rot in hell. We see him piously burning a mock grave of the WM3 and loudly preaching about eternal damnation.

Byers is the only member of the victims' families to participate in the second installment, *Revelations*, because the others were displeased with the original film's bias. Byers is now on a crusade to thwart Berlinger and Sinofsky's and the WM3 support group's exoneration efforts, but, like Kratz and Kachinsky in *Making a Murderer*, he is portrayed as having mixed motives. He is shown energized and animated by the national attention, and his mission is cast as ego-driven and performative.

In an unexpected and moving twist, after seeing *Revelations* and coming to understand the significance of the new DNA evidence, John Byers becomes convinced of the teens' innocence, supporting the WM3's exoneration efforts with just as much fervor as he had trying to prevent them. His transformation is documented in the third installment, *Purgatory*, in which another victim's mother says that her confidence in the WM3's guilt has also now wavered. She is no longer sure and supports a new trial for them. Her ex-husband is the man whom Berlinger and Sinofsky point the finger at in *Purgatory*, and she concedes this theory is plausible. In all, the bias attributed to the first film becomes less of an issue by the end of the third, when the WM3 enter *Alford* pleas, in large part because the state no longer has a case against them. Because of these transformations, the films grow less biased and more rooted in objective truth.

Finally, an important exception to the way these series may lack objectivity in how they represent victims is the two series on the Atlanta murders. Both can be seen as doing justice to the feelings of victims' families, which they feel were not served by the prosecutor's office or the system. Because the families do not consider their children's cases solved and do not believe that Williams was the perpetrator, these particular series can be seen as explorations of the theories of the victims' families, more than the defendant's. The series take these theories seriously and investigate every claim and possible explanation. On Reddit, many people felt that both series are biased in Williams's favor, and they do in some ways start from the premise that he may be innocent. However, after probing all the elements, neither comes to firm conclusions, and they do not make a strong case for him. This may in part be due to the fact that neither Lindsey nor Berg is able to paint a truly sympathetic picture of Williams, who in both series exhibits arrogance and changes his story.

The Presumption of Innocence and Reasonable Doubt

Unlike the traditional whodunnits of crime entertainment, when it comes to who actually did it, the New True may leave us wanting more, since often we do not really know and we cannot really agree. In lieu of this kind of resolution, the New True call forth the concept of reasonable doubt. Reasonable doubt, the presumption of innocence, and the burden of proof are closely intertwined and often used synonymously.[36] Simply put, the standard of proof beyond a reasonable doubt requires that the prosecution bear the burden of proving to juries that the defendant is not in fact innocent, which the jury must initially presume them to be. Pamela Ferguson differentiates the presumption of innocence from the burden of proof by explaining how the presumption ideally pressurizes the work of the prosecutor and establishes the proper disposition of the jury:

> The presumption of innocence requires that the starting point is for one side of the scales to be tipped in favor of the accused. This means that rather than the prosecution presenting its case to jurors who are "neutral" or open-minded about the accused's guilt or innocence, it faces an

uphill struggle to change their minds from believing the accused did *not* commit the crime, to being convinced of the opposite. The requirement for proof of guilt to be established "beyond a reasonable doubt" tells the jurors where they must end up in order to convict. The presumption of innocence tells them from where they must begin—with our scale pans on the side of "not guilty."[37]

Adopting this view of the presumption of innocence centers it as a robust protection against the overreach of the government and wrongful convictions, as opposed to a mere technical stipulation. Richard Lippke, like Ferguson, argues that the prosecution has a responsibility to act with the presumption of the defendant's innocence even before trial, during all stages of the criminal justice process.[38] Adopting an expansive view of the presumption of innocence would guard against the dangers of tunnel vision and reduces the likelihood of *Brady* violations. Lippke links this responsibility to the integrity of the criminal justice system and its perceived legitimacy, arguing that there is a societal need for "moral assurance" that the state will only inflict the pains of imprisonment when truly justified.[39]

If jurors are truly able to adopt this stance—which is doubtful, given that often jurors generally believe that the accused would not be in court unless the state had considerable evidence—then they would be more likely to see reasonable doubt as favoring the defendant.[40] Reasonable doubt means that if there is any chance the defendant is innocent, as they are presumed to be, then the state has not sufficiently proved its case.

Many defendants in the New True lament the lack of presumption of innocence and identify it as pivotal in their wrongful conviction. When Michael Peterson's brother optimistically points out that the defense does not have the burden of proof, Peterson responds, "Innocence until proven guilty is horse shit—you're guilty the minute they arrest."[41] In fact, a vein of cynicism runs through the New True as the criminal justice system repeatedly falls short of its ideals. An appellate attorney in

Tommy Ward's case also expresses that although the uphill battle should be the prosecution's, it is actually the defense's: "We talk all the time about the presumption of innocence; we act like there's a huge burden on the prosecution to overcome that presumption of innocence, but the fact is jurors tend to think, 'Why would they have charged him if there wasn't the evidence? He's got to be guilty.'"[42] From this perspective, the prosecution only has to do just enough to reinforce the jury's existing belief. Echoing this sentiment, one of Avery's trial attorneys says that even if he were acquitted, he has permanently lost his presumption of innocence: "There's nowhere for Steve to go to win his reputation back if he wins his trial. . . . To be accused is to lose."[43]

While "presumption of innocence" is not expressly stated in the US Constitution, it is widely and commonly recognized as implied and protected in the Fifth, Sixth, and Fourteenth Amendments.[44] The burden of proof beyond a reasonable doubt is protected in the Due Process Clauses of the Fifth and Fourteenth Amendments and has been held to play a vital role in US democracy, giving "concrete substance" to the presumption of innocence and symbolizing the significance that society attaches "to liberty itself."[45] Reasonable doubt is understood as the requirement that when a juror "harbors a doubt that prevents his conscientiously voting guilty, that doubt will be expressed in a vote of acquittal."[46]

Of the New True, *Serial* most consciously functions as an elaboration of the concept of reasonable doubt; it most openly operates as an exercise in uncertainty, as Koenig engages in a Socratic dialogue with herself, posing more questions than answers and trying out various hypotheses without landing on any of them—except reasonable doubt. That is where she lands. She considers the problem of Syed's motive from multiple angles. By many accounts, he seemed to have moved on from the breakup with Lee. But what, Koenig asks, if he wasn't really over it? He did at one point express to a friend that he thought they might get back together. What if Syed held out hopes that were crushed when it sunk in that Lee was seeing someone else? But no one she talks to saw him that way. Koenig concludes that one cannot really speculate. So what if she can come up with one likely explanation, when she can posit so many others that are equally likely? She reflects that "even the soberest, most likely scenario holds no more water than the most harebrained."[47]

Confounded, Koenig wonders if she just spent a year on a perfectly ordinary case, but when she asks one of her experts about this, the former detective Jim Trainum tells her that most cases do not have this degree of ambiguity and so many holes. Other experts she consults say the same thing. Her conclusion: "this case is a mess." An innocence lawyer who looks at the case also concludes that "there are mountains of reasonable doubt." Koenig began the project feeling that "certainty seemed so attainable," but she ends a year later feeling "like shaking everyone by the shoulders": "We didn't have the facts fifteen years ago, and we still don't have them now."[48]

Audiences that decry the guilty verdicts in the New True often seem acutely aware of the importance of the presumption of innocence in the US legal system and the necessity of the standard of proof beyond a reasonable doubt. For most of these series, Redditors upheld its importance even when they thought the defendant did it. One Redditor said of Syed, "Is he guilty beyond a reasonable doubt, on the evidence presented at trial? No, he's not. Did he do it? That's a very different question and precisely why *Serial* is so riveting from start to finish." Another Redditor said, "If somebody wants to think hes guilty thats fine, but there is absolutely no way that the belief is 100%. There is way too much reasonable doubt." Many echoed the Redditors who said, "I think Adnan is probably guilty, but have, what I believe to be reasonable, doubts," or "It's one of those cases where he shouldn't have been convicted based on the evidence alone, there was so much reasonable doubt, but I think he did it."[49] In *The Case against Adnan Syed*, we watch a radio broadcaster, two weeks before his second appeal hearing, say, "I don't know 100 percent that he's not guilty. . . . What I do know is they didn't prove he was guilty, and that's what anyone is entitled to."[50]

In Lindsey's *Atlanta Monster*, the emotional certainty characteristic of the victims' families that believe in Williams's innocence is continually juxtaposed with law enforcement's certainty of his guilt. The former officers whom Lindsey interviews consider the case "airtight," while the victims' families believe they have not had justice.[51] Like Koenig, Lindsey explores each hypothesis as far it takes him, but he is not able to conclude if the murders actually stopped when Williams was arrested.

On Reddit, many people concluded, like Lindsey, that there is not one Atlanta monster. Listeners were left thinking that there is not enough evidence to prove he murdered all the victims but there is not enough to prove he did not either. *Atlanta's Missing and Murdered* opens and closes with scenes of a community meeting where victims' families speak about the lack of closure they were given by the system, and the unending trauma of the community is at the heart of both narratives. Redditors were able to debate which of the twenty-eight murders Williams might have committed or land on reasonable doubt, like one who said that Wayne is "sketchy for sure" but that the HBO series "has shed serious doubts on the trial witnesses and fiber evidence": "I haven't seen anything that would sway me beyond a reasonable doubt."[52] But the impoverished Black community feels that it has been deeply neglected. Regardless of Williams's guilt or innocence, the community has suffered from racial injustice and economic inequality, and it is hard to see these wounds healing without larger, systemic social change.

Fuhs says that *The Staircase* does not claim to provide "an objective account of what happened in the Peterson house" but rather that it "asserts claims about social prejudice and the prosecutorial bias that create reasonable doubt."[53] In the last episode of the first installment, as the verdict approaches, David Rudolf explains reasonable doubt to Lestrade, saying, "Not guilty is not the same as innocent." He elaborates that he does not have the onus to prove innocence: "If I spend my time trying to prove he's innocent, I relieve the state of their burden of proof. I invite the jury to weigh in. . . . That's giving up a tremendous legal advantage that all defendants have and should have . . . to avoid innocent people going to prison."[54] Here, reasonable doubt makes actual innocence beside the point. At the end of the series, when they discuss the *Alford* plea, Rudolf says that in most cases, "you can't know for sure what happened. Best is reasonable doubt. It's rare that you can prove someone innocent."[55]

Redditors had a strong distaste for Peterson that buttressed their sense of his guilt. Those who thought he was innocent did not point to his character but rather pointed to reasonable doubt or, as two Redditors put it, "a tsunami of reasonable doubt." Another said, "Any rational human should be able to come to the conclusion that there is enough reasonable doubt to not convict." As with Syed, several Redditors believed that Peterson was probably guilty but still acknowledged that the state had not made its case, for example, "I lean slightly more toward guilty than innocent but do not believe there is proof beyond a reasonable doubt" and "I don't think he's innocent. But I also don't think there is proof beyond a reasonable doubt." One Redditor acknowledged the importance of the presumption of innocence, the burden of proof, and reasonable doubt, saying, "This is America, we have a system."[56]

Innocence operates differently in *Making a Murderer* than in the other series because Steven Avery had already been exonerated for a wrongful conviction when filming started. The series begins by chronicling his first case and how he had never had a presumption of innocence in Manitowac. His exoneration shocked the state, and an assemblyman passed the Avery Bill and formed an Avery Task Force devoted to investigating wrongful convictions in Wisconsin (these were renamed following his arrest for the Halbach murder). From the perspective of the filmmakers, that wrongful conviction, stemming from the presumption of innocence that he was denied, was the original sin that set the state's events in motion when Halbach disappeared. That wrongful conviction is posited as the state's motive for framing him. In a way, prosecutors' resentment of his actual innocence becomes their reason for again refusing to grant him the presumption of innocence in the new case.

One of Avery's attorneys says that both cases show "a tragic lack of humility of everyone who participates in our criminal justice system," and, as if to prove this point, Kratz, the prosecutor, says in his closing arguments, somewhat astonishingly, "Reasonable doubts are for innocent people."[57] This statement exemplifies the arrogance that Avery's attorney was referring to and is the source of much outrage. One journalist retorts, "They are not. And procedural protections like access to defense counsel and freedom from coerced interrogations extend to both the innocent and the guilty."[58] A Redditor's response to this statement was more blunt: "Go fuck yourself you unbelievable piece of shit."[59] As we have seen, Kratz emerges as one of several villains in this series with "punchable" faces (in fact, he claims to have received death threats).[60] Another Redditor linked Kratz's unseemly conduct to their sense of reasonable doubt for Avery and their inability to believe that Kratz was a sincere actor: "Personally, I have no idea if SA is guilty, but I do not think he should have been convicted based on the evidence presented. . . . Kratz played a game and he tainted the jury pool, planted his own creepy fantasy in everyone's minds and made it look like SA came up with it. It's completely insane to me how anyone can look at this and think the state had justice for TH in mind."[61]

One of Avery's trial attorneys, Dean Strang, elucidates the importance of reasonable doubt as he, like Rudolf, troubles the idea of knowable truth: "Human endeavors are muddy. They are imperfect by definition, and a chase for truth in a criminal trial can be in vain. Justice, it seems to me, is staying true to the set of principles we have about what we do when confronted with uncertainty. Do we err on the side of depriving a human being of their liberty, or do we err on the side of a human being sustaining his claim to liberty when we are uncertain, as we almost always are?"[62] Strang is evoking Blackstone's maxim, the assertion that it is better that ten guilty people go free than that one innocent person be sent to prison. That is why doubt should equal an acquittal. The maxim expresses a commitment to moral assurance when the state deprives one of liberty as a means of punishment and the idea "that while we accept that no justice system can be infallible, we regard wrongful convictions as a particularly grave injustice."[63]

Perhaps Strang and Rudolf and all the series makers considered here are making an assumption about the American public that is itself untrue. As an unexplored matter of fact, do people think it is better that the guilty are freed than that the innocent are convicted? Many Redditors who posted about the series seem to, but there is no reason to think that their sentiments are generalizable. The punitive turn in criminal justice, with its emphasis on crime control over due process, is set up to ward against the guilty going free, with less concern for the innocent, who might in this model be seen as collateral damage.

The *Alford* Plea

An *Alford* plea is a subset of guilty pleas that allows the defendant to plead guilty while maintaining their innocence. A traditional guilty plea requires the defendant to admit to committing the crime in an allocution statement before the judge, who requires this to establish the factual basis of the plea. The vast majority of criminal cases are resolved through a plea bargain, which accounts for as many as 94 percent of state convictions.[64] The *Alford* plea was upheld by the US Supreme Court in 1970, in a case in which a man facing the death penalty entered a guilty plea without admitting guilt. In "The *Alford* Plea Turns Fifty: Why It Deserves Another Fifty Years," Michael Conklin argues that like all guilty pleas, an *Alford* plea is "highly coercive. . . . The average sentence disparity between what is offered in a plea and what would result from a trial conviction is 500%."[65] *Alford* pleas have been praised for increasing efficiency in the system, but many scholars and court actors are opposed to *Alford* pleas, which give the state permission to punish an individual who has neither been found guilty by a jury nor admitted guilt in court.[66] *Alford* pleas have been critiqued on a number of other grounds, including concerns that it muddies the moral message of punishment and permits "equivocation and ambiguity when clarity is essential" and does not provide victims with closure or an acknowledgment of wrongdoing.[67]

In a study of 2004 data from the Bureau of Justice Statistics, Alison Redlich and Asil Ali Ozdogru found that *Alford* pleas amounted to 6.5

percent of all pleas entered (including not guilty). It is generally believed (but not empirically known) that most people who enter *Alford* pleas are guilty but will not admit it out of "embarrassment, shame, and psychological denial—reasons that relate to one's guilt rather than innocence."[68]

Another study found that innocent defendants rarely enter *Alford* pleas.[69] It is not possible to know how many actually innocent defendants enter these pleas, and Redlich and Ozdogru report that the majority of exonerees pleaded not guilty and were convicted by a jury. However, given the sheer number of guilty pleas (such as the seventy-six thousand that Redlich and Ozdogru look at), if even a small number were innocent, it would be significantly concerning. As Syed's appellate attorney says, "It's easy to say, 'Well why would anyone ever plead guilty to something they didn't do.' But it literally happens every day. Our criminal justice system is not always fair, and it's not always right. This is reality."[70] In the New True, *Alford* pleas allow guilt and innocence to coexist; they suspend the notion of truth, freezing the legal narrative in a state of uncertainty and ambiguity.

Normally, *Alford* pleas are entered at sentencing. For three of the New True cases, *Alford* pleas are raised as a possible outcome only after years of imprisonment during postconviction processes, representing an uneasy compromise that can be likened to settlements in civil court, where money is paid to the plaintiff but no wrongdoing is admitted. In the cases of the WM3 and Peterson, *Alford* pleas were offered at a stage when new trials seemed likely and the state faced a danger of losing its conviction. In the *Paradise Lost* trilogy and *The Staircase*, they are offered in exchange for time served. The WM3 will be freed, and Peterson will not have to face another trial and the prospect of returning to prison to die. In these series, the defendants face a deep moral and emotional crisis in the face of this option, because entering the plea means losing the chance to be acquitted or exonerated in court.

In *The Case against Adnan Syed*, we learn that Syed would consider an *Alford* plea with time served, should it be offered. Although he does not see it as a desirable outcome, he can live with it as an acceptable one.

In this series, we see how the movement around his innocence since *Serial* has impacted his family. During the time Koenig was interviewing Syed, he had been maintaining his innocence for nearly fifteen years, and he and his family were deeply invested in it. Syed tells Koenig that it would be easier on his family if he were guilty, because even though it would be heart-rending for them, they would understand he deserved to be there. One of the experts Koenig interviews says that at this point it would be impossible for Syed to admit guilt because of what his family has been through. All this is amplified after the airing of the podcast and the immense public attention and support Syed receives. A large segment of the audience believes in him, and this arguably impacts the postconviction process.

Berg shows us how on the basis of evidence that Koenig acquired, Syed's attorney are able to win a new trial, but then the prosecution appeals the ruling. As everyone awaits the circuit court ruling—will he or will he not get a new trial with the new evidence?—the prosecution offers Syed a deal: plead guilty for time served plus four years. Syed knows that if he turns it down and loses the ruling, he will remain in prison for the rest of his life. Worse, he would be living with the knowledge that he turned down the chance for freedom. He grapples with the decision and in the end feels that he cannot bear to lose his integrity and plead guilty to something he did not do. Unfortunately, Syed loses this gamble, and the judge rules in favor of the prosecution.

Of the New True cases, the West Memphis Three came closest to a DNA exoneration. In the third film, *Purgatory*, Berlinger and Sinofsky follow the WM3's case after DNA testing excludes them from the crime scene and includes a match with one of the victims' stepfathers (not Byers). The film centers on an upcoming evidentiary hearing for a new trial on the basis of this evidence, which would allow for all of the new evidence to be submitted, and the filmmakers and supporters are caught off guard when a hearing is suddenly held for the men to enter *Alford* pleas.

By this time, Echols has been in solitary confinement on death row for eighteen years. The WM3's lawyers had quietly negotiated the plea, which would give them time served and allow them to be immediately released. Although they most certainly would have been granted a new trial, which they would most likely win, the process could take years. Berlinger and Sinofsky film them individually entering their pleas, while each makes a statement maintaining his innocence. This outcome is cathartic and creates a great sense of relief but also of anger and frustration. One scholar writes that because there was so much evidence of their innocence, the court should not have accepted the pleas. There was not the necessary factual basis of guilt: "Courts should not accept guilty pleas when enough compelling evidence exists that clearly shows that an individual is not linked to the crime for which he or she has been charged. . . . The Echols court's allowance of an *Alford* plea was inappropriate because there was enough evidence to establish the West Memphis Three's innocence but not enough of a factual basis for the *Alford* plea."[71] Byers, who had been passionately, melodramatically, and performatively convinced of their guilt, only to become equally passionate about their innocence following the DNA results, is outraged at the outcome, shouting angrily at the cameras about the injustice and how they should have been exonerated.

Yet the scene of the three men emerging from court newly free is, at least for me, the most emotional scene in all the New True. All three are conflicted about the plea, but Baldwin expresses this most acutely. He says, with evident pain, that he would not have entered the plea if his friend Echols had not been facing execution; he says, "They were going to kill Damien. I did it for him."[72]

When Lestrade returns eight years after the verdict to follow Michael Peterson's postconviction hearings after he has won a motion for a new trial, we see Peterson as an aged and broken man. Although he gets released from prison while his case is pending, his optimism is tempered by an air of despair and a great sense of loss. As the process drags on for two more years, the prosecution finally offers him an *Alford* plea, which he and his family debate. His children are divided, with one of his daughters saying that an *Alford* plea will not bring them justice. In contrast, one of her brothers poses a cynical argument: "What's the point of winning a game that is not a fair game?" His wife continues the thought: "As much as I want justice for you, I'm scared to ask for justice again when every time we've been screwed."[73]

Peterson asks for a show of hands: Who believes in justice? No one raises their hand. Peterson is angry and bitter about accepting the *Alford* plea because he believes the state "played dirty" and would do so again. Rudolf informs him that even were the state willing to dismiss the charges, at this point, it is not able to, because "they've been captive to Candace."[74]

When Peterson does enter the *Alford* plea, Candace is outraged, and the concession violates her sense of justice. On the courthouse steps, she says in anger, "Alford Schmalford! You will be treated as guilty and live as a convicted felon. An innocent man does not plead guilty, and Mr. Peterson pled guilty today." In the end, Rudolf laments the millions and millions of dollars the state spent to convict an innocent person. No one ends up winning in this story, and Peterson, with sorrow at the futility of it all, quotes from the final scene of *Romeo and Juliet*: "All are punish'd."[75]

The Will to Punish

So, really, binge-watching TV has really led me to be a
humanitarian.

—Emily Simpson, *Real Housewives of Orange County*

N an episode of *The Real Housewives of Orange County* in March
2022, cast member Emily Simpson showcased her volunteer work
with the California Innocence Project, crediting her interest
in wrongful conviction to documentaries and her television binge-
watching habit. An attorney, Simpson offered her legal expertise to the
organization and now contributes to its efforts by reviewing applications.
She explained, "I get sent a case, and then I make my own personal decision as to whether it should go forward that we can represent them and
actually help them. And I have read through cases where it is so clear
to me that this person is not guilty that it breaks my heart." She used
her platform as a Bravo Housewife to raise awareness, and the episode
featured her having lunch with an exoneree who had served fourteen
years of a thirty-year sentence for rape and murder before being exonerated based on DNA evidence. We get to hear a little bit of his story and
witness her expressing empathy for him and indignation at the injustice.

The Real Housewives of Orange County first aired in 2006 and inspired numerous, if not seemingly ubiquitous, spin-offs in different cit-
ies. The series showcase the "conspicuous consumption, privilege, and
pampered excess" of women whose "self-interest [borders] on solip-
sism."[1] The *Housewives* franchise is hardly prestige TV and functions as
lowbrow camp, gleefully offering up the cast members for ridicule and
opprobrium, while seeming to celebrate vapid and narcissistic visions
of women. Often individual Housewives will use the show to highlight

hastily thrown-together business ventures, trying to sell products such as handbags, face creams, makeup, and candles—all of which are associated with traditional, if not old-fashioned, female gender norms organized around beauty and presentation. Social justice issues and critical inquiry are usually nowhere to be seen in the Housewives universe, falling far outside what producers have believed to be their viewers' interests.

So Simpson championing the innocent marks something new, not only for *Housewives* but for American popular culture more generally. It indicates that innocence issues are now inarguably mainstream, no longer confined to critical criminology, academia, and elite journalism. This shift is part of a cultural moment when critiques of criminal justice and demands for reform are widespread through different segments of society. The popularity of innocence narratives in the past decade coincides with a growing understanding of systemic injustice that began to emerge around 2010, when the insights of critical criminologists started to disseminate more broadly. That year saw the federal government's Justice Reinvestment Initiative and the publication of the massively popular and influential *The New Jim Crow: Mass Incarceration in the Era of Colorblindness*, by Michelle Alexander, representing a cultural pivot from the "punitive turn" toward a critical, reform-minded movement. For the general public, innocence seems to be an important access point to these issues. As Emily Simpson explains on one of her social media accounts, focusing on wrongful conviction not only helps free the innocent but can "work to reform the criminal justice system, and train students to become zealous advocates."[2]

Throughout this book, I have examined the New True as a twenty-first-century iteration of true crime that rejects the de facto portrayal of the defendant as a dangerous deviant and instead implicates state actors as potential perpetrators of injustice. I now consider the representation of innocence issues in these long-form docuseries in the context of the larger culture, situating them within ongoing discourses about punishment in US society and changing views about who, how, and why we punish.

Mass Incarceration and Popular Culture

Critiques of criminal justice are increasingly a feature of popular culture, where the fact that the US makes up 5 percent of the world's population but houses 25 percent of the world's prisoners is now frequently cited in the media.[3] The general public now has greater knowledge about the ways the system operates, the ways it is flawed, and the devastating impacts these have on communities of color. Criminal justice is increasingly understood as an arm of oppression. Today, for many people, mass incarceration—not crime—is a social crisis. Our punishment practices, not our crime rates, are increasingly understood as the problem.

The criminologists Todd R. Clear and Natasha A. Frost identify 2009 as marking the change in how we talk about incarceration and when we began to recognize mass incarceration as a grave problem.[4] Frost declared the 2013 "the beginning of the end of mass incarceration."[5] This understanding first took shape in the mid-1990s as scholars began sounding the alarm about the dramatic increase in the size of the United States' prison population since the 1970s—a sevenfold increase between 1970 and 2004, with the US now having nearly two million people behind bars and another five million people under community supervision.[6] The United States has the highest incarceration rate in the world and holds one-fifth of the world's prisoners.[7] During the 1990s, scholars identified "the punitive turn" and "the new penology" and explained the various extralegal factors contributing to "the prison binge."[8] These authors point to the convergence between global capitalism, the rise of the neoliberal state and the destruction of the social safety net, and political realignments stoked by racism and fear. They do not attribute policies such as the war on crime and the war on drugs to crime rates or increased substance use but rather to reactionary political strategies designed to hobble the civil rights movement and other radical calls for social change.[9]

The politicization of crime issues resulted in support of a number of policies that together account for the historic increase in the criminal justice population. Well-funded police forces empowered with zero-tolerance tactics led to massive increases in drug arrests, while the federal government and the states introduced an array of highly popular, harsh sentencing policies that extended the sentences for drug-related convictions and intensified existing racial disparities. The 1990s saw media amplification of violent crime and harsher sentencing for repeat offenders, including a shift from indeterminate to determinate sentencing and mandatory minimum sentencings, as well as the introduction of three-strikes laws.[10] This era also marked a rise in community surveillance technologies that brought more people into the web of social control. In addition, labeling juvenile offenders "super-predators" led to more young people being tried as adults to face longer sentences.[11]

Mass incarceration has also been recognized as first and foremost a form of racial social control. Looking at the disproportionate rate of imprisonment for Black communities, Loïc Wacquant sees Black "hyper-incarceration" as an instrument designed to create and enforce caste.[12] With one out of every nine Black men ages twenty to thirty-four behind bars and a steadily increasing gap in incarceration rates between Black people and white, Wacquant argues that incarceration is serving an "extra-penological" function of "defining, confining, and controlling African Americans in the United States."[13] Wacquant analyzes mass incarceration as a hyperghetto entwined with the prison, which has replaced other "peculiar institutions" that control and oppress Black people, specifically slavery (1619–1865), Jim Crow (1865–1965), and the urban ghetto in the North (1915–1968).

This historical analysis is chronicled in more detail, and for a broader audience, by Michelle Alexander in her best-selling *The New Jim Crow: Mass Incarceration in the Era of Colorblindness*, which, in 2010, catapulted the crisis of mass incarceration into the general public's consciousness. Promoting its release, Alexander made media appearances on progressive outlets such as *Democracy Now*, NPR, and MSNBC. She has also since been featured in several documentaries, including *The House I Live In*, about the war on drugs, and *The 13th*, about the role of criminal justice in racial oppression.[14] The book has sold over one million copies, has been cited in important legal decisions, and has been quoted by celebrities at the Academy Awards.[15] Alexander's work has been compared to W. E. B. Du Bois's, and, attesting to its power and influence, it has actually been banned in several prisons.[16] Its ten-year anniversary was celebrated by the comedian Ellen DeGeneres on her popular daytime talk show. Since its publication, mass incarceration has become a "commonplace concern," and a range of journalists and popular historians have joined criminal justice scholars in writing about these issues.[17] This wave of nonacademic general-nonfiction books critical of the criminal justice system looks at the militarization of law enforcement, the political organization of prisoners, private prisons, prosecutorial misconduct, restorative justice, and prison abolition.[18] Taken together, these books offer the public sophisticated, well-researched, nuanced critiques of key aspects of criminal justice. Like the New True, they provide case examples, explanations of procedures and legal concepts, and sociohistorical analysis.

Criticism of criminal justice is now a regular feature of left-leaning popular media, from straight news programs like *All In with Chris Hayes* to progressive-learning infotainment such as the late-night comedy show *The Daily Show with Trevor Noah* and comedy/talk shows like *Real Time with Bill Maher*. On John Oliver's weekly comedy/news show on HBO Max, *Last Week Tonight*, the comedian has devoted a number of his main story segments to different aspects of the criminal justice system's problems. In addition to a 2022 segment on wrongful conviction in which he stated that Black men are seven times more likely to be wrongfully convicted than white men, Oliver has devoted segments to prison, lethal injection, bail and pretrial detention, mandatory minimums, elected judges, for-profit policing, public defenders, reentry issues, municipal violations, and civil asset forfeiture. These segments inform and educate viewers about the system's procedures and methods while framing arguments about how they contribute to social injustice.

Wrongful conviction is an important part of this growing, increasingly impactful, popular movement focused on the system's massive and destructive failures, with the New True emerging as the one of the more visible criminal-justice-reform-conscious media products. Exemplifying the synergy between innocence issues and popular culture is the reality television star and celebrity businesswoman Kim Kardashian, who has been making a new name for herself as an advocate for the wrongfully convicted. She met with Donald Trump in the Oval Office during his presidency to lobby for shorter sentences and petition for a wrongfully convicted woman, and she has used her Twitter platform (with over seventy million followers) to advocate for other cases. She is also enrolled in a law school program in order to more effectively pursue this work, and her efforts to study for the bar exam may be chronicled in the renewed reality show about her family, produced for Hulu.[19]

Penal Harm and the Will to Punish

Existing within a culture that has become conscious of the relationship between punishment and racism and injustice, and consumed simultaneously as entertainment and journalism, the New True may function dually as catalysts for reform and as palliatives for anxieties and ambivalences about punitiveness. US society is charged with conflicting currents of punishing sentiments and the desire to see itself as modern, civilized, rational and just. I believe the New True create a space where these opposing orientations can coexist, with stories of innocence bridging a gap between warring societal concerns about crime, punishment, and social justice.

Docuseries about wrongful conviction tend to focus on trial processes, looking at how someone can be wrongfully convicted. They do not, however, look at the nature and mechanisms of punishment. Prison furnishes the backdrop of these narratives but does not claim the spotlight. Yet the stories these series tell are deeply tied to the ways we punish and the ways we justify punishment, and wrongful convictions take place within a larger culture shaped by punitive sentiments.

In a paper analyzing the difference between innocent defendants who were identified and released (near misses) and those who were eventually convicted, Jon Gould et al. examine the effects of cultural punitiveness on wrongful conviction. For the purpose of analysis, they use the number of executions in each state as a marker of punitiveness. They found that defendants in more punitive states were at a higher risk of conviction. In states with a more punitive legal culture, "police and prosecutors may be more interested in obtaining a conviction *at all costs* (leading to greater *Brady* violations, etc.), and community pressure may encourage overly swift resolutions to cases involving serious crimes like rape and murder. Additionally, officials in more punitive states may be more likely to assume the defendant's guilt. This culture eventually works against the innocent defendant, as state agents overlook or undervalue evidence that contradicts the assumption of guilt."

They find that in contrast, "defendants in less punitive jurisdictions might benefit from a law enforcement or legal community willing to consider exculpatory theories or evidence": "Among the near misses in our study, there were many examples of prosecutors in less punitive jurisdictions who actively questioned the case prepared by the police or another prosecutor, as well as judges who rigorously vetted evidence, such as confessions, during pretrial hearings."[20] Laying out the differences in how prosecutors approach cases, this work places the causes of wrongful conviction that I have already examined within a broader cultural context and points to the significance of popular punitiveness in wrongful conviction.

The policies that led to mass incarceration were fueled by an intensification of harsh public sentiments about perceived offenders. For much of the twentieth century, crime was addressed through progressive-minded efforts to reform and reintegrate offenders, and until the 1970s, Americans professed some commitment to a rehabilitative framework geared toward treating the offender and addressing the underlying causes of crime, such as poverty. From the earliest days of the penitentiary, this perspective has fluctuated, with prisons being viewed as failures in one decade, only to be seen as having promising potential, with reformation, in the next.

But in the 1970s, the rehabilitative ideal took a blow that it has not since recovered from. The 1974 publication of Robert Martinson's article "What Works? Questions and Answers about Prison Reform" is often seen as a definitive marker of this shift in thinking. Politicians embraced the cynical belief that nothing works and incorporated it into fear-stoking rhetoric and campaigns built around tougher sentencing, while adopting a neoliberal framing of crime and poverty as the result of the free choices of dangerous and unrestrained individuals and weak social control. They used "gonzo" language to "justify exaggerated acts of punishment . . . and . . . make the extreme seem necessary through compelling narratives of institutional failure and unnecessary victimization."[21] Punitive sentiment was freely expressed, giving way to what John Pratt calls a "decivilizing" of punishment, in which it is "made to be a public spectacle again; punishments are to be made more unpleasant rather than ameliorated; much of the rhetoric and ideology associated with them is based around brutalizing language and images; there is a sense of anxiety, crisis, and fear which allows non-modern and explicitly coercive and punitive strategies . . . to gain acceptance as a crime fighting strategy."[22]

Punishment practices began to move backward, away from rationalization and bureaucratization. Todd R. Clear's elaboration of the phrase "penal harm" brings into focus an aspect of punishment that is often overlooked, although always operative: "it is supposed to hurt." He frames punishment as "a planned governmental act whereby a citizen is harmed," which "implies that harm is justifiable precisely because it is an offender who is suffering."[23] This fundamental characteristic of punishment is often downplayed because of cultural ambivalences about the infliction of suffering.[24] Penal harm may certainly be necessary for utilitarian goals such as community safety/incapacitation and deterrence, but it is particularly critical to retribution, where harm is expressly stated as the goal of punishment.

Nietzsche's concept of the will to power is useful here, as it points to a universal orientation to dominate, master, and be obeyed. In his philosophy, punishment (like true crime) is related to pleasure.[25] Revenge, like anger, can be a powerful, consuming emotion, and punishment can be seen as the manifestation of this drive. It is controlled and constrained through our criminal justice institutions and practices. The will to punish is a deep human instinct that is collectively expressed in penal harm.

Popular punitiveness entails a denigration and Othering of the offender, who is increasingly less likely to be seen as deserving of rights and who must be framed in such a way as to justify their casting out. The rise of the victims' rights movement in the 1980s, which merged some of the goals of the feminist movement with those of conservative think tanks, is an important example of how due process protections became degraded. The movement posits a zero-sum game between victims' and offenders, where defendants' legal protections are "articulated as coming at the expense of the victims' well-being"; conversely, limiting these rights and expanding harsh punishments "affirm the value of the victims' life."[26] Rafael Ginsberg argues that victims' rights are part of a neoliberal project that rejects the societal goals of punishment and societal solutions to problems and are part of the array of practices that have led to mass incarceration. Individually and collectively, the policies that created mass incarceration shut down any possibilities of meaningful integration of offenders and deny "the importance of societal relations generally."[27] Victims' rights goals cast out the offender, not just as irredeemable but as not even worthy of redemption efforts. Important due process protections of the innocent against wrongful convictions are seen as violations of the victims and, by extension, the populace. Victims' rights are a populist manifestation of punitiveness. Traditional true crime is often aligned with the goal of retribution, as it valorizes the victim, arouses disgust for the perpetrator, and demands vindication for those who have been harmed.

Revenge and retribution are the principal emotional register of penal harm; they animate the victims' rights movement and are personified in some of the New True in the figures of victims' family members such as Kathleen Peterson's sister Candace and Teresa Halbach's brother. Yet retribution as a motive for punishment makes people in modern society uneasy. We want to mask our will to punish. Revenge themes in popular culture are "one more manifestation of the gap between private feelings about revenge and the public pretense that justice and vengeance have nothing, perish the uncivilized thought, to do with each other."[28] Indeed, vengeance and the infliction of suffering are often perceived as at odds with civilized, democratic ideals, "regarded as the sick vestige of a more punitive stage of human development."[29] Historical changes in the modes of punishment have entailed increasing rationalization and bureaucratization, and punitive sentiments began to be seen as shameful, negative, and irrational.[30] We like to believe that as a society we have risen above base emotions and have mastered primitive needs to inflict suffering. Because of this, the New True are able to cast victims' family members as villains. Their unabashed will to punish is at odds with how we like to see ourselves.

Punishment is emotional, and the will to punish is possibly as strong as the need to see ourselves as civilized. The New True evoke strong emotions in audiences, which form an identification with the defendant and a sense of outrage against the state, and innocence may act as a cathexis for contradictory sentiments around punishment. In *Punishment and Culture*, Philip Smith explores the ways in which dark needs and negative passions geared toward righteously inflicting suffering continually need to be concealed in order to mitigate our ambivalence. Specific forms of punishment lose their appeal when their methods reveal themselves to be too barbarous for the sensibilities of the times.[31] For example, the electric chair was once widely viewed as more "humane" than previous forms of execution, such as hanging. Intended to "cleanse judicially sanctioned death," the electric chair eventually began to be seen as gruesome and tortuous, "an icon of barbarousness, a symbol of oppression, a relic of the past, and the carrier of a ghoulish charisma."[32] In other words, when the harms of punishment become too visible and hard to ignore, people feel conflicted and seek another means of punishment that better masks the underlying will to punish.

For the same reason that the electric chair emerged, it eventually gave way to a seemingly more sanitized medical procedure: the lethal injection. Yet this method, too, is now beginning to be understood as inhumane. In a 2019 segment of *Last Week Tonight*, John Oliver expressed views similar to Smith's, arguing that lethal injection seems humane compared to "the horrors of the electric chair."[33] People may think the person goes gently into sleep. But Oliver explained that the three-part injection method does not include adequate anesthesia and that the paralytic and cardiac arrest components are tortuous. He concluded his segment by saying that the methods of execution are about our sensibilities, not the experiences of the person being executed: "It is a show, designed not to minimize the pain of people being executed but *to maximize the comfort of those who want to support the death penalty without confronting the reality of it*, which is that it's violent and it's brutal and it's never going to be anything other than that."

I see the New True as offering an imperfect reconciliation between the will to punish and the need to see oneself as "civilized." The will to punish must always be expressed in ways that seem rational and just to the observer; but punishment, when scrutinized, often reveals itself to be brutal. Through dramatic narratives that foster an identification between the audience and the defendant, the New True provide an opportunity to feel moral outrage against a perceived wrong perpetrated by the state without asking audiences to take a close look at the methods of punishment themselves. The narratives are about defendants who are living within prisons during much of the filming and who have been stripped of their rights and banished from their communities. Yet none of the series highlight the inhumanity of prisons. The documentarians work to reinstate the defendants' status as rightful members of civil society, yet in arguing their innocence, the documentarians sidestep an examination of what the US does to those we have deemed guilty and thus "deserving" of punishment. Solitary confinement, boot camps, chain gangs, long sentences, the conditions within prison—none of these are held up to scrutiny, and the ways we treat the majority of people under control of the criminal justice system who are in fact guilty are left beyond the scope of the series.

Although the series do not explicitly examine mass incarceration and penal harm, some innocence scholars have suggested that the punitive turn may have helped make innocence issues more broadly and culturally salient. The rise in the numbers of people incarcerated created a greater urgency to help offenders and scrutinize the system.[34] The catalogue of errors identified by wrongful-conviction scholars and activists suggests reforms that would create a much more just, more perfect criminal justice system, one in which all defendants—including the guilty—would be afforded robust due process, including well-funded and zealous attorneys, oversight of each step of investigations, and mechanisms for preventing and responding to agents of the state abusing their power. Each type of reform is unconditionally necessary. However, innocence as a vehicle for criminal justice reform falls short of addressing other systemic problems, the underlying punitive culture, and the horrors of what we actually do to the people we consider deserving of punishment. Innocence narratives leave contradictory beliefs about crime and punishment unreconciled.

Expanding the Concept of Innocence and Reckoning with Injustice

Some innocence scholars foreground economic inequality and systemic racism in their analysis of wrongful conviction. In "Finding the Causes in the Contexts: Structural Sources of Wrongful Conviction," William S. Lofquist looks at the concentrated disadvantage faced by Black people, arguing that the structural factors creating wrongful conviction should be understood in terms of "the larger contexts in which particular groups become vulnerable to being defined as suspects, to being arrested, and to having their arrests transformed into convictions."[35] He considers wrongful conviction in relation to the criminalization of poor, Black communities and the construction of crime as "a primary problem . . . to be resolved through the direct application of policy resources, rather than also secondarily and indirectly, as a byproduct of investments in employment, community building, and education, as crime control had previously been understood."[36] Here Lofquist links wrongful-conviction issues to the decline of the rehabilitative ideal and the punitive turn and posits, in Ginsberg's terms, a *societal* view of crime issues rather than a neoliberal one. When criminal justice issues are seen as social justice issues and racial justice issues, education, employment, housing, and health care are all part of the solution. From this standpoint, wrongful convictions cannot be addressed in a vacuum by focusing on specific flawed procedures because those procedures are deeply entwined with systemic racism and structures that maintain inequality.

An antidote or companion piece to the New True is *Free Meek*, a 2019 documentary series available on Amazon Prime Video about the long-term negative consequences of criminal conviction. This series reimagines innocence and unties it from its legal definition. Meek Mill is a successful Black rap artist from South Philadelphia who was arrested and convicted in his youth on drugs and weapons charges. Following a short term in prison, he was released on parole for five years. The documentary shows the numerous obstacles and legal entanglements that being under this supervision created for Mill. Mill did in fact commit the original crime, and in what is in some ways a radical departure for true crime, *Free Meek* attacks the criminal justice system for the way it oppresses poor people, particularly people of color, entrapping them within a carceral control apparatus that works in tandem with economic and racial injustice—regardless of innocence.

In a critique of traditional true crime, Rangan Pooja and Brett Story praise *Free Meek* for pointing to a "form of abolition documentary that relinquishes . . . its investments in the category of crime altogether." They maintain that "crime and criminality are invented and mutable constructs" that "authorize a set of violent and punitive intrusions by the state into the lives of its citizens, and, increasingly, non-citizens."[37] *Free Meek* is radical in that it bestows the mantle of innocence on Mill "despite his guilt." He is innocent "relative to the harsh and unreasonable punishment that does not fit the crime." Pooja and Story bring attention to the potential danger of innocence narratives that may "reify *guilt* as justifications for often severe punitive action."[38] Others have also noted as problematic the ways the New True leave "unchanged the oppressive treatment of legally and factually guilty defendants and prisoners" and "untouched the question of why incarceration is so devastating."[39] *Free Meek* perhaps marks important new iterations of innocence narratives with the potential to challenge the will to punish and to expand the range of our empathy in ways that could transform our visions of justice and point to radical compassion.

By highlighting wrongful punishment instead of *excessive* punishment, innocence has the capacity to let us off the hook, to allow us to view the system as imperfect but amenable to reform. Innocence projects offer numerous concrete ways of reducing wrongful convictions, all of which would make a more just system generally, at least with regard to who is convicted. But what happens to people after convictions, even rightful ones, is left in the shadows.

Although the New True leave us nowhere with regard to how we treat the guilty, and injustice is framed as a wrong done to the innocent, by generating some empathy for their subjects, the series open the door to new ways for framing the guilty. The documentarians leave room to believe that the defendants still might actually be guilty of the murders they were convicted of and, in so doing, complicate our feelings by presenting the defendants with dignity and humanity regardless of their innocence. If they are guilty, if they are in fact where they "should" be, can we, as members of an audience and as members of a society, be pressed to reconsider our will to punish?

The will to punish is exemplified in the figure of the angriest, most vindictive victim, the victim who wants as most punishment as possible. This figure is easy to demonize, easy to pathologize, and easy to characterize as "grieving by punishment."[40] At the other end of the spectrum are stories such as that of Katie Kitchen, who forgave her father's murderer and advocated for his release without asking for him to show remorse or accountability. Kitchen had a deep sense of her own privilege as a middle-class white woman and an understanding of racial injustice informed by antiracist writers such as Ibram X. Kendi. Her commitment to social justice inspired her to press for the release of the disadvantaged Black man.[41] Restorative justice programs, such as the one Kitchen participated in, work with a range of cases between such extremes and recognize that "mercy alone often fails to acknowledge the suffering of those harmed or to take seriously the responsibility of those who caused pain."[42] They honor and acknowledge the pain and suffering of survivors while seeking solutions to violent crime that repair harm. These programs are intended to address mass incarceration and the failures of prison, and they are receiving greater attention and have been featured in a CNN series, *The Redemption Project*, with Van Jones.

The death penalty is the ultimate punitive sanction, and it inspires intense emotion and intense debate. It represents the will to punish in its starkest, purest form. Innocence has played a critical role in some lawmakers' decisions to reconsider it. But for me, the most persuasive arguments I have heard on the subject are those made in opposition to it not on grounds of innocence but on grounds of mercy. These have been most powerfully made by murder victims' friends and family, who have formed groups advocating for the abolition of capital punishment. One such group made forceful, heart-rending statements that influenced Governor George Ryan of Illinois. They did not believe that the death of a murderer would heal their loss or do justice to their loved ones' memories. These victims' families stand in contrast to the unflattering images of the vindictive families in the New True, such as Candace.

Advocacy groups such as California Crime Victims for Alternatives to the Death Penalty tell the stories of those whose lives were deeply, unalterably impacted by violent crime. In their words, we hear anguished calls for the "healing power of forgiveness." One parent of a twenty-three-year-old murder victim states, "We do not think that the execution of [our son's] killer will make the world a better place. We honor [our son's] life by working for peace and social justice—goals that were important to him." A parent of another young victim states, "For the past 16 years I've continued working for peace. I believe where the wounds are, the gift lies."[43] While mercy is a theme far less prominent in popular culture than retribution is, if we look, we can find such stories. I believe more of these would make a powerful, truly new, more radical addition to our true-crime pantheon alongside the contemporary narratives of innocence.

Wrongful Conviction and Society

N 2005, the legal scholar Richard A. Leo called for a criminology of wrongful conviction, inviting criminologists and empirical social scientists to develop "a coherent academic field of study" with generalizable precepts.[1] I believe that the study of wrongful convictions should include sociocultural perspectives and that representations of wrongful convictions in popular culture are an important component of this sociology. In this chapter, I suggest ways several interrelated theoretical orientations can be engaged in developing a robust sociology of wrongful conviction that applies a conflict perspective along with an examination of cultural and symbolic meanings.

A Critical Criminology of Wrongful Conviction

Adopting a pluralist understanding of conflict among social groups in society guides us to questions about whose interests benefit from the policies and culture of punitiveness. Given that punishment policies over the past forty years have devastated low-income communities of color, it is impossible to see this transformation as serving the interests of the economically and socially marginalized; it instead suggests that those policies might serve the interests of those who benefit from inequality.

Those who are most often criminalized come from powerless groups that are considered "problem populations" for those who benefit from established economic relations.[2] This includes some subjects of the New True—the impoverished men in *The Innocent Man*, the *Paradise Lost* trilogy, and *Making a Murderer*, as well the middle-class Wayne Williams. Preserving the economic and social status quo is an ever-animating priority for the same conservative politicians who employ tough-on-crime rhetoric in their campaigns and enact punitive policies while in office. The financial and corporate elite associated with center-right politics benefit from establishing and maintaining a general populace focused on cultural issues rather than economic ones, who can be easily riled by a politics of fear. Racism and white supremacy have a stake in the punitive state, which has been described by Michelle Alexander as enforcing a separate caste system that maintains these. Additionally, various state actors, such as police officers and their departments and prosecutors and their offices, need to be well funded and ideologically supported to maintain their status. Their jobs, budgets, available resources, and social power are on the line in contests over punishment.[3]

The interests of these diverse groups coalesce in the criminal justice goals of deterrence, incapacitation, and retribution, which are best effected in what has been called a "crime control" model, as opposed to a "due process" model. These models impact innocence issues in society in the same way that Gould et al.'s study was able to link differing outcomes to the state's overall punitiveness. The crime-control model prioritizes the repression of crime as the paramount, overriding function of the criminal justice system.[4] Swiftly catching the bad guys and severely punishing them is important above all else. "The punitive turn" has meant a hard shift to the crime-control model, with its "tougher punishments, greater efficiency in processing offenders, and fewer constitutional constraints on police power."[5] Emphasizing the need for public safety, which is most keenly felt when the media stoke fears of crime, this model aligns with conservative ideology, maintenance of the status quo, and management of problem populations. It is achieved through harsh treatment of offenders and little concern for their rights. As previously discussed, in this model, protections of defendants are seen as obstacles to the goals of justice.

The interests of economic elites, politicians, and criminal justice professions are best served when the criminal justice system is designed to punish down, away from those in power. The due-process model, in contrast prioritizes protecting the individual from abuses of state power. Freedom from injustice requires procedural safeguards such as "the presumption of innocence, transparency of police and judicial proceedings, and credible appeals processes."[6] This view upholds constitutional protections that guard against wrongfully convicting the innocent and keep government overreach and absolute authority in check. It has the greater potential to serve the interests of the socially vulnerable.

A crime-control model designed to catch the bad guys above all else can entail a high tolerance for collateral consequence because the ends are believed to justify the means, and we have seen how such a culture in prosecutors' offices contributes to the likelihood of *Brady* violations, as Gould et al. and others have demonstrated.[7] Such a system cannot be overly concerned with errors because such focus would hinder its overall effective functioning.[8] It is true that wrongful-conviction issues can be reframed as necessary to community safety, in that they call for making sure the actual criminal is really off the streets, but in fact, wrongful convictions are more usually used as calls for more robust due process.[9] Because of this, wrongful-conviction narratives push back on the crime-control emphasis and, indirectly, the interests that support it.

The crime-control model, aligned with political agendas and the self-generating demands of a growing "prison industrial complex," is set up to reduce Type II errors (false negatives, i.e., releasing a guilty person), even at the expense of more false positives (i.e., convictions of the innocent, or Type I errors).[10] What amount of which type of error is considered acceptable is a matter for debate.[11] Blackstone's often-quoted ratio that "it is better that ten guilty persons escape than that one innocent suffer" is by no means set in stone or in any way collectively agreed on.[12] In fact, one study has found that jurors are more reluctant to let a guilty person go free than they are to err in the other direction, and another found a decline over time in the belief that convicting an innocent person is worse than releasing a guilty one.[13] In these scenarios, the ratio is one to one, far smaller than the relatively liberal ten to one expressed by Blackstone. This suggests that when the goal is to maximize punitiveness, as in the crime-control model, wrongful convictions may be considered an unfortunate, though acceptable, by-product. Narratives of innocence, which dramatize individual cases and create an emotional identification with the defendant, call this situation into question, asking if it is in fact acceptable.

By bringing the existence of Type I errors to the general public and explaining them as the consequences of inadequate due process, the New True narratives provide a way to consider these tensions and consciously think about the goals of justice. They offer the public a granular view of some aspects of the working of justice from the perspective of people who believe they were wronged. They put a human face on "false positives" and show the consequences of these errors on the lives of individuals. Turning the criminological gaze toward the state, these stories make claims about the importance of the presumption of innocence and push back on the premises of crime-control perspectives. Framing the convicted as victims of the state, these series are public pleas to reduce the societal tolerance of these errors.

Social constructionist perspectives highlight the work in which competing groups engage in contests to define the situation and position the status quo, or resistance to change, as serving the interests of "government, crime control agencies, and social elites."[14] In the much-anthologized article "Conflict and Criminal Law," Joseph F. Sheley posits that criminal definitions are relative and subject to change over time. This idea is rooted in the sociology of deviance that rejects the notion that deviance is inherent in the individual and instead argues that it is a function of social definitions and processes.[15] In this discussion of the New True, the deviance in question is both the state's actions that lead to wrongful convictions, what has been called "official deviance," and the alleged crimes of the defendants. The New True are sites of negotiation between opposing views of reality and wrongdoers, contests between prosecutors and defense attorneys over the ascription of deviance to the defendants' characters. A social constructionist perspective helps elucidate how the meanings given to these issues are contested by different social groups with conflicting perspectives.

With the rise of the "DNA revolution," innocence issues have gained prominence in the cultural landscape, and the innocence movement has grown from a handful of lawyers and journalists to a more organized, impactful force in criminal justice.[16] Wrongful conviction stories have been taking up greater space in a number of media spheres, and their producers have emerged as claims-makers in an arena of shifting definitions of criminal justice that is shaped by "political influence, social sentiment, cultural values, and the interests of powerful groups in society."[17] The New True have come to represent a greater proportion of true-crime storytelling on streaming platforms, along with some of the episodic series, such as *The Innocence Files* and *The Confession Tapes* on Netflix, and episodic podcasts such as *Wrongful Conviction*—all of which contribute to the social movement and a more critical popular criminology.

In Richard Leo's 2017 look back at progress made since his 2005 article calling for a criminology of wrongful conviction, he discusses a number of significant books written by journalists and lawyers, as opposed to academic social scientists, including "big picture" ones that revisit the existing "familiar plots" of wrongful conviction (e.g., eyewitness misidentification, false confessions, etc.) and case-study-type works that are similar to the New True in that "they humanize the problem of wrongful conviction by documenting the history of many individual case tragedies. . . . These books are written to reach a popular audience and have often been the basis for television documentaries, shows, plays, and even movies. They tell gripping stories of the reality of wrongful convictions that poignantly illustrate the discrepancy between our legal ideals and the ongoing failures of the criminal justice system."[18] Humanizing accounts of wrongful conviction represent one side of the public contest over how to define this issue, with documentarians advocating for greater oversight of criminal justice actors and evidence-based reforms of existing practices. They speak up to power and challenge the status quo.

Narratives of wrongful conviction are proliferating at a moment when popular punitiveness seems to be giving way to popular resistance. Clear and Frost observe that "the emotional and practical energy for punitive harshness, seemingly irresistible just a short time ago, now is oddly passé."[19] Criminal justice is increasingly recognized as a race-creating and inequality-maintaining system that needs to be dismantled in the name of racial and social justice. Antiracist critiques of law enforcement and its routine practices are now regularly featured in the media. The enormous public outcry following the murder of George Floyd has inspired younger generations to fight against racism and dismantle white supremacy, with an understanding of the critical role criminal justice plays in maintaining oppression. Wrongful convictions have a part to play in this movement. Bryan Stevenson's 2014 book *Just Mercy* and the subsequent 2020 feature film are an example of how innocence can help illuminate broader, systemic injustice. Stevenson frames wrongful conviction in the context of the brutality of poverty and racism in the South and recounts his tireless work advocating for the innocent as a quest for racial justice and equality. This popular book has been read as a call for action and has been praised for its potential to inspire social change.[20]

Wrongful convictions are also important to critical criminology because they threaten the legitimacy of the state. When wrongful convictions are in the spotlight, as they are in the New True, the attention shifts from the criminality to the ways the state harms its citizens. Saundra D. Westervelt and Kimberly J. Cook have contributed to the wrongful-conviction field in their studies of the lives of released exonerees. They have argued that these men are victims of state harm, using a framework outlined by David Kauzlarich et al., who claim that victims of state crimes experience "economic, cultural, or physical harm, pain, exclusion, or exploitation because of tacit or explicit state actions or policies which violate the law or generally defined human rights."[21] The New True narrate state actors' law violations and subject this wrongdoing to scrutiny.

Richard Lippke argues that the presumption of innocence "is a legal protection which reflects the proper relationship which should apply between citizen and State."[22] Inadequate due process, or a commonly held belief that individuals are insufficiently protected, is inconsistent with the ethos of a functioning democracy. Ideal democracy is dependent on equality among its citizens and a state that is by, for, and of the people, not a state that is run by powerful elites focused on maintaining their power. When the public is not afforded the "moral assurance" intended by the presumption of innocence and the state's burden of proof beyond a reasonable doubt, it becomes difficult to conceive of the state in this ideal sense. In other words, wrongful convictions undermine citizens' belief in the adequate functioning of democracy.

Cultural Criminology: Meanings, Myths, and Reproduction

The limits on the New True's ability to inspire robust reform, as we have seen in reactions on Reddit and other social media, may be rooted in the ease with which consumer capitalism co-opts resistance. As entertainment, the series can be seen as repackaging critiques of criminal justice into consumable commodities in the media marketplace. Like the for-profit platforms on which they air, the New True are products of consumer capitalism. As such, they are part of an existing array of punishment-themed amusements.

Critical and cultural criminologists explore the relationship between criminal justice practices, representations, and power relations under late-stage capitalism. This perspective highlights the media among the social institutions that reproduce class relations in a way that makes power and inequality seem natural and right.[23] These representations are themselves products—packaged, bought, sold—in the entertainment market, where they have the potential to become sites of ideological struggle and competing views.[24]

Although imprisonment is a form of punishment largely kept out of view, we—as consumers of culture—have a working knowledge of aspects of it, furnished through signs and symbols and visual images, what Michelle Brown calls a "prison iconography" that repeats through various iterations of crime media.[25] The tower and concertina razor wire against a clear sky, the striped or orange uniforms, the shackled foot, the hands gripping bars, the long, dystopic tiers of cells—these are all visual staples of fiction and documentary that are just as likely to be featured on a John Oliver graphic on mandatory minimums, a drama about prison, or the cover of books on mass incarceration, such as *The New Jim Crow* or *The Culture of Control*. Signaling "the prison," this iconography becomes a shorthand for the regimes of social control that have emerged in the modern world through the crime-control policies that created the crisis of mass incarceration. It is in the entertainment marketplace that we clearly see the "circulating cultural fluidity" of the late modern world, where representations and reality become confounded with each other.[26] Brown has noted that the prison often functions as a metaphor for the bureaucratic dehumanization characteristic of the late modern world, calling forth the mind-numbing monotony of the workplace and even futuristic visions of "industrial entrapment."[27]

The prison is a constant specter in the New True. It is what the series' subjects are desperately trying to get out of, what the documentarians and defense attorneys are fighting against. It is the series' raison d'être. The glimpses that the filmmakers give of the prison and that Koenig engages at the beginning of each episode with the audio of the prisons' Global Tel Link recording ping audiences' knowledge receptors developed over time through a multitude of prison films and television shows, many of which "build audience empathy for the prisoner."[28]

As such, the New True are yet another iteration of punishment as popular culture. I have noted that the detective work in them serves to stimulate the audience. It creates a kind of "fun." Punishment-themed entertainments are even geared for children. A Lego City Prison Island instills children aged six to twelve with images and archetypes of crime and justice, along with a learning objective of "creative thinking." This 754-piece set was marketed as "a cool building toy" and features numerous props of social control such as a helicopter with spinning rotors, binoculars, walkie-talkies, handcuffs, and so on.[29] Although the product

was retired in 2019, while it was available, it received positive, even ef-
fusive, reviews on Amazon ("Lots of trapdoors and endless fun!").[30] The
incarcerated figure is de facto guilty; the convict is a plaything.

Should one look further for prison-themed toys, one will find a number of others, although geared for adults. These include a jigsaw puzzle
depicting "Prison Mike"—a photo of the character Michael Scott, the
boss on *The Office*, who in one episode ("The Convict") becomes so
discomfited when his coworkers compare their workplace to prison that
he tries to "scare them straight" by wearing a bandana and speaking in
some sort of accent, emulating the people he assumes are in prison. This
same image, now apparently iconic, is also available in a sequined pillow,
a celebration of this fictional character's comically distorted representation of the reality of prison.

A particularly strange merging of punishment and entertainment is
a variety of true-crime "activity books" and *The Steven Avery Coloring
Book*. Also worth noting, *The Real Housewives of New York* featured the
cast members attending a workout session called "ConBody," provided
by a company of that name that offers in-person and video on-demand
classes. The workout regimen and fitness inspiration is also available in
a book by Coss Marte, *ConBody: The Revolutionary Bodyweight Prison
Boot Camp Born from an Extraordinary Story of Hope* (2018). The boot
camp offers "pointless labor, humiliating haircuts, instant obedience to
commands, Spartan living conditions"; the justification is "their very
unpleasantness rather than their crime-reducing potential."[31] Yet for
middle-class and wealthy women, these experiences can be transformed
into consumable products promising an improved body and mind via
the rigorous and the purportedly transformative potential of prison
regimes.

Lego City Prison Island and ConBody workouts are examples of how
punishment is embedded in leisure practices. The signs and symbols that
make criminal justice legible and recognizable are diffuse throughout
society. Representations of criminal justice, punishment, and innocence
do not exist apart from an overarching social context but are in fact

intrinsic to that context, and they are laden with the properties of myth. Although in contemporary society punishment itself is usually hidden from public view, the ritual quality of the law and its consequences is continually witnessed and experienced through its representations in the news, particularly in the case of high-profile crimes, as well as fictionalized legal dramas and true-crime stories, including documentaries about wrongful conviction. These are saturated with myths about criminal justice, human behavior, and social norms, which are repeated with an almost compulsive quality throughout popular culture. The word "obsessed" is frequently used in relation to crime stories, and a platform devoted to several podcasts on the subject is aptly named "The Obsessed Network."

Crime stories form a cultural mythology. In their various forms, they express views on morality and ideology, character and identity, and the rightful order of the world. They draw from the monstrous archetypes of folk and fairy tales. True crime, from classic Victorian detective mysteries to contemporary forensic- and technology-driven serial-killer hunts, will continue to evolve at the same time key features continue to endure. They will stick to old scripts at the same time that they branch into new territory. The past decade has seen the emergence of stories of wrongful conviction and critiques of criminal justice. In this way, innocence narratives are adding to the existing mythology of justice.

Myths communicate meanings and require deciphering.[32] My analysis of the series that I have called the New True provides an examination of this mythology. In the previous chapters, I have focused on how narrative elements create social meaning and have in some ways sketched out the beginnings of a semiotics of innocence. At the center of the New True is the transgressive deed, the taking of a life, the dead body of the innocent victim. The bodily horror at the center of most crime stories is continually reproduced in crime-scene photos within the familiar structure of the criminal trial. Each player assumes their traditional role in the competition over the definition of the situation, which they try to establish through the presentation of "facts" as no longer fixed and immutable. From blood stains to phone records, items of evidence are believed to contain truths. While the constraints of the jury trial in the New True present mythologies of solvable mysteries, within the broader life of the docuseries, these are troubled and problematized and rendered disputable.

The New True represent myths about the monsters in our midst and employ repetitive cultural devices used to address questions about character. Mythologies tied to inequality and racial and class oppression are mobilized and inscribed onto the legal subject in efforts to establish the truth of their being. Social categories merge with embedded archetypes of evil and, in contemporary US society, are transformed or reformed through a medicalized vocabulary of psychopathology that aligns with conservative ideology and crime-control models as opposed to societal views of problems.

The New True series, by making arguments on behalf of their subjects' innocence, turn the tables on perceptions of villainy, moving the criminological gaze from the alleged murderer to the state. Often in popular culture, the prosecutor is the savior, as in the classic *Law & Order* TV series, which has been credited with inspiring a generation of aspiring attorneys.[33] In innocence narratives, however, prosecutors may be the real lawbreaker, violating our shared community beliefs about due process and the protection of individual rights. Changing the lens, the documentarians posit the dangers of an authoritarian, unconstrained government apparatus in narratives that coexist with darker, dystopic conspiracy themes in popular culture.

The six cases I have focused on are by no means the only contemporary stories of wrongful conviction. While I do see these popular, long-form, detailed series as having unique characteristics, I recognize that they exist within a still-growing field of critical documentary projects on criminal justice. Wrongful convictions are the subject of popular episodic podcasts such as some of the ones already mentioned, like *Wrongful Conviction* and *Undisclosed*, as well as illustrative episodic series on Netflix, such as *The Innocence Files* and *The Confessions Tapes*.

Interestingly, in 2021, a long-form, investigative podcast enlisting the work of an innocence organization, the twenty-episode *Murder in Alliance*, points to a possible new direction in this storytelling. On the episodic podcast *Unjust and Unsolved*, the journalist Maggie Freleng takes a deep dive into wrongful conviction each week. *Murder in Alliance* grew from one of those episodes, but after months of investigation uncovering shoddy police work and unfollowed leads, she eventually concedes that she and her team ultimately came up empty-handed. The man they sought to exonerate is most likely guilty, a far different conclusion from the ones the New True documentarians leave their audiences with. The conventions of innocence storytelling can lead to new ways of narrating guilt.

Conclusion

Truth and Consequences

Adnan's case contains just about every chronic problem our
system can cough up: police using questionable interview
methods, prosecutors keeping crucial evidence from the defense, slightly junky science, extreme prison sentences, juveniles treated as adults, [and] how grindingly difficult it is to
get your case back in court once you've been convicted.
—Sarah Koenig in *Serial*'s final episode, "Adnan Is Out" (2022)

T HERE are reasons to be hopeful about the direction the United
States is heading with regard to popular punitiveness, to think that
as empathy for the accused combines with demands for social and
racial justice, we will see a renewed commitment to meaningful, systemic criminal justice reforms tied to investments in public, societal
solutions. *Serial* was released in 2014, around the time "the beginning
of the end" of mass incarceration was starting to be proclaimed. Adnan
Syed's exoneration in 2022 was a result not only of the attention that
Serial brought to the case but also of recent reforms in the criminal
justice system, such as Conviction Integrity Units, and Maryland's Juvenile Restoration Act.[1] The economic crisis of 2008 made addressing
the financial burden of mass incarceration more urgent, contributing
to bipartisan support for postrelease programs.[2] Journalistic and social
science accounts depicting the hardships of individuals, families, and
communities impacted by criminal justice became more and more
common, and the zero-sum, get-tough views exemplified by the victims'
rights movement became tempered with a widespread perception that

the system had gotten out of control.[3] And, as I have argued, by arousing deep emotional identification with defendants, popular innocence narratives have contributed to this developing awareness.

Testament to the fact that the reform movement has moved into the mainstream is the bipartisan 2018 First Step Act, signed into law by President Donald Trump. The First Step Act includes sentencing reforms such as reducing mandatory minimums for second felonies and redefining serious violent and serious drug felonies. It allows for the retroactive application of the provisions of President Obama's 2010 Fair Sentencing Act, which reduced the sentencing disparity between crack and powder cocaine. To focus on better postrelease outcomes, it incentivizes participation in prison recidivism-reduction programs, and it reauthorized the 2007 Second Chance Act, which grants states support for more reentry programs. The First Step Act also addresses a number of issues associated with penal harm and the cruel treatment of inmates, at least in federal prisons. For example, it limits the use of shackles on pregnant inmates, prohibits solitary confinement for juveniles, expands the compassionate release guidelines, encourages placing inmates in prisons closer to their primary residence, and mandates deescalation training for prison staff.

Yet at the moment of this writing, in the middle of 2022, I do not have confidence in the direction that criminal justice is going and believe we are witnessing an unspooling of the potential for progress. For one, the media have been reporting spikes in crime that are having direct influence on politics. Mayor Eric Adams was elected in New York City in 2021 on a platform promising more support of law enforcement, and in 2022, the progressive San Francisco district attorney, Chesa Boudin, was recalled because he was not perceived as being tough enough on crime. Equally worrying is the new, chaotic, "post-truth" era we find ourselves in and how that shapes our understanding of social problems.

The representations of innocence and wrongful conviction that constitute the New True are stories of doubt that are shaped by the contemporary volatilization and polarization of truth characteristic of contemporary life. All the series are made available through streaming services that have contributed to a fractured viewership. Americans are now no longer watching the same things. In spite of the attention and buzz that accompany so much of today's programming, none has been watched by such a large a segment of the population as traditional twentieth-century sitcoms once were.[4] Content providers do not need to reach all at once but rather increase business by catering to, and creating, niche viewers. Internet-distributed content providers have enormous amounts of data on our private viewing habits. Netflix knows what we watch, when we watch, and how much we watch, and its home screens direct us to specific content that their algorithms have curated for us. This means our "content utopias" are simultaneously content bubbles, insulating and isolating us.[5] What I click on determines what is later available for me to click on. My Netflix home screen is not the same as yours. Few of us are seeing the same things when we turn on our smart TVs. The same is true for the news just as much for entertainment: CNN viewers are not seeing the same news as Fox News viewers. The media I have relied on in my analysis of the series is limited by the cultural echo chamber I exist in.

The New True projects mistrust the conclusions of the original fact finders: the juries. The series are premised on the idea that their conclusions are not certain, undermining the finality of the courts. The New True construct stories in which audiences can decide guilt or innocence for themselves, with the suggestion that truth is merely in the eye of the beholder. The epistemological anxieties that run through the New True also seep across American culture to the extent that Americans are more and more living in separate versions of reality.

During the time I have spent closely reading these docuseries, I have become increasingly unsettled by unfolding political events and view the ambiguity and uncertainty that these series present with more concern. While they provide important lessons about flaws in every aspect of the criminal justice system, which gives them great reform potential, it is perhaps more important to consider what it means that they leave audiences deeply divided, with some people feeling just as passionately convinced of one defendant's innocence as others do of their guilt. Koenig's observation that the same piece of evidence can be interpreted in completely opposite ways holds true when it comes to how facts are given meaning in the larger culture. Right now, the American public is riven in how it construes seemingly every single news event. The instability of truth that characterizes the New True has become a disturbing characteristic of the US political and media landscapes since Donald Trump rose to power and transformed our conversations about where truth lies.

In defending the patently false statements that then–White House Press Secretary Sean Spicer made about the size of the crowd at President Trump's 2017 inauguration, the president's counselor Kelly Ann Conway famously justified them as "alternative facts." The brazen denial of the notion of truth reignited sales of George Orwell's dystopic *1984* and opened the door for ever-more-outlandish statements by politicians and others that increasingly defy reason.[6] US politics has not been the same since.

Following the announcement of Joe Biden as the winner of the 2020 presidential election, President Trump, Republican lawmakers, and far-right commentators proclaimed "the big lie" that the election was "stolen," despite the election results repeatedly being independently verified. Since the 2020 elections, questioning election results has evolved from being a strategy to secure power to a whole new way of seeing reality, with Republicans using belief in "the big lie" as a kind of purity test to weed out party members.[7] Alternative facts have successfully inflamed easily riled emotions in such a way that truth is irrelevant. Writing in 2017 following false statements about voter fraud and inauguration turnout, Adam Gopnik explained that no one around Donald Trump believed his lies about three million illegal votes, but that was beside the point: "The lie is not a claim about specific facts; the lunacy is a deliberate challenge to the whole larger idea of sanity. Once a lie that big is in circulation, trying to reel the conversation back into the territory of rational argument becomes impossible."[8]

Five years later, the Congressional Select Committee investigating the January 6 insurrection is providing evidence that no one around the president believed the 2020 election was stolen either. But what is true does not matter. Large segments of the electorate, including the insurrectionists, profess to believe it and are inflamed by it. Trump's alternate reality animates a populist resentment that traditional politicians previously managed to contain. Gopnik argues this is the key to Trump's success: "His base loves craziness, incompetence, and contempt for reason because sanity, competence, and the patient accumulation of evidence are things that allow educated people to pretend that they are superior. Resentment comes before reason."[9]

The New True produce innocence stories that occupy an ambiguous position in a world where truth has lost its finality and objectivity, where reality is tribal, and where emotion outplays reason. They serve multiple functions. They champion the poor, rural, and uneducated against powerful elites, a narrative that can support both populist resentment politics and progressive reform ideology. They also express cynicism and paint pictures of routine government corruption that can contribute to apathy. As representations of crime issues and empathy-generating projects, they provide a framework that could advance a critical criminology. But by undermining the finality of jury verdicts, they present truth as contestable, which resonates with the hall-of-mirrors quality that our public life has taken on. In providing sophisticated explications of wrongful-conviction issues, they help create an informed, critical public, although, and at the same time, they resist consensus and leave innocence suspended.

In 2022, HBO Max released a dramatized, scripted series based on the Michael Peterson case, also titled *The Staircase*. The show is a strange reenactment of the documentary. Actors perform scenes from it, which are augmented with imagined dramatizations of events that took place beyond what Lestrade filmed. This version-of-a-version of real events shies away from committing to a theory of the case. While the director,

Antonio Campos, was not constrained by the same journalistic standards of documentary filmmaking and had far more freedom to present a point of view, he instead chose to suggest three possible explanations for Kathleen's death: an accidental fall, an owl attack, or a beating. The truth may never be known and can be endlessly debated. One reviewer observes that at this point, *The Staircase* is an "Escherian" metaphor, and for me, Peterson emerges in this show as more inscrutable, less real.[10]

We are not even attempting to get at the truth of a story; we are storytelling around it. While this may be an enjoyable form of entertainment, "fake news" and "alternative facts" have dangerously degraded American discourse to the extent that up is down and down is up. As it continues to emerge that no one who promoted the obvious, proven lies about the 2020 election really believed them, it remains unclear how public debate will meaningfully return to reason or how such a polarized nation will come to an agreement about what is true in politics, journalism, documentary, or popular entertainment.

Acknowledgments

THIS project first began to take shape as I prepared for a presentation at a faculty salon at Borough of Manhattan Community College, CUNY, when I realized that my work as a punishment scholar needed to examine the intersections between crime policy and popular culture, and so I thank the Faculty Salon Committee for that opportunity.

I am also grateful to the gang at my local coffee shop, Café Martin, particularly Jen and Jake, for the lively conversations and debate about some of the series I focus on.

Some of this work was developed during summer 2020, when I participated in an Incarceration and the Humanities seminar at La Guardia Community College, CUNY, which was funded by the National Endowment for the Humanities. I am always appreciative of Barbara Katz Rothman and Lynn Chancer for their intellectual inspiration and support.

For a close, attentive read of my manuscript and editorial guidance, I thank Tony Amato. I also thank Samara Michaelson for her help with later versions of the manuscript. Ilene Kalish and everyone at NYU Press have been invaluable.

Karen Starr must be credited not only for her support but for her help brainstorming chapter titles. I have her to thank for "Where Truth Lies."

Larisa Honey was an important sounding board as I began my research. Rebecca Tiger and Jessie Daniels played a large role in helping me focus my ideas and develop the shape of the book. Jessie's feedback on a number of chapters was invaluable, as was her friendship, advice, and encouragement through every stage of my writing process. I am indebted to Emily Pugh for turning my attention to historical accounts of grisly high-profile crimes.

Finally, I am grateful to friends and family for listening to me, sharing ideas and recommendations, making suggestions, and, again, listening. I know I talked a lot about this for a long time! All my thanks and gratitude to my A-team: Alex Exposito, Gillian McCain, Meridith McNeal, Laura Migdal, Lee Olin, David Ricard, Sarah Ricard, and Shari Sperling.

Notes

Introduction

1. Koenig et al., 2014 ("The Alibi").
2. Bolin, 2018.
3. Bruzzi, 2016.
4. Rafter, 2006, ix.
5. Berg, 2019 ("Time Is the Killer").
6. Kennedy, 2018, 391.
7. Brown, 2009, 12.
8. Beckett, 1999, 62.
9. Gabler, 1998, 59.
10. Jewkes, 2015, 49.
11. Chancer, 2005, 59.
12. Beckett, 1999, 65
13. Ferrell et al., 2015, 70.
14. Jewkes, 2015, 45.
15. Yardley et al., 2019, 509.
16. Chancer, 2005, 213.
17. Rafter, 2006, vii.
18. Rafter, 2006, 63.
19. Rafter, 2006, 76.
20. Ferrell et al., 2015, 133.
21. Gabler, 1998, 96.
22. Ferrell et al., 2015, 130.
23. Warden, 2014, 39, 42, 46.
24. Rafter, 2006, 11; Brown, 2009, 78.
25. Jarvis, 2007, 326.
26. Ferrell et al., 2015, 11.
27. Seltzer, 2007, 48.
28. Norris, 2017a, 13.
29. Acker, 2017, 8.
30. Maddy deLone, quoted in Norris, 2017a, 166.
31. Norris, 2017a, 27.
32. Norris, 2017a, 27.
33. Norris, 2017a, 3.

34. Carrano & Zalman, 2014, 11.
35. Carrano & Zalman, 2014, 13.
36. Lofquist, 2014, 19; Norris, 2017a, 95.
37. Acker, 2017, 10.
38. Lofquist, 2014, 19.
39. See Lippke, 2014.
40. Bazelon, 2019, xxvi.
41. Zalman & Marion 2014, 26.
42. Godsey, 2017, 87.
43. Godsey, 2017, 67.
44. Doyle, 2014, 59.
45. Zalman & Marion 2014, 30.
46. Norris & Bonventre, 2015, 929.
47. Lofquist, 2014, 21.
48. Carrano & Zalman, 2014, 11.
49. Gross et al., 2020.
50. Hale, 2015.

Chapter 1. True Crime

1. Chancer, 2005, 213.
2. Murley, 2008, 111.
3. Jewkes, 2015, 64.
4. Rafter, 2006, 5; Halttunen, 1998, 61.
5. Browder, 2006, 933.
6. Rafter, 2006, 8.
7. Murley, 2008, 110.
8. Dean, 2016.
9. See Halttunen 1998; and Punnett, 2018.
10. Gabler, 1998, 61.
11. Gabler, 1998, 61; Murley, 2008, 9.
12. Dowler et al., 2006, 837.
13. Gabler, 1998, 74.
14. Gabler, 1998, 70.
15. Chancer, 2005, 270; Gabler, 1998, 77.
16. Jewkes, 2015, 45.
17. Beckett & Sasson, 2004, 80.
18. Dowler & Fleming, 2006, 839.
19. Jewkes, 2015, 46.
20. Jewkes, 2015, 49–65.
21. Chancer, 2005, x.
22. Dowler & Fleming, 2006, 841.
23. Johnson & Johnson, 2021; Bolin, 2018.

24. Quoted in Chancer, 2005, 34.

25. Jewkes, 2015, 54.

26. Maratea & Monahan, 2013, 265.

27. Maratea & Monahan, 2013, 261, 263.

28. Maratea, & Monahan, 2013, 263.

29. Warden, 2014, 39.

30. Yant, 2014, 79–80.

31. Yant, 2014, 80.

32. Warden, 2014, 39.

33. Warden, 2014, 40.

34. Warden, 2014, 49.

35. Murley, 2008, 109.

36. Murley, 2008, 110.

37. Murley, 2008, 120.

38. Seltzer, 2007, 40.

39. Rhineberger-Dunn et al., 2017, 532.

40. Rafter, 2006, 63.

41. Daniels et al., 2018, 338, 340.

42. Rosenberger & Callanan, 2011, quoted in Berryessa & Goodspeed, 2019, 964.

43. Beckett & Sasson, 2004, 84.

44. Beckett & Sasson, 2004, 84.

45. Beckett & Sasson, 2004, 86–87.

46. Rafter, 2006, ix.

47. Rafter, 2006, 74.

48. Rafter, 2006, 74.

49. Rafter, 2006, 111.

50. Beckett & Sasson, 2004, 88.

51. See, for example, Grubb & Posick, 2021.

52. Murley, 2008, 110.

53. Seltzer, 2007, 37.

54. Berryessa & Goodspeed, 2019, 964; Murley, 2008, 112; Rhineberger-Dunn et al., 2017, 532.

55. Rhineberger-Dunn et al., 2017, 532.

56. R. Pratt, 2003, 259.

57. Murley, 2008, 118.

58. Seltzer, 2007, 2.

59. Murley, 2008, 13.

60. Murley, 2008, 13.

61. Murley, 2008, 12.

62. Murley, 2008, 27.

63. Murley, 2008, 16.

64. Murley, 2008, 4.

65. Murley, 2008, 4.

66. Murley, 2008, 17.
67. Quoted in Green, 2020.
68. Green, 2020.
69. Murley, 2008, 20.
70. Green, 2020 (emphasis in original).
71. Walter Lowe Jr., quoted in Green, 2020.
72. Chestnut, 2018; Monroe, 2019.
73. Dean, 2016.
74. Murley, 2008, 14; Monroe, 2019, 4.
75. Monroe, 2019, 4.
76. Monroe, 2019.
77. Monroe, 2019, 1.
78. Monroe, 2016, 6.
79. Murley, 2008, 59.
80. Halttunen, 1998, 160.
81. Murley, 2008, 74.
82. Murley, 2008, 74.
83. Browder, 2006, 929.
84. Browder, 2006, 932.
85. Browder, 2006, 932.
86. Browder, 2006, 935.
87. Browder, 2006, 937, 928.
88. These include Truman Capote's *In Cold Blood* (1966), Joseph Wambaugh's *The Onion Field* (1973), Vincent Bugliosi's *Helter Skelter* (1974), Norman Mailer's *The Executioner's Song* (1975), Ann Rule's *The Stranger Beside Me* (1980) and *Small Sacrifices* (1988), and Joe McGinnis's *Fatal Vision* (1983).
89. Murley, 2008, 44.
90. Murley, 2008, 4.
91. Murley, 2008, 45
92. Browder, 2006, 936.
93. Browder, 2006, 944.
94. Murley, 2008, 73.
95. Murley, 2008, 73.
96. Murley, 2008, 56.
97. Bruzzi, 2006, 15.
98. Bruzzi, 2006, 10.
99. Bruzzi, 2006, 74.
100. Druick, 2008, 441.
101. Fuhs, 2014, 787.
102. Fuhs, 2014, 786.
103. Manzella, 2011.
104. Weinberg 2005, 19.

Chapter 2. The New True

1. Steiner, 2017, 142.
2. Wayne, 2018, 728.
3. Poniewozik, 2015.
4. Mittel, 2016.
5. Wayne, 2018, 728.
6. Kenny, 2017.
7. Wayne, 2018, 726.
8. Baker, 2017, 31.
9. Grandinetti, 2017, 13; Steiner, 2017, 45.
10. Baker, 2017, 43.
11. Baker, 2017, 31; Steiner, 2017, 143.
12. Berry, 2006, 144.
13. Aufderheide et al., 2020, 1683.
14. Berry, 2016, 664.
15. Quoted in Kenny, 2017.
16. Murphy, 2018.
17. Bolin, 2020, 228.
18. For example, see Quah, 2022.
19. Paquet, 2018, 75.
20. Schulz, 2016.
21. Mnookin, 2005, 154.
22. Bruzzi, 2016, 280; Chestnut, 2018.
23. Marsh, 2016, 8.
24. Chestnut, 2018.
25. Buozis, 2017, 258.
26. Ferrell et al., 2015, 155.
27. Mnookin, 2005, 172.
28. Hale, 2012.
29. Mnookin, 2005, 179.
30. Adkins, 2008, 18.
31. Mnookin, 2005, 174.
32. Adkins 2008, 18.
33. Adkins, 2008, 17.
34. Monroe, 2019, 144.
35. Monroe, 2019, 145.
36. Seltzer, 2007, 36.
37. Seltzer, 2007, 53.
38. Monroe, 2019, 151.
39. Mnookin 2005, 154.
40. Mnookin, 2005, 154.
41. Itzkoff, 2012.

42. Adkins, 2008, 17.

43. Ryan, 2018.

44. Lestrade, 2018 ("A Prosecution Trickery").

45. Gilbert, 2018.

46. Gilbert, 2018.

47. Marsh, 2016, 7; McDonell-Parry, 2018b.

48. Lestrade, 2018 ("Reopening the Case").

49. Saraiya, 2018a.

50. Saraiya, 2018a; Ryan, 2018.

51. Fuhs, 2014, 798; Bruzzi, 2016, 254.

52. Boling & Hull, 2018, 92; Garner, 2014.

53. Bruzzi, 2016, 273.

54. Koenig et al., 2014 ("The Breakup").

55. LaFrance, 2014; Buozis, 2017, 260.

56. Marsh, 2016, 10.

57. Koenig et al., 2014 ("What We Know").

58. Yardley et al., 2019, 519.

59. Berg, 2019 ("Forbidden Love").

60. Berg, 2019 ("Time Is the Killer").

61. Koenig et al., 2022 ("Adnan Is Out").

62. Levenson, 2022.

63. Yardley et al., 2017, 472.

64. Yardley et al., 2017, 479.

65. Starr, 2018.

66. Shattuck, 2015.

67. McPhate, 2016; Starr, 2018; Victor, 2016b.

68. McPhate, 2016.

69. Murphy, 2015.

70. La Chance & Kaplan, 2019, 87; Marsh, 2016, 10.

71. Ricciardi & Demos, 2015 ("Plight of the Accused").

72. Hale, 2015.

73. La Chance & Kaplan, 2019, 86.

74. Ricciardi & Demos, 2015 ("Indefensible").

75. Ricciardi & Demos, 2015 ("Lack of Humility"; "The Great Burden").

76. Murphy, 2018.

77. Schulz, 2016.

78. Marsh, 2016, 11; Shattuck, 2015.

79. Ricciardi & Demos, 2018 ("Special Care").

80. Murphy, 2018.

81. Hale, 2018.

82. Hale 2018.

83. Hale, 2015.

84. Saraiya, 2018b; Schulz, 2016; Victor, 2016a.
85. Saraiya, 2018b.
86. Saraiya, 2018b.
87. Larson, 2018.
88. Baldwin, 1985, 10.
89. Baldwin, 1985, 12.
90. Williamson, 2021, 24.
91. Larson, 2018.
92. Miller, 2020.
93. Lindsey, 2018 ("Loose Ends").
94. Pollard et al., 2020 ("Part 2").
95. Miller, 2020.
96. Stevens, 2020.
97. Pollard et al., 2020 ("Part 5").
98. Tweel, 2018 ("Debbie and Denice").
99. Fitz-Gerald, 2018.
100. Gilbert, 2018.
101. Clay, 2021.

Chapter 3. Exhibit A

1. As in *An Angel Betrayed: How Wealth, Power, and Corruption Destroyed the JonBenet Ramsey Murder Investigation*, by David Hughes (2014).
2. Fuhs, 2014, 783; Fiske & Glynn, 1995, 505.
3. Silbey, 2007, 558.
4. Chancer, 2005, 117.
5. Hutson, 2017, 145.
6. Lestrade, 2018 ("Secrets and Lies").
7. Paquet, 2018, 72.
8. LaFrance, 2014.
9. Marsh, 2016, 7; Yardley et al., 2018, 82.
10. Murley, 2008, 5, 19.
11. Garrett, 2015, 258.
12. Adler, 2015, 242.
13. Murley, 2008, 5.
14. Douglas, 1966,
15. Halttunen, 1998, 65.
16. Halttunen, 1998, 66.
17. Seltzer, 2007, 10.
18. Yardley et al., 2017, 471.
19. Ginsberg, 2014, 924.
20. Yardley et al., 2017, 471.
21. Yardley et al., 2017, 471.

22. Barthes, 1981, 26.

23. Tweel, 2018 ("Debbie and Denice").

24. Tweel, 2018 ("Debbie and Denice").

25. Seltzer, 2007, 17.

26. Baldwin, 1985, 62.

27. Bernstein, 2011, 16.

28. Penfold-Mounce, 2016, 21, 28.

29. A. Jarecki, 2015 ("The State of Texas v. Robert Durst").

30. Seltzer, 2007, 41.

31. Lestrade, 2018 ("A Weak Case").

32. Hornshaw, 2018.

33. LaFrance, 2014.

34. Berg, 2019 ("In Between the Truth").

35. Foucault, 1977.

36. Garrett, 2015, 263.

37. Toobin, 2007, 32.

38. Toobin, 2007, 32.

39. Garrett, 2015, 261.

40. Pollard et al., 2020.

41. Lestrade, 2018 ("A Weak Case").

42. National Registry of Exonerations, 2022.

43. Ricciardi & Demos, 2018 ("What + Why = Who").

Chapter 4. Where the Devil Truly Resides

Portions of this chapter are also presented in Rickard, 2022a.

1. Berlinger & Sinofsky, 1996.

2. Jewkes, 2015, 22.

3. J. Young, 1999, 111.

4. J. Young, 1999, 112.

5. Weinstock, 2020b, 359.

6. Weinstock, 2020b, 359.

7. Cohen, 2020, 49.

8. Garfinkel, 1959.

9. Agamben, 1995, 131.

10. Yardley et al., 2019, 507.

11. Yant, 2014, 80.

12. Berlinger & Sinofsky, 1996.

13. Berlinger & Sinofsky, 2011.

14. Allison, 2018, vii.

15. Godsey, 2017, 161.

16. Ricciardi & Demos, 2015 ("18 Lost Years").

17. Hale, 2015.

18. Soderman & Carter, 2008, 21.

19. Manzella, 2011, 1232; La Chance & Kaplan, 2019, 86.

20. Tweel, 2018 ("Debbie and Denice").

21. Gilbert, 2018.

22. Tweel, 2018 ("Debbie and Denice").

23. Tweel, 2018 ("Corpus Delicti").

24. Lestrade, 2018 ("The Verdict").

25. Lestrade, 2018 ("Crime or Accident").

26. Lestrade, 2018 ("The Verdict").

27. Szymanski, 2012, 442.

28. Bruzzi, 2016, 251.

29. Lestrade, 2018 ("The Blow Poke Returns").

30. Lestrade, 2018 ("The Verdict").

31. Bernstein, 2011, 16.

32. Lindsey, 2018 ("CIA").

33. Pollard et al., 2020 ("Part 3").

34. Whitty, 2008, 1708.

35. Goffman, 1959, 141.

36. Lindsey, 2018 ("CIA").

37. Lestrade, 2018 ("Secrets and Lies").

38. Lestrade, 2018 ("Secrets and Lies").

39. Koenig et al., 2014 ("What We Know").

40. Koenig et al., 2014 ("The Case against Adnan Syed").

41. Smith, 2008, 179.

42. Kennedy, 2018, 399.

43. Mnookin, 2005, 164.

44. Mnookin, 2005, 165 (emphasis in original).

45. Giddens, 1991, 51.

46. Giddens, 1991, 58.

47. Halttunen, 1998, 133.

48. Weinstock, 2020a, 22.

49. Frankfurter, 2006, xiii.

50. Murley, 2008, 8.

51. Berlinger & Sinofsky, 1996.

52. Ricciardi & Demos, 2015 ("Fighting for Their Lives").

53. Ricciardi & Demos, 2015 ("Indefensible").

54. Frankfurter, 2006, 137.

55. Berryessa & Goodspeed, 2019, 963.

56. McMurty, 2016, 306.

57. Weinstock, 2020b, 359.

58. Weinstock, 2020b, 359.

59. Frankfurter, 2006, 134 (emphasis added).

60. Cohen, 2020, 49.
61. Weinstock, 2020b, 363.
62. Freud, 2020, 76.
63. Berryessa & Goodspeed, 2019, 965.
64. Lindsey, 2018 ("The Trial").
65. Buozis, 2017, 263.
66. Koenig et al., 2014 ("To Be Suspected").
67. Bruzzi, 2016, 253.
68. Godsey, 2017, 161.
69. Pollard et al., 2020 ("Part 3").
70. Baldwin, 1985, 10.
71. Baldwin, 1985, 75.
72. Malcolm, 1990, 74.
73. Yant, 1991, 78.
74. Koenig et al., 2014 ("Rumors").
75. Stout, 2005, 106.
76. Malcolm, 1990, 75.
77. Punnett, 2018, 46.
78. Seltzer, 2007, 41.
79. Buozis, 2017, 258.
80. Jewkes, 2015, 53; Punnett, 2018, 4.
81. Dayan, 2001, 22.
82. Kennedy, 2018, 400.

Chapter 5. Conviction and Wrongful Conviction

1. Medwed, 2017.
2. Leo, 2017, 83.
3. Leo, 2017, 85.
4. Bornstein & Green, 2011, 63.
5. Bornstein & Green, 2011, 63.
6. Neuschatz et al., 2008, 142.
7. Neuschatz et al., 2008, 142.
8. Rodriguez et al., 2019, 429.
9. Rodriguez et al., 2019, 431.
10. Lestrade, 2018 ("Secrets and Lies").
11. Bornstein & Greene, 2011, 65.
12. R. Pratt, 2003, 257.
13. Lofquist, 2014, 19.
14. National Registry of Exonerations, 2022.
15. Zalman & Marion, 2014, 26; Godsey, 2017, 87.
16. Gould, 2014, 2; Lofquist, 2014, 21.
17. Lofquist, 2014, 21; Leo, 2017, 88.

18. Doyle, 2014, 59.
19. Stohr & Walsh, 2015, 18.
20. Worden et al., 2014, 210–211.
21. Godsey, 2017, 67.
22. Godsey, 2017, 75; Leo & Davis, 2010, 33.
23. Norris & Mullinix, 2020, 329.
24. Godsey, 2017, 136; Lackey, 2020, 45; National Registry of Exonerations, 2022; Starr, 2013.
25. Leo & Davis, 2010, 25; National Registry of Exonerations, 2022.
26. Petersen, 2016; Starr, 2013.
27. Petersen, 2016; Starr, 2013.
28. Starr, 2013.
29. Godsey, 2017, 136.
30. Petersen, 2016.
31. Lackey, 2020, 48.
32. Leo & Davis, 2010, 25.
33. Starr, 2013; Leo & Davis, 2010, 45.
34. Leo & Davis, 2010, 15, 19.
35. Leo & Davis, 2010, 25.
36. Leo & Davis, 2010, 50 (emphasis in original).
37. Neuschatz et al., 2008, 137.
38. Carrano & Zalman, 2014, 11; Petersen, 2016; Leo & Davis, 2010, 48; Starr, 2013.
39. Neuschatz et al., 2008, 139.
40. Ricciardi & Demos, 2015 ("Indefensible").
41. Barthes, 1981, 42.
42. Ricciardi & Demos, 2015 ("Indefensible").
43. Ricciardi & Demos, 2015 ("Indefensible").
44. Ricciardi & Demos, 2015 ("Indefensible").
45. Leo & Davis, 2010, 23–24.
46. Ricciardi & Demos, 2015 ("Fighting for Their Lives").
47. Ricciardi & Demos, 2015 ("Indefensible").
48. Lackey, 2020, 60. This phenomenon is the focus of a recent docuseries on HBO Max, *Mind Over Murder* (2022).
49. When the charges against Syed were dropped in 2022, this was in part because there was evidence that the state had not turned over pertinent evidence.
50. Gross et al., 2020, 11.
51. National Registry of Exonerations, 2022.
52. Schoenfeld, 2005, 251.
53. Bazelon, 2019, 29.
54. Godsey, 2017, 63.
55. Scheck et al., 2003, 252.
56. Stacey, 1991, quoted in Lofquist, 2014, 24.

57. Gould et al., 2014, 80.
58. Scheck et al., 2003, 231; Bazelon, 2019, 191.
59. Scheck et al., 2003, 231.
60. Bazelon, 2019, 19.
61. Worden, 2014, 210.
62. Gould et al., 2014, 74; Scheck et al., 2003, 252.
63. Gould et al., 2014, 84.
64. Doyle, 2014, 64.
65. Doyle, 2014, 64; Scheck et al., 2003, 225.
66. Bazelon, 2019, 19; Weintraub, 2020, 1198.
67. Westervelt & Cook, 2010, 264.
68. Bornstein & Greene, 2011, 65.
69. *Brady v. Maryland*, 373 U.S. 83, 87 (1963).
70. Bazelon, 2019, 105; Scheck et al., 2003, 222.
71. Bazclon, 2019, 105.
72. Bazelon, 2019, 189.
73. Gross et al., 2020, 92.
74. Gross et al., 2020, 65.
75. Gross et al., 2020, 35.
76. Although prosecutorial misconduct was not a focus of either Koenig's or Berg's series on Adnan Syed, his release in 2022 was based in part on a *Brady* violation, as notes were found in his file indicating that the prosecutor had evidence of another possible suspect.
77. Kjeldgaard-Christiansen, 2019, 68.
78. Ricciardi & Demos, 2015 ("Testing the Evidence").
79. Ricciardi & Demos, 2018 ("Friday Nite").
80. Ricciardi & Demos, 2018 ("Special Care").
81. Pollard et al., 2020 ("Part 5").
82. Pollard et al., 2020 ("Part 4").
83. Pollard et al., 2020 ("Part 5").
84. Tweel, 2018 ("Corpus Delicti").
85. Tweel, 2018 ("Smoking Guns").
86. National Registry of Exonerations, 2022; Neuschatz et al., 2008, 138, 142.
87. Tweel, 2018 ("Snow Storm").
88. Westervelt & Cook, 2010, 261.
89. Westervelt & Cook, 2010, 261.
90. Westervelt & Cook, 2010, 263.
91. Stratton, 2015, 24.
92. Norris & Mullinix, 2020, 329.

Chapter 6. Judging the Jury

1. Marantz, 2018.
2. Marantz, 2018.
3. Marantz, 2018.
4. Rodriguez et al., 2019, 432.
5. Andrew D. (2020).
6. Unless otherwise indicated, all the quotes in this section are from posts and comments on r/MakingaMurderer, www.reddit.com. Users' handles have been omitted.
7. Rodriguez et al., 2019, 435.
8. Unless otherwise indicated, all the quotes in this section are from posts and comments on r/serialpodcast, www.reddit.com. Users' handles have been omitted.
9. Gavin H. (2020).
10. Unless otherwise indicated, all the quotes in this section are from posts and comments on r/TheStaircase, www.reddit.com. Users' handles have been omitted.
11. Fuhs, 2014, 798.
12. Unless otherwise indicated, all quotes about either the *Atlanta Monster* podcast or the HBO Max series *Atlanta's Missing and Murdered: The Lost Children* are from the following subReddits: r/serialkillers, r/TrueCrimePodcasts, or r/MindHunter, www.reddit.com. Users' handles have been omitted.
13. Unless otherwise indicated, all the quotes in this section are from posts and comments on r/WestMemphisThree, www.reddit.com. Users' handles have been omitted.
14. Unless otherwise indicated, all the quotes in this section are from posts and comments on r/TheInnocentMan and r/MakingaMurderer, www.reddit.com. Users' handles have been omitted.
15. Gould et al., 2014, 82.

Chapter 7. Where Truth Lies

This chapter is derived in part from an article published in *Law and Humanities* (Rickard, 2022b), copyright Taylor & Francis, available online: www.tandfonline.com.

1. Fiske & Glynn, 1995, 505.
2. Fiske & Glynn, 1995, 509.
3. Chancer, 2005, 5.
4. Malcolm, 1990, 63.
5. Buozis, 2017, 257–258.
6. Fuhs, 2014, 804.
7. Paquet, 2018, 84; Buozis, 2017, 255.
8. Marsh, 2016, 9.
9. Koenig et al., 2014 ("The Alibi").
10. Baldwin, 1985, 100.

11. Rothbart, 2012.
12. Griffin, 2016.
13. Bruzzi, 2006, 56.
14. Bruzzi, 2006, 36.
15. Bruzzi, 2006, 74.
16. Bruzzi, 2006, 78.
17. Bruzzi, 2006, 13.
18. Fuhs, 2014, 784.
19. Malcolm, 1990, 32.
20. Modell, 2018.
21. Gruttadaro, 2018; Modell, 2018.
22. Modell, 2018.
23. Modell, 2018.
24. Schulz, 2016.
25. Schneider, 2018.
26. Schulz, 2016.
27. Schulz, 2016.
28. Bradley, 2018.
29. Lestrade, 2018 ("Reopening the Case").
30. Yardley et al., 2017, 479.
31. Yardley et al., 2017, 477.
32. Yardley et al., 2017, 480.
33. Yardley et al., 2017, 479.
34. Ricciardi & Demos, 2018 ("Special Care").
35. Clay, 2021.
36. Ferguson, 2016, 132.
37. Ferguson, 2016, 146 (emphasis in original).
38. Lippke, 2014.
39. Lippke, 2014, 340.
40. Lippke, 2014, 339.
41. Lestrade, 2018 ("Secrets and Lies").
42. Tweel, 2018 ("Corpus Delicti").
43. Ricciardi & Demos, 2015 ("The Great Burden").
44. Ferguson, 2016, 133.
45. Shapiro & Muth, 2021, 1029.
46. Shapiro & Muth, 2021, 1034.
47. Koenig et al., 2014 ("What We Know").
48. Koenig et al., 2014 ("What We Know").
49. From r/serialpodcast, www.reddit.com.
50. Berg, 2019 ("Time Is the Killer").
51. Lindsey, 2018 ("Air Tight").
52. From r/MindHunter, www.reddit.com.

53. Fuhs, 2014, 799, 800.

54. Lestrade, 2018 ("The Verdict").

55. Lestrade, 2018 ("Flawed Justice").

56. From r/TheStaircase, www.reddit.com.

57. Ricciardi & Demos, 2015 ("The Lack of Humility").

58. Griffin, 2016.

59. From r/MakingaMurderer, www.reddit.com.

60. Victor, 2016a.

61. From r/MakingaMurderer, www.reddit.com.

62. Ricciardi & Demos, 2015 ("The Last Person to See Theresa Alive").

63. Ferguson, 2014, 147.

64. Yoffe, 2017.

65. Conklin, 2020, 9.

66. Conklin, 2020, 8.

67. Conklin, 2020, 14, 15.

68. Redlich & Ozdogru, 2009, 472.

69. Conklin, 2020, 11.

70. Berg, 2019 ("Time Is the Killer").

71. Vota, 2012, 1021.

72. Berlinger & Sinofsky, 2011.

73. Lestrade, 2018 ("Flawed Justice").

74. Lestrade, 2018 ("Flawed Justice").

75. Lestrade, 2018 ("Flawed Justice").

Chapter 8. The Will to Punish

1. Leonard, 2020, 278.

2. Vena, 2022.

3. See E. Jarecki, 2012; and DuVernay, 2016.

4. Clear & Frost, 2014.

5. Clear & Frost, 2014, xiii.

6. Western, 2007, xvii.

7. Clear & Frost, 2014, 17.

8. Garland, 2001; Feeley & Simon, 1992; Parenti, 1999/2008.

9. Parenti, 1999/2008, 13.

10. Clear & Frost, 2014, 74.

11. Clear & Frost, 2014, 75.

12. Wacquant, 2001, 98.

13. Wacquant, 2001, 96, 98.

14. E. Jarecki, 2012; DuVernay, 2016.

15. Bromwich, 2018.

16. Bromwich, 2018.

17. Gopnik, 2019.

18. See Radley Balko's *Rise of the Warrior Cop: The Militarization of America's Police Forces* (2014), Bryan Stevenson's *Just Mercy: A Story of Justice and Redemption* (2014), Naomi Murakawa's *The First Civil Right: How Liberals Built Prison America* (2014), Dan Berger's *Captive Nation: Black Prison Organizing in the Civil Rights Era* (2016), Elizabeth Hinton's *From the War on Poverty to the War on Crime: The Making of Mass Incarceration in America* (2016), Shane Bauer's *American Prison: A Reporter's Undercover Journey into the Business of Punishment* (2018), James Forman Jr.'s Pulitzer Prize–winning (and controversial) *Locking Up Our Own: Crime and Punishment in Black America* (2018), Emily Bazelon's *Charged: The New Movement to Transform American Prosecution and End Mass Incarceration* (2019), Danielle Sered's discussion of restorative justice in *Until We Reckon: Violence, Mass Incarceration, and a Road to Repair* (2019), Victoria Law's *"Prison Makes Us Safer": And 20 Other Myths about Mass Incarceration* (2021), and Mariame Kaba's *We Do This till We Free Us: Abolitionist Organizing and Transforming Justice* (2021).
19. Respers France, 2021.
20. Gould et al., 2014, 80 (emphasis in original).
21. Maratea & Monahan, 2013, 270.
22. Pratt, 1998, 487.
23. Clear, 1994, 4.
24. Clear, 1994, 5.
25. Nietzsche, 1965, 12; Garland, 1990, 63.
26. Ginsberg, 2014, 919.
27. Ginsberg, 2014, 927.
28. Jacoby, 1983, 8.
29. Jacoby, 1983, 17.
30. Garland, 1990, 189.
31. Smith, 2008, 144.
32. Smith, 2008, 142.
33. Season 6, episode 10.
34. Norris, 2017a, 135.
35. Lofquist, 2014, 22.
36. Lofquist, 2014, 25.
37. Pooja & Story, 2021.
38. Pooja & Story, 2021(emphasis in original).
39. La Chance & Kaplan, 2019, 85.
40. Sered, 2019, 21.
41. Orbey, 2022.
42. Sered, 2019, 94.
43. Murder Victims Families Reconciliation, Death Penalty Focus, and American Civil Liberties Union of Northern California, 2008.

Chapter 9. Wrongful Conviction and Society

1. Leo, 2017, 82.
2. Spitzer, 1975.
3. Kraska & Brent, 2011, 153.
4. Kraska & Brent, 2011, 93.
5. Kraska & Brent, 2011, 97.
6. Kraska & Brent, 2011, 93.
7. Gould et al., 2014.
8. Zalman, 2014, 285.
9. Acker, 2017, 17.
10. Kraska & Brent, 2011, 197.
11. Xiong et al., 2017, 20.
12. Shapiro & Muth, 2021, 1042.
13. Shapiro & Muth, 2021, 1042; Xiong et al., 2017, 19.
14. Kappeler, 2011, 187.
15. Sheley, 1991.
16. See Norris, 2017a and 2017b.
17. Kappeler, 2011, 186.
18. Leo, 2017, 85.
19. Clear & Frost, 2014, 3.
20. Conover, 2014.
21. Westervelt & Cook, 2012, 260.
22. Lippke, 2014, 348.
23. Jewkes, 2015, 21.
24. Jewkes, 2015, 28.
25. Brown, 2009, 50.
26. Ferrell et al., 2015, 130.
27. Brown, 2009, 66.
28. Global Tel Link refers to the communications company that provides phone services (at exorbitant cost) to inmates; Brown, 2009, 59.
29. Lego, n.d.
30. Customer review on Lego Prison Island 60130, October 29, 2018, Amazon.com.
31. J. Pratt, 1998, 501.
32. Barthes, 1972, 121.
33. Norris, 2017a, 201.

Conclusion

1. Hellgren, 2022; Levenson, 2022.
2. Clear & Frost, 2014, 3.
3. Clear & Frost, 2014, 3.
4. Manjoo, 2017.
5. Crouch, 2016.

6. De Freytas-Tamura, 2017.
7. Levine, 2021.
8. Gopnik, 2017
9. Gopnik, 2017.
10. St. Felix, 2022.

References

Acker, J. R. (2017). Taking stock of innocence: Movements, mountains, and wrongful convictions. *Journal of Contemporary Criminal Justice, 33*(1), 8–25.

Adkins, K. (2008). *Paradise Lost*: Documenting a southern tragedy. *Journal of Film and Video, 60*(1), 14–22.

Adler, A. (2015). The pleasures of punishment: Complicity, spectatorship, and Abu Ghraib. In C. J. Ogletree & A. Sarat (Eds.), *Punishment in popular culture* (pp. 236–256). New York University Press.

Agamben, G. (1995). *Homo sacer: Sovereign power and bare life.* Stanford University Press.

Alexander, M. (2010). *The new Jim Crow: Mass incarceration in the era of colorblindness.* New Press.

Allison, D. (2018). Stubborn girls and mean stories. In *Trash* (pp. vii–xvi). Penguin Books.

Andrew D. (2020, October 20). Making a Murderer: Season 1 reviews: All audience. *Rotten Tomatoes.* www.rottentomatoes.com.

Aufderheide, P., Lieberman, D., Alkhallouf, A., & Ugboma, J. M. (2020). Podcasting as public media: The future of US news, public affairs, and educational podcasts. *International Journal of Communication, 14*, 1683–1704.

Baker, D. (2017). Terms of excess: Binge-viewing as epic-viewing in the Netflix era. In C. Barker & M. Wiatrowski (Eds.), *The age of Netflix: Critical essays on streaming media, digital delivery and instant access* (pp. 31–45). McFarland.

Baldwin, J. (1985). *Evidence of things not seen.* Henry Holt.

Barthes, R. (1972). *Mythologies* (A. Lavers, Trans.). Hill and Wang.

Barthes, R. (1981). *Camera lucida: Reflections on photography* (R. Howard, Trans.). Hill and Wang.

Bazelon, E. (2019). *Charged: The new movement to transform American prosecution and end mass incarceration.* Random House.

Beal, T. (2020). Introduction to *Religion and Its Monsters.* In J. A. Weinstock (Ed.), *The monster theory reader* (pp. 295–302). University of Minnesota Press.

Beckett, K. (1999). *Making crime pay: Law and order in contemporary American politics.* Oxford University Press.

Beckett, K., & Sasson, T. (2004). *The politics of injustice: Crime and punishment in America.* Sage.

Berg, A. (Director). (2019). *The case against Adnan Syed* [Film]. HBO.

Berlinger, J., & Sinofsky, B. (Directors). (1996). *Paradise lost: The child murders and Robin Hood Hills* [Film]. HBO.

Berlinger, J., & Sinofsky, B. (Directors). (2000). *Paradise lost 2: Revelations* [Film]. HBO.

Berlinger, J., & Sinofsky, B. (Directors). (2011). *Paradise lost 3: Purgatory* [Film]. HBO.

Bernstein, R. (2011). *Racial innocence: Performing American childhood from slavery to civil rights*. New York University Press.

Berry, R. (2006). Will the iPod kill the radio star? *Convergence: The International Journal of Research into New Media Technologies, 12*(2), 143–162.

Berry, R. (2016). Part of the establishment: Reflecting on 10 years of podcasting as an audio medium. *Convergence: The International Journal of Research into New Media Technologies, 22*(6), 661–671.

Berryessa, C., & Goodspeed, T. (2019). The brain of Dexter Morgan: The science of psychopathy in Showtime's season 8 of *Dexter. American Journal of Criminal Justice, 44*, 962–978.

Bolin, A. (2018). *Dead girls: Essays on surviving an American obsession*. William Morrow.

Bolin, A. (2020). The ethical dilemma of highbrow true crime. In S. Weinman (Ed.), *Unspeakable acts: True tales of crime, murder, deceit, and obsession*, 227–240. Ecco.

Boling, K. S., & Hull, K. (2018). "*Undisclosed* information—*Serial* Is *my favorite* murder: Examining motivations in the true crime podcast." *Journal of Radio and Audio Media, 25*(1), 92–108.

Bornstein, B. H., & Greene, E. (2011). Jury decision making: Implications for and from psychology. *Current Directions in Psychological Science, 20*(1), 63–67.

Bradley, L. (2018, October 9). Why *Making a Murderer's* creators made part 2. *Vanity Fair.* www.vanityfair.com.

Bromwich, J. E. (2018, January 18). Why are American prisons so afraid of this book? *The New York Times.* www.nytimes.com.

Browder, L. (2006). Dystopian romance: True crime and the female reader. *The Journal of Popular Culture 39*(6), 928–953.

Brown, M. (2009). *The culture of punishment: Prison, society and spectacle.* New York University Press.

Bruzzi, S. (2006). *New documentary* (2nd ed.). Routledge.

Bruzzi, S. (2016). Making a genre: The case of the contemporary true crime documentary. *Law and Humanities, 10*(2), 249–280.

Buozis, M. (2017). Giving voice to the accused: *Serial* and the critical potential of true crime. *Communication and Critical/Cultural Studies, 14*(3), 254–270.

Carrano, J., & Zalman, M. (2014). An introduction to innocence reform. In M. Zalman & J. Carrano (Eds.), *Wrongful conviction and criminal justice reform: Making justice* (pp. 11–23). Routledge.

Chancer, L. (2005). *High-profile crimes: When legal cases become social causes.* University of Chicago Press.

Chestnut, Rachel (2018, June 1). Is true crime as entertainment morally defensible? *The New York Times*. www.nytimes.com.

Clay, N. (2021, February 8). Family of victim in infamous Oklahoma murder lashes out at Netflix. *The Oklahoman*. www.oklahoman.com.

Clear, T. R. (1994). *Harm in American penology: Offenders, victims, and their communities*. State University of New York Press.

Clear, T. R., & Frost, A. (2014). *The punishment imperative: The rise and failure of mass incarceration*. New York University Press.

Cohen, J. J. (2020). Monster culture (seven theses). In J. A. Weinstock (Ed.), *The monster theory reader* (pp. 37–58). University of Minnesota Press.

Conklin, M. (2020). The *Alford* plea turns fifty: Why it deserves another fifty years. *Creighton Law Review*, 54(10), 1–18.

Conover, T. (2014, October 17). "Just Mercy" by Brian Stevenson. *The New York Times*. www.nytimes.com.

Crouch, I. (2016, January 7). The image of Netflix as content utopia. *The New Yorker*. www.newyorker.com.

Daniels, J., Netherland, J. C., & Lyons, A .P. (2018). White women, US popular culture, and narratives of addiction. *Contemporary Drug Problems*, 45(3), 329–346.

Dayan, J. (2001). Legal slaves and civil bodies. *Nepantla: Views from the South*, 2(1), 3–39.

Dean, M. (2016, June 23). "True crime addict" and the serious problem of internet sleuths. *The New Yorker*. www.newyorker.com.

De Freytas-Tamura, K. (2017, January 25). George Orwell's "1984" is suddenly a best seller. *The New York Times*. www.nytimes.com.

Douglas, Mary. 1966. *Purity and Danger: An Analysis of Concepts of Pollution and Taboo*. Routledge and Kegan Paul.

Dowler, K., Fleming, T., & Muzzatti, S. (2006). Constructing crime: Media, crime, and popular culture. *Canadian Journal of Criminology and Criminal Justice*, 48(6), 837–850.

Doyle, J. (2014). An etiology of wrongful convictions: Error, safety, and forward-Looking accountability in criminal justice. In M. Zalman & J. Carrano (Eds.), *Wrongful conviction and criminal justice reform* (pp. 56–72). Routledge.

Druick, Z. (2008). The courtroom and the closet in *The Thin Blue Line* and *Capturing the Friedmans*. *Screen*, 49(4), 440–448.

DuVernay, A. (2016). *The 13th* [Film]. Netflix.

Feeley, M. M., & Simon, J. (1992). The new penology: Notes on the emerging strategy of corrections and its implications. *Criminology*, 30 (4), 449–474.

Ferguson, P. (2016). The presumption of innocence and its role in the criminal process. *Criminal Law Forum*, 27, 121–158.

Ferrell, J., Hayward, K., & Young, J. (2015). *Cultural criminology: An invitation*. 2nd ed. Sage.

Findley, K. A., & Scott, M. (2006). The multiple dimensions of tunnel vision in criminal cases. *Wisconsin Law Review*, 2, 291–397.

Fiske, J., & Glynn, K. (1995). Trials of the postmodern. *Cultural Studies*, 9(3), 505–521.

Fitz-Gerald, S. (2018, December 18). Netflix's newest true-crime series will make you question the justice system (again). *thrillist*. www.thrillist.com.

Foucault, M. (1977). *Discipline and punish: The birth of the prison*. Vintage Books.

Frankfurter, D. (2006). *Evil incarnate: Rumors of demonic conspiracy and satanic abuse in history*. Princeton University Press.

Freud, S. (2020). The uncanny. In J. A. Weinstock (Ed.), *The monster theory reader* (pp. 59–94). University of Minnesota Press.

Fuhs, K. (2014). The legal trial and/in documentary film. *Cultural Studies*, 28(5–6), 781–808.

Gabler, N. (1998). *Life: The movie: How entertainment conquered reality*. Vintage Books.

Garfinkel, H. (1956). Conditions of successful degradation ceremonies. *American Journal of Sociology*, 61(5), 420–424.

Garland, D. (1990). *Punishment and modern society: A study in social theory*. University of Chicago Press.

Garland, D. (2001). *The culture of control: Crime and social order in contemporary society*. University of Chicago Press.

Garner, D. (2014, December 18). "Serial" podcast finale: A desire for "eureka" as the digging ends. *The New York Times*. www.nytimes.com.

Garrett, B. I. (2015). Images of injustice. In C. J. Ogletree & A. Sarat (Eds.), *Punishment in popular culture* (pp. 257–286). New York University Press.

Gavin H. (2020, January 30). The Staircase: Season 1 reviews: All audience. *Rotten Tomatoes*. www.rottentomatoes.com.

Giddens, A. (1991). *Modernity and self-identity: Self and society in the late modern age*. Stanford University Press.

Gilbert, S. (2018). *The Innocent Man* tells half a story. *The Atlantic*. www.theatlantic.com.

Ginsberg, R. (2014). Mighty crime victims: Victims' rights and neoliberalism in the American conjuncture. *Cultural Studies*, 28(5–6), 911–946.

Godsey, M. (2017). *Blind injustice: A former prosecutor exposes the psychology and politics of wrongful convictions*. University of California Press.

Goffman, E. (1959). *The presentation of self in everyday life*. Anchor Books.

Gopnik, A. (2017, January 27). Orwell's 1984 and Trump's America. *The New Yorker*. www.newyorker.com.

Gopnik, A. (2019, April 3). How we misunderstand mass incarceration. *The New Yorker*. www.newyorker.com.

Gould, J. B. (2014). Introduction. In M. Zalman & J. Carrano (Eds.), *Wrongful conviction and criminal justice reform: Making justice* (pp. 1–10). Routledge.

Gould, J. B., Carrano, J., Leo, R. A., & Hail-Jares, K. (2014). Innocent defendants: Divergent case outcomes and what they teach us. In M. Zalman & J. Carrano (Eds.), *Wrongful conviction and criminal justice reform: Making justice* (pp. 73–89). Routledge.

Grandinetti, J. (2017). From primetime to anytime: Streaming video, temporality and the future of communal television. In C. Barker & M. Wiatrowski (Eds.), *The age of Netflix: Critical essays on streaming media, digital delivery and instant access* (pp. 11–30). McFarland.

Green, E. (2020, August 21). The enduring, pernicious whiteness of true crime. *The Appeal.* www.theappeal.com.

Griffin, L. K. (2016, January 12). *Making a Murderer* is about justice, not truth. *The New York Times.* www.nytimes.com.

Gross, S. R., Possley, M. J., Jackson Roll, K., & Huber Stephens, K. (2020). *Government misconduct and convicting the innocent: The role of prosecutor, police, and other law enforcement.* National Registry of Exonerations.

Grubb, J. A., & Posick, C. (Eds.) (2021). *Crime TV: Streaming criminology in popular culture.* New York University Press.

Gruttadaro, A. (2018, June 9). "What about the truth?": *Staircase* director Jean-Xavier de Lestrade on the Michael Peterson case. *The Ringer.* www.theringer.com.

Hale, M. (2012, January 11). Third film on killings shows toll of time. *The New York Times.* www.nytimes.com.

Hale, M. (2015, December 16). *Making a Murderer,* true crime on Netflix. *The New York Times.* www.nytimes.com.

Hale, M. (2018, October 19). "Making a Murderer Part 2": What's next for Steven Avery. *The New York Times.* www.nytimes.com.

Halttunen, K. (1998). *Murder most foul: The killer in the American gothic imagination.* Harvard University Press.

Hellgren, M. (2022, September 23). Adnan Syed is one of many: A look at MD defendants who have had murder convictions thrown out. *CBS News Baltimore.* www.cbsnews.com.

Hornshaw, P. (2018, June 8). "The Staircase": What the heck is blow poke, the supposed murder weapon? *The Wrap.* www.thewrap.com.

Hughes, D. (2014). *An angel betrayed: How wealth, power, and corruption destroyed the JonBenet Ramsey murder investigation.* Strategic Book Publishing.

Hutson, L. (2017). Proof and probability: Law, imagination, and the forms of things unknown. In E. S. Anker & B. Meyler (Eds.), *New directions in law and literature* (pp. 144–159). Oxford University Press.

Itzkoff, D. (2012, January 6). Filmmakers take dual roles in quest for truth. *The New York Times.* www.nytimes.com.

Jacoby, S. (1983). *Wild justice: The evolution of revenge.* Harper Colophon Books.

Jarecki, A. (Director). (2015). *The jinx: The life and deaths of Robert Durst* [TV Series]. HBO Documentary Films.

Jarecki, E. (Director). (2012). *The house I live in* [Film]. Abramorama.

Jarvis, B. (2007). Monsters Inc.: Serial killers and consumer culture. *Crime, Media, Culture: An International Journal, 3*(3), 326–344.

Jewkes, Y. (2015). *Media and crime* (3rd ed.). Sage.

Johnson, T. L., & Johnson, N. N. (2021, October 4). Despite skewed media image, Black men are more likely to be victimized than other groups. *USA Today*. www.usatoday.com.

Kappeler, V. E. (2011). Inventing criminal justice: Myth and social construction. In P. B. Kraska & J. J. Brent, *Theorizing criminal justice: Eight essential orientations* (2nd ed., pp. 185–195). Waveland.

Kauzlarich, D., Matthews, R., & Miller, W. (2001). Toward a victimology of state crime. *Critical Criminology*, 10(3), 173–194.

Kennedy, L. (2018). "Man I'm all torn up inside": Analyzing audience responses to *Making a Murderer*. *Crime, Media, Culture: An International Journal*, 14(3), 391–408.

Kenny, G. (2017, March 9). Netflix casts a wider net for original documentaries. *The New York Times*. www.nytimes.com.

Kjeldgaard-Christiansen, J. (2019). A structure of antipathy: Constructing the villain in narrative film. *Projections*, 13(1), 67–90.

Koenig, S., Snyder, J., Chivvas, D., & Condon, E. (Producers). (2014). *Serial* (Season 1) [Podcast].

Koenig, S., Snyder, J., Chivvas, D., & Condon, E. (Producers). (2022, October 11). "Adnan Is Out." *Serial* [Podcast].

Kraska, P. B., & Brent, J. J. (2011). *Theorizing criminal justice: Eight essential orientations* (2nd ed.). Waveland.

La Chance, D., & Kaplan P. (2019). Criminal justice in the middlebrow imagination: The punitive dimensions of making a murderer. *Crime, Media, Culture: An International Journal*, 1(16), 81–96.

Lackey, J. (2020). False confessions and testimonial injustice. *The Journal of Criminal Law and Criminology*, 110(1), 43–68.

LaFrance, A. (2014, November 8). Is it wrong to be hooked on *Serial*? *The Atlantic*. www.theatlantic.com.

Lancaster, R. (2011). *Sex panic and the punitive state*. University of California Press.

Larson, S. (2018, February 12). "Atlanta Monster": In pursuit of justice and a hit podcast. *The New Yorker*. www.newyorker.com.

Lego. (n.d.) "Prison Island." www.lego.com.

Leo, R. A. (2017). The criminology of wrongful conviction: A decade later. *Journal of Contemporary Criminal Justice*, 33(1), 82–106.

Leo, R. A., & Davis, D. (2010). From false confession to wrongful conviction: Seven psychological processes. *The Journal of Psychiatry & Law*, 38 (Spring–Summer), 9–56.

Leonard, S. (2020). *The real housewives of Beverly Hills*: Franchising femininity. In E. Thompson & J. Mittell (Eds.), *How to watch television* (2nd ed., pp. 278–286). New York University Press.

Lestrade, J. X. de (Director). (2004). *The staircase* (Fr. *Soupcons*) [TV series].

Lestrade, J. X. de (Director). (2013). *The staircase: Last chance* [TV series].

Lestrade, J. X. de (Director). (2018). *The staircase III* [TV series].

Levenson, M. (2022, September 19). Judge vacates murder conviction of Adnan Syed of "Serial." *The New York Times*. www.nytimes.com.

Levine, S. (2021, June 13). How Republicans came to embrace the big lie of a stolen election. *The Guardian*. www.theguardian.com.

Lindsey, P. (Producer). (2018). *Atlanta monster* [Podcast]. Tenderfoot TV.

Lippke, R. L. (2014). The prosecutor and the presumption of innocence. *Criminal Law and Philosophy*, 8, 337–352.

Lofquist, W. S. (2014). Finding the causes in the contexts: Structural sources of wrongful conviction. In A. D. Redlich, A. R. Acker, R. J. Norris, & C. L. Bonventre (Eds.), *Examining wrongful convictions: Stepping back, moving forward* (pp. 19–34). Carolina Academic Press.

Malcolm, J. (1990). *The journalist and the murderer*. Vintage Books.

Manjoo, F. (2017, January 11). How Netflix is deepening our cultural echo chambers. *The New York Times*. www.nytimes.com.

Manzella, A. G. (2011). "*Pharakos*-logical" panic: The narrative logic of *Capturing the Friedmans*. *The Journal of Popular Culture*, 44(6), 1228–1247.

Marantz, A. (2018, March 12). Reddit and the struggle to detoxify the internet. *The New Yorker*. www.newyorker.com.

Maratea, R. J., & Monahan, B. A. (2013). Crime control as mediated spectacle: The institutionalization of gonzo rhetoric in modern media and politics. *Symbolic Interaction*, 36(3), 261–274.

Marsh, L. (2016). Murder, they wrote. *Dissent*, 63(2), 7–11.

McDonell-Parry, A. (2018, July 25). *The Staircase*: Inside wild theory that could solve docuseries mystery. *Rolling Stone*. www.rollingstone.com.

McMurty, L. G. (2016). "I'm not a real detective: I only play one on radio": *Serial* as the future of audio drama. *The Journal of Popular Culture*, 49(2), 306–324.

McPhate, M. (2016, February 3). Record number of false convictions overturned in 2015. *The New York Times*. www.nytimes.com.

Medwed, D. (2017). *Wrongful conviction and the DNA revolution: Twenty-five years of freeing the innocent*. Cambridge University Press.

Mill, M., & Jay-Z (Producers). (2019). *Free Meek* [Film]. Amazon Prime Video.

Miller, L. (2020, April 16). HBO's latest true-crime documentary is driven more by twists than by truth. *Slate*. www.slate.com.

Mittell, J. (2016, February 23). Why Netflix doesn't release its ratings. *The Atlantic*. www.theatlantic.com.

Mnookin, J. I. (2005). Reproducing a trial: Evidence and its assessment in *Paradise Lost*. In A. Sarat, L. Douglas, & M. M. Umphrey (Eds.), *Law on the screen* (pp. 153–200). Stanford University Press.

Modell, J. (2018, June 11). *The Staircase* director Jean-Xavier de Lestrade on the Peterson case, his ethical struggle, and the owl theory. *Vulture*. www.vulture.com.

Monroe, R. (2019). *Savage appetites: Women, crime, and obsession.* Scribner.

Murder Victims Families Reconciliation, Death Penalty Focus, and the American Civil Liberties Union of Northern California. (2008, January). *Voices from California crime victims for alternatives to the death penalty.* California Crime Victims for Alternatives to the Death Penalty.

Murley, J. (2008). *The rise of true crime: 20th century murder and American popular culture.* Praeger.

Murphy, M. (2015, December 20). Behind "Making a Murderer," a new documentary series on Netflix. *The New York Times.* www.nytimes.com.

Murphy, M. (2018, October 17). Making "Making a Murderer," again. *The New York Times.* www.nytimes.com.

National Registry of Exonerations. (2022). *2021 annual report.* www.law.umich.edu.

Neuschatz, J. S., Lawson, D. S., Swannter, J. K., & Meissner, C. A. (2008). The effects of accomplice witnesses and jailhouse informants on jury decision making. *Law and Human Behavior,* 32(2), 137–149.

Nietzsche, F. (1965). *Beyond good and evil: Prelude to a philosophy of the future* (W. Kaufmann, Trans). Vintage Books.

Norris, R. J. (2017a). *Exonerated: A history of the innocence movement.* New York University Press.

Norris, R. J. (2017b). Framing DNA: Social movement theory and the foundations of the innocence movement. *Journal of Contemporary Criminal Justice,* 33(10), 26–42.

Norris, R. J., & Bonventre, C. L. (2015). Advancing wrongful conviction scholarship: Toward new conceptual frameworks. *Justice Quarterly,* 32(6), 929–949.

Norris, R. J., & Mullinix, K. J. (2020). Framing innocence: An experimental test of the effects of wrongful conviction on public opinion. *Journal of Experimental Criminology,* 16(2), 311–334.

Orbey, E. (2022, January 17). A daughter's quest to free her father's killer. *The New Yorker.* www.newyorker.com.

Paquet, L. (2018). Literary forensic rhetoric: Maps, emotional assent, and rhetorical space in *Serial* and *Making a Murderer. Law and Humanities,* 12(1), 71–92.

Parenti, C. (2008). *Lockdown America: Police and prisons in the age of crisis,* New Edition. Verso Books. (Original work published 1999)

Penfold-Mounce, R. (2016). Corpses, popular culture and forensic science: Public obsession with death. *Mortality,* 21(1), 19–35.

Petersen, G. (2016, December 16). Wrongful convictions, exoneration, and criminal justice with with Samuel Gross. *The Economics Detective.* www.economicsdetective.com.

Pollard, S., Cermayeff, M., Dupre, J., & Bennett, J. (Directors). (2020). *Atlanta's missing and murdered* [TV series]. HBO.

Poniewozik, J. (2015, December 16). Streaming TV isn't just a new way to watch. It's a new genre. *The New York Times.* www.nytimes.com.

Pooja, R., & Story, B. (2021). Four propositions on true crime and abolition. *World Records Journal*, 5(16). https://worldrecordsjournal.org.

Pratt, J. (1998). Towards the "decivilizing" of punishment? *Social and Legal Studies*, 7(4), 487–515.

Pratt, R. (2003). Theorizing conspiracy. *Theory and Society*, 32(2), 255–271.

Punnett, I. C. (2018). *Toward a theory of true crime narratives: A textual analysis*. Taylor and Francis.

Quah, N. (2022, October 13). The best true-crime podcasts of 2022 (so far). *Vulture*. www.vulture.com.

Rafter, N. (2006). *Shots in the mirror: Crime films and society* (2nd ed.). Oxford University Press.

Redlich, A. D., & Ozdogru, A. A. (2009). *Alford* pleas in the age of innocence. *Behavioral Sciences and the Law*, 27, 467–488.

Respers France, L. (2021, May 26). Kim Kardashian says she failed the "baby bar" exam. *CNN Entertainment*. www.cnn.com.

Rhineberger-Dunn, G., Briggs, S. J., & Rader, N. E. (2017). The CSI effect, DNA discourse, and popular crime dramas. *Social Science Quarterly*, (98)2, 532–547.

Ricciardi, L., & Demos, M. (Directors). (2015). *Making a murderer* (Season 1) [TV series].

Ricciardi, L., & Demos, M. (Directors). (2018). *Making a murderer* (Season 2) [TV series].

Rickard, D. (2022a). The devil resides in comfort: Constructs of evil in contemporary true crime stories. *Journal of Popular Culture*, 55(6).

Rickard, D. (2022b). Truth and doubt: Questioning legal outcomes in true crime documentaries. *Law and Humanities*, 16(2).

Rodriguez, L., Agrarap, S., Boals, A., Kearns, N. T., & Bedford, L. (2019). Making a biased jury decision: Using the Steven Avery murder case to investigate potential influences in jury decision-making. *Psychology of Popular Media Culture*, 8(4), 429–436.

Rosenberger, J. S. & Callanan, V. J. (2011). The influence of media on penal attitudes. *Criminal Justice Review*, 36(4), 435–455.

Rothbart, D. (2012, January 15). Bruce Sinofsky and Joe Berlinger: Bonus questions. *Grantland*. www.grantland.com.

Ryan, M. (June 7, 2018). *The Staircase* on Netflix revisits a genre-defining trial. *The New York Times*. www.nytimes.com.

Saraiya, S. (2018a, June 8). Whether old or new *The Staircase* offers no easy answers. *Vanity Fair*. www.vanityfair.com.

Saraiya, S. (2018b, October 19). *Making a Murderer* season 2 can't make a case for itself. *Vanity Fair*. www.vanityfair.com.

Scheck, B., Neufeld, P., & Dwyer, J. (2003). *Actual innocence: When justice goes wrong and how to make it right*. New American Library.

Schneider, M. (2018, October 18). With "Making a Murderer Part 2" its filmmakers are ready to take on their critics. *IndieWire*. www.indiewire.com.

Schoenfeld, H. (2005). Violated trust: Conceptualizing prosecutorial misconduct. *Journal of Contemporary Criminal Justice*, 23(3), 250–271.

Schulz, K. (2016, January 25). Dead certainty: How "Making a Murderer" went wrong. *The New Yorker*. www.newyorker.com.

Seltzer, M. (2007). *True crime: Observations on violence and modernity*. Routledge.

Sered, D. (2019). *Until we reckon: Violence, mass incarceration, and a road to repair*. New Press.

Shapiro, J. A., & Muth, K. T. (2021). Beyond a reasonable doubt: Juries don't get it. *Loyola University Chicago Law Journal*, 52, 1029–1044.

Shattuck, K. (2015, December 31). "Making a Murderer": Watched it all? Share your theories. *The New York Times*. www.nytimes.com.

Sheley, J. (1991). Conflict and criminal law. In J. Sheley (Ed.), *Criminology* (pp. 21–39). Wadsworth.

Silbey, J. (2007). Truth tales and trial films. *Loyola of Los Angeles Law Review*, 40, 551–586.

Smith, P. (2008). *Punishment and culture*. University of Chicago Press.

Soderman, B., & Carter, R. (2008). The auto salvage: A space of second chances. *space and culture*, 11(1), 20–38.

Spitzer, S. (1975). Toward a Marxian theory of deviance. *Social Problems*, 22(5), 638–651.

Stacy, T. 1991. The search for truth in constitutional criminal procedure. *Columbia Law Review*, 91, 1369–1451.

Starr, D. (2013, December 9). The interview: Do police interrogation techniques produce false confessions? *The New Yorker*. www.nytimes.com.

Starr, D. (2018, June 6). In the "Making a Murderer" case, the Supreme Court could help address the problem of false confession. *The New Yorker*. www.newyorker.com.

Steiner, E. (2017). Binge-watching in practice: The rituals, motives and feelings of streaming video viewers. In C. Barker & M. Wiatrowski (Eds.), *The age of Netflix: Critical essays on streaming media, digital delivery and instant access* (pp. 141–161). McFarland.

Stevens, A. (2020, April 5). "Atlanta's Missing and Murdered" is a sharp, somber survey of a case marred by unanswered questions. *Salon*. www.salon.com.

Stevenson, B. (2014). *Just mercy: A story of justice and redemption*. One World Trade.

St. Felix, D. (2022, June 9). "The Staircase" deconstructs a true-crime genre. *The New Yorker*. www.newyorker.com.

Stohr, M. K., & Walsh, A. (2015). *Corrections: From research to practice*. Sage.

Stout, M. (2005). *The sociopath next door: The ruthless versus the rest of us*. Harmony Books.

Stratton, G. (2015). Wrongfully convicting the innocent: A state crime? *Critical Criminology*, 23, 21–37.

Szymanski, M. (2012). Bi film-video review: The Staircase. *Journal of Bisexuality*, 12, 442–443.

Toobin, J. (2007). The CSI effect. *The New Yorker*, 83(11), 30–35.

Tweel, D. (Director). (2018). *The innocent man* [TV series]. Campfire Productions.

Vena, J. (2022, March). Emily Simpson posts some interesting news on her legal career. *The Daily Dish*, Bravo. www.bravotv.com.

Victor, D. (2016a, January 5). "Making a Murderer" left out crucial facts, prosecutor says. *The New York Times*. www.nytimes.com.

Victor, D. (2016b, January 8). No "Making a Murderer" pardon from Obama, White House says. *The New York Times*. www.nytimes.com.

Vota, K. (2012). Comment: The truth behind *Echols v. State*: How an *Alford* guilty plea saved the West Memphis Three. *Loyola of Los Angeles Law Review*, 45(3), 1003–1021.

Wacquant, L. (2001). Deadly symbiosis: When ghetto and prison meet and mesh. *Punishment and Society*, 3(95), 95–133.

Warden, B. (2014). The role of the media and public opinion on innocence reform: Past and future. In M. Zalman & J. Carrano (Eds.), *Wrongful conviction and criminal justice reform: Making justice* (pp. 39–55). Routledge.

Wayne, M. L. (2018). Netflix, Amazon, and branded television content is subscription video on-demand portals. *Media, Culture & Society*, 40(5), 725–741.

Weinberg, S. (2005). Unlocking justice: An interview with Ofra Bikel. *Columbia Journalism Review*, 44(4), 19.

Weinstock, J. A. (2020a). Introduction: A genealogy of monster theory. In J. A. Weinstock (Ed.), *The monster theory reader* (pp. 1–36). University of Minnesota Press.

Weinstock, J. A. (2020b). Invisible monsters: Vision, horror, and contemporary culture. In J. A. Weinstock (Ed.), *The monster theory reader* (pp. 358–373). University of Minnesota Press.

Weintraub, J. N. (2020). Obstructing justice: The association between prosecutorial misconduct and the identification of true perpetrators. *Crime and Delinquency*, 66(9), 1195–1216.

Western, B. (2007). Introduction. In G. M. Sykes, *The Society of Captives: A Study of a Maximum Security Prison* (pp. ix–xxix). Princeton University Press.

Westervelt, S. D., & Cook, K. J. (2010). Framing innocents: The wrongfully convicted as victims of state harm. *Crime, Law, and Social Change*, 58(3), 259–275.

Whitty, S. (2008). Revealing the "real" me, searching for the "actual" you: Presentations of self on an internet dating site. *Computers in Human Behavior*, 24(4), 1707–1723.

Williamson, T. L. (2021). Of serial murder and true crime: Some preliminary thoughts on Black feminist research praxis and the implications of settler colonialism. *EPD: Society and Space*, 39(1), 22–29.

Worden, A. P., Blaize Davies, A. L., & Brown, E. K. (2014). Public defense in an age of innocence: The innocence paradigm and the challenges of representing the accused. In M. Zalman & J. Carrano (Eds.), *Wrongful conviction and criminal justice reform: Making Justice* (pp. 209–225). Routledge.

Xiong, M., Greenleaf, R. G., & Goldschmidt, J. (2017). Citizen attitudes towards errors in criminal justice: Implications of the declining acceptance of Blackstone's ration. *International Journal of Law, Crime and Justice*, 48, 14–26.

Yant, M. (2014). The media's muddled message on wrongful convictions. In A. D. Redlich, A. R. Acker, R. J. Norris, & C. L. Bonventre (Eds.), *Examining wrongful convictions: Stepping back, moving forward* (pp. 71–89). Carolina Academic Press.

Yardley, E., Kelly, E., & Robinson-Edwards, S. (2019). Forever trapped in the imaginary of late capitalism? The serialized true crime podcast as a wake-up call in times of criminological slumber. *Crime, Media, Culture: An International Journal*, 15(3), 503–521.

Yardley, E., Thomas-Lynes, A. G., Wilson, D., & Kelly, M. (2018). What's the deal with "websleuthing"? News media representations of amateur detectives in networked spaces. *Crime Media Culture: An International Journal*, 14(1), 81–109.

Yardley, E., Wilson, D., & Kennedy, M. (2017). "To me its [*sic*] real life": Secondary victims of homicide in newer media. *Victims and Offenders*, 12, 467–496.

Yoffe, E. (2017, September). Innocence is irrelevant. *The Atlantic*. www.theatlantic.com.

Young, J. (1999). *The exclusive society*. Sage.

Zalman, M. (2014). Theorizing wrongful conviction. In A. D. Redlich, A. R. Acker, R. J. Norris, & C. L. Bonventre (Eds.), *Examining wrongful convictions: Stepping back, moving forward* (pp. 283–300). Carolina Academic Press.

Zalman, M., & Marion, N. E. (2014). The public policy process and innocence reform. In M. Zalman & J. Carrano (Eds.), *Wrongful conviction and criminal justice reform: Making justice* (pp. 24–38). Routledge.

Index

Page numbers in *italics* indicate Table

advocates, audiences as, 3, 41, 43–44, 46
Alexander, Michelle, 209, 211–12, 225
Alford pleas, 71, 203; of Peterson, M., 51,
189, 204, 206–7; Syed consideration for,
56, 204–5; of WM3, 47, 204–6
America's Most Wanted (1988-present), 21,
22, 190
assumption of guilt, 20, 22, 134, 142–43,
214. *See also* presumption of innocence
Atlanta Monster (2018), 3, 41, 63–68, *72*,
156; crime-scene photos in, 83; deviance and guilt in, 112–13; elusiveness
of truth in, 181–86; experimental
recreation of splash in, 67, 98–99; fiber evidence in, 65, 94; Ku Klux Klan
theory and, 65, 66, 67, 149, 174; official misconduct in, 135, 141, 144–45,
148–50; pedophile ring theory and,
66–67; postmodernism and, 181–86;
racial role in, 64–65; Reddit views on,
171–75, 200; Sanders clan or Sanders brothers, 149; victim families
on child unsolved cases, 64–65, 174,
195–96, 199–200; victim visual portrayal in, 81. *See also* Lindsey, Payne;
Williams, Wayne
Atlanta murders, 64–65; mayor Lance Bottoms federal action request for, 67–68;
of 28 Black children and 2 men, *72*
Atlanta's Missing and Murdered (2020), 65–
67; Bennett, Charmayeff, Dupre, and
Pollard as directors of, 64, *72*; official
misconduct in, 135, 141, 144–45, 148–50;

racial role in, 64, 68, 171–75; Reddit
views on, 171–75, 200; victim visual
portrayal in, 81. *See also* Williams,
Wayne
AT&T agreement, in *Serial*, 91–92
attorneys: Buting as trial attorney of Avery,
72, 145, 146; dominant narratives in trials by, 75; Kachinsky as first attorney of
Dassey, 60, 61, *72*, 195; Kratz as district
attorney in *Making a Murderer*, 60–62,
72, 148, 163–64, 181, 201–2; Kunstler
and Cook, B., representation of Williams, 66, 68, 148; Rudolf as defense
attorney to Peterson, M., 49, 51, 52, *72*,
74, 75, 188–89, 200–203, 207; storyteller
role of, 74; Strang as trial attorney
of Avery, *72*, 145–46, 202–3. *See also*
defense counsel; prosecutors; Zellner,
Kathleen
audiences, of true crime: as advocates, 3,
41, 43–44, 46; *America's Most Wanted*
crime solving with, 21, 22, 190; binge
watching preference of, 2, 38–39,
208; case outcomes influenced by, 3,
7; crime news and, 16, 17; forensic-
based television shows and, 26; ideological messages about punishment
from, 4; New True documentary
activated, 43–44; objects of evidence
fixation of, 85; *Paradise Lost* trilogy
web technology response, 48; on presumption of innocence, 199; social
media and, 3, 155–56; white women
fan base of literature for, 30–31. *See
also* Reddit

Avery, Steven: *Brady* violation and, 59; Buting as trial attorney of, 72, 145, 146; civil suit against county by, 59, 145; Dassey false confession and, 58, 59, 63, 137–41, 147–48, 162–63; deviance and true self of, 118–19; DNA evidence and exoneration of, 58; Halbach alleged rape and murder by, 59, 201; life without parole sentence of, 58; official misconduct and, 60, 72, 95, 99, 145–48, 163; portrayal of family of, 193; Ricciardi and Demos support of, 190–91; sexual assault conviction of, 58. *See also* Zellner, Kathleen

Baldwin, James, 64–65, 81, 125, 185
Baldwin, Jason, 45–47, 72, 131, 183, 206
Barthes, Roland, 80, 82, 139
Beal, Timothy, 103
Bennett, Joshua, 67–68
Berg, Amy, 56–57, 72, 84, 192, 196, 205
Berlinger, Joe, 48–49, 107, 119, 122; Byers, J., and, 63, 195; on innocence of subjects, 186, 206; on media influence, 132; as *Paradise Lost* trilogy director/producer, 45–46, 72, 186; as WM3 advocate, 47, 186, 205
Bernstein, Robin, 81
Bikel, Ofra, 36–37
binge watching, 2, 38–39, 208
bisexuality, of Peterson, M., 50, 51, 75, 110, 113
Black Americans: Atlanta murders of 28 Black children and 2 men, 72; high rates of victims in, 29; *Just Mercy* on death penalty of, 27, 229; de Lestrade on Butler wrongful conviction of, 34–35; Wacquant on mass incarceration of, 211; Wilds negative racial associations of, 54
Black Lives Matter Movement, criminal justice reform and, 13

blood: EDTA testing for, 95; forensic science evidence of, 95–98; *Making a Murderer* absence of, 84, 161, 162; at scene, in *The Staircase*, 49, 50, 83–84, 95–97, 168–70
blow poke, in *The Staircase*, 85–87, 135
body of evidence and corpse, 80–81, 84; crime-scene photos of victim body, 8, 74, 77–79, 82–83
Bolin, Alice, 15, 73
Borchard, Edwin, 9
Brady violations, 134, 214, 226; Avery and, 59; examples of, 144; for Fontenot and Ward, 70; official misconduct of, 12; presumption of innocence and, 197; Williams and, 149
Brady v. Maryland, 144
brain fingerprinting, 62, 93
Branch, Steve, 72, 81
Brown, Michelle, 4, 230–31; on prison films of modern suffering, 8
Bruzzi, Stella, 33, 187
Buting, Jerome, 72, 145, 146
Butler, Brenton, 34–35
Byers, Christopher, 72, 81
Byers, John Mark, 72, 122; melodramatic religious presentation of, 46; as *Paradise Lost* possible suspect, 46; *Purgatory* on WM3 innocence and support by, 47, 195; *Revelations* fall from grace of, 46

California Crime Victims for Alternatives to the Death Penalty, 222
Candace, as Peterson, M., sister-in-law, 72, 217; on blow poke, 86; on Peterson, M., *Alford* plea, 207; *The Staircase* response from, 191
Capturing the Friedmans documentary (2003), 35
Carter, Debbie, 68, 72, 194; crime-scene photos of, 82; visual portrayal of, 80

The Case against Adnan Syed (2019), 52–
55, 57, *72*; on evidence revisited and
hearing for new trial, 6; media impact
on, 56; Reddit views on, 165–67, 179–
80. *See also* Berg, Amy; Lee, Hae Min;
Syed, Adnan

The Case for Innocence documentary
(2000), 36–37

cases: audience influence on outcomes
for, 3, 7; exonerations for trial, 10;
plea bargained, 10, 11, 130, 203; Reddit
comments on, 3, 156–58; true-crime
documentary role in solving, 49

cell phone records, pings, in *Serial*, 53, 54,
89–91

Center for Wrongful Convictions, 63, 153

The Central Park Five documentary
(2012), 20, 35–36

Chancer, Lynn, 5, 182

Chermayeff, Maro, 67–68

Clear, Todd R., 210, 215, 229

coerced confessions. *See* false confessions

Colburn, Andrew, 60, *72*, 145–47, 148, 163

Cold Case Files (1999–2017), 21

The Confessions documentary (2010), 37

The Confession Tapes (2017), 42, 228, 234

confirmation bias, 147; juries and, 144;
official misconduct and, 134–36

"Conflict and Criminal Law" (Sheley),
227

conservative ideologies, about crime, 5,
19–20

Constitution, US, 10, 198, 226

Convicting the Innocent (Borchard), 9

Conviction (film), 9, 27

Conviction Integrity Units, 237

convictions: Avery sexual assault, 58;
death penalty, 10, 21, 37, 218, 222–23;
DNA evidence in postconviction
testing, 9; Fontenot murder, 69;
Fontenot overturn of, 70, 178; *Free
Meek* on negative consequences of,

220–21; Fritz murder, 68; of jury
based on forensic science evidence,
26; New True on innocence issues
and, 43; Ward murder, 69; Ward
overturn of, 70, 178; Williamson
murder, 68. *See also* wrongful
convictions

Cook, Bobby Lee, 66, 68, 148

Cook, Kimberly, 152–53, 229

corpse. *See* body of evidence and corpse

county law enforcement, in *Making of
a Murderer*, *72*; Colburn and Lenk
official misconduct by, 60, 145–47, 148,
163

crime: cause of, 23; conservative ideologies about, 5; crime news depiction
of, 19; gonzo rhetoric portrayal of,
19, 20, 215; politicization of, 210–11;
public information from movies and
television dramas on, 6; reporting
absence on crime against people of
color, 30; violence and entertainment
from, 7–8, 16

crime-control model, 225; Type II errors
reductions and, 226–27

crime entertainment: crime news and,
17–22, 73, 78–79; of fictional crime
drama, 15, 22–28; on ideal victims,
78–79

crime news, 17–22, 73, 78–79

crime-scene photos, of victims, 8, 74, 77–
79, 82–83

crime stories, 15, 21, 22; causal explanations of crime, 23; cultural mythology of, 233–34; cultural norms and
expectations in, 79; media and, 4–8;
murder victim crime-scene photos in,
74; reporter sources for, 17–18; serial
killer popularity in, 8; violence and
pleasure of, 16

criminal justice reform, 11, 13; legislation
for, 9, 237–38

criminal justice system, 11; constitutional protections in, 10; crime-control model in, 225, 226; crime shows information on, 22; criticism of, 212; due-process model in, 225–26; *Frontline* documentaries on, 36–37; innocence issues in, 3; mass incarceration and, 134, 210–15, 219, 237; mass-media consumers educated on, 16; New True critiques of, 41; poverty impact in, 113; punishment practices in, 4, 14, 23, 104, 208–23; rehabilitative perspective in, 214–15; true-crime documentaries critique of, 33. *See also* presumption of innocence

criminology: problem populations and, 224–25; social constructionist perspectives, 227–28; wrongful conviction critical, 224–30

CSI effect, 26, 93

cultural criminology, 233–35; Brown on, 230–31; prison and, 230–32; punishment in leisure practices, 231–32

The Culture of Punishment (Brown), 4

Dassey, Brendan: Avery and false confession of, 58, 59, 63, 137–41, 147–48, 162–63; Center for Wrongful Convictions for, 63; Kachinsky as first attorney of, 60, 61, 72, 195; life in prison sentence for, 58; portrayal of family of, 193

Dateline NBC, 190; Kratz appearance on, 62; wrongful conviction special report of, 22

Dead Girls (Bolin), 15, 73

death penalty convictions, 37; debate over, 222–23; exoneration rates of, 10; Grumman on wrongful, 21; punishment practices for, 218

defense counsel: event accounts of, 75–76; exoneration from perfunctory access

to, 10; experts use by, 76; in *Paradise Lost*, 46; wrongful conviction from inadequate, 11, 133–35, 180

de Lestrade, Jean Xavier, 49, 72, 124, 169, 206; on Butler wrongful conviction, 34–35; as *Murder on a Sunday Morning* director, 34–35, 50; on objectivity, 187, 189; Peterson, M., presentation by, 51–52, 110–11, 188; on Peterson, M., truth, 188–90; on wrongful conviction, 186

Demos, Moira, 58, 61, 72, 119, 186; on Avery and official misconduct, 156; Avery support by, 190–91; Zellner and, 63, 100, 147, 194

deviance and guilt, 227; alternative suspects and, 70–71, 114; in *Atlanta Monster*, 112–13; in *The Innocent Man*, 109–10; in *Making a Murderer*, 108–9; in *The Paradise Lost* trilogy, 106–8, 176–77; in *Serial*, 111–12; social, 104, 113, 128; sociopath and, 104, 123–27; in *The Staircase*, 110–11

deviance and true self, 19, 114–15, 120; Avery and, 118–19; defense perspective on, 119; in *Making a Murderer*, 118; in *Paradise Lost*, 118; in *Paradise Lost* trilogy, 119–20; of Peterson, M., 116–17; of Syed, 116, 117–18; of Williams, 116

directors/producers: Bennett, Chermayeff, Dupre, and Pollard as *Atlanta's Missing and Murdered*, 67–68; Berlinger and Sinofsky as *Paradise Lost* trilogy, 45–49, 63, 72, 107, 119, 122, 132, 186, 195, 205, 206; Koenig as *Serial*, 1, 53–57, 72, 79–80, 82, 89–91, 101, 111–12, 117–18, 123, 124, 126, 180, 184–85, 198–99, 205, 231, 237; de Lestrade as *The Staircase*, 34–35, 49–52, 72, 110–11, 124, 169, 186, 188–90, 206; Lindsey as *Atlanta Monster*, 63–64, 66–67, 72, 98–99, 184–85, 184–86, 196, 200; Ricciardi and Demos as *Making a Murderer*, 58, 61, 63, 72, 100, 119, 147, 156, 186, 190–91, 194; Tweel as *The Innocent Man*, 68, 70, 71, 72, 80, 109, 122, 138, 150, 186, 194

DNA evidence: availability in 1989, 7–8; innocence movement and, 8–9, 228; postconviction testing for, 9; Syed and prison release, 57, 237; of WM3 testing in *Purgatory*, 47, 205–6

DNA exoneration, 2, 8–9, 129; of Avery, 58; *The Case for Innocence* documentary and, 36–37; of Dotson, 21; Innocence Project on, 12; in *Making a Murderer*, 2, 59; for sexual assault and homicide, 10; of Williamson and Fritz, 68; WM3 and, 205–6

documentarian: event accounts of, 75–77; on juries, 131–33

documentaries. *See* true-crime documentaries

documentation, as object of evidence, 89–92

Dotson, Gary, 21

The Dreams of Ada (Mayer), 70, 186

due-process model, 225–26

Dupre, Jeff, 67–68

Echols, Damien, 156; *Alford* plea and, 206; death by lethal injection sentence of, 45; as *Paradise Lost* defendant, 45, 72, 103; Reddit views on, 176–77; trial presentation of, 46, 107–8; Wicca practice and occult exploration of, 45, 107, 122

"The Enduring Pernicious Whiteness of True Crime" (Green), 29

Evidence of Things Not Seen (Baldwin, James), 64–65

evil and true identity, 120–22; sociopathy in documentaries, 104, 123–27

Evil Incarnate (Frankfurter), 121

Exhibit A (2019), on forensic science evidence flaws, 27, 93

exonerations: death penalty conviction rates of, 10; for defense council perfunctory access, 10; with DNA evidence, 2, 8–10, 12, 21, 36–37, 58, 68, 129, 205–6; Innocence Project of Williamson and Fritz for, 68; misapplied forensics for, 97; from official misconduct, 12, 142; from plea bargain use, 10; revictimization of released, 153, 229; sexual assault rates of, 10

experimental recreations: in *Atlanta Monster*, 67, 98–99; in *Making a Murderer*, 99–100; in *Serial*, 54, 92, 101; in *The Staircase*, 96, 98

experts: defense use of, 76; documentarian reliance on, 97–98; false testimony of, 50–51; on forensic science evidence, 92–101; Rule as law enforcement and criminologists, 33; on *The Staircase* blow poke, 86, 135; wrongful conviction and testimony of, 12

eyewitness misidentification, as wrongful conviction factor, 11, 36, 37, 133, 180

Facebook: crime-centric groups of, 48; *Making A Murderer* followers on, 156; *The Staircase* followers on, 156

Fair Sentencing Act (2010), 238

false confessions, 37, 80, 133, 134; of Butler, 35; of Central Park Five, 36; in *The Innocent Man*, 11, 58, 59, 63, 69, 88–89, 137–41, 147–48, 162–63; interrogation strategies and, 135–36; in *Making a Murderer*, 11, 58, 61, 137, 139, 162–63; in *Paradise Lost*, 11, 45, 137–38

Fatal Vision (McGinnis), 32

fiber evidence, in *Atlanta Monster*, 65, 94

fictional crime drama, 15, 22–28

Fifth Amendment, US Constitution, 198

films: Brown on prison, 8; of innocence movement, 9, 27; multiepisode documentaries in, 42

"Finding the Causes in the Contexts" (Lofquist), 219–20

The First 48 (2004-present), 21

Fiske, John, 181–82

Fontenot, Karl: *Brady* violation for, 70; conviction overturn for, 70, 178; false confession of, 69, 137–39; on Haraway flowered blouse, 88–89, 151; life in prison sentence, 69; murder conviction of, 69; official misconduct and, 150

forensic-based television shows, 26

forensic experts. *See* experts

Forensic Files (1996–2011, 2022–present), 21, 73

forensic science evidence, 94–97, 102; of blood, 95–98; in DNA testing, 21; of experimental re-creations, 54, 67, 92, 98–101; in expert testimony, 12, 50–51; of fiber, 65, 94; junk science critique and, 26–27; jury conviction based on, 26; misapplication as wrongful conviction factor, 11, 12, 26, 36, 133, 134, 180; persuasive quality of, 12; practitioner mistakes, 12; in unreliable or invalid specific field, 12, 92–93

48 Hours and *48 Hours Mystery* (1988-present), 21, 190

Fourteenth Amendment, US Constitution, 198

Frankfurter, David, 121, 123

Free Meek: on criminal conviction negative consequences, 220–21; on minor crime and probation oppressive features, 43

Frist Step Act (2018), 238

Fritz, Dennis, 69, 72, 178, 194; DNA evidence and exoneration of, 68; Innocence Project and exoneration of, 68; murder conviction of, 68; official misconduct and, 150, 152

Frontline documentaries, of PBS, 36–37

Frost, Natasha A., 210, 229

Fuhs, Kristen, 187

Gabler, Neal, 5, 17

Giddens, Anthony, 120

Ginsberg, Rafael, 216

Glynn, Kevin, 181–82

Goffman, Erving, 115

gonzo rhetoric, 19, 20, 215

Gore, Glen, 152

Gould, Jon, 213–19, 225

government misconduct. *See* official misconduct

graphic revolution, Gabler on, 5

Grisham, John, 70, 151, 178

Grumman, Cornelia, 21

Halbach, Teresa, 63, 72; absence of blood for, 84, 161, 162; Avery alleged rape and murder of, 59, 201; family on media coverage of, 61–62; Hillegas as ex-boyfriend of, 62, 162, 194; RAV4 vehicle of, 59–60, 62, 85, 87–88, 99–100, 146–47, 161–62; visual portrayal of, 80

Halttunen, Karen, 16

Haraway, Denice, 72, 81; flowered blouse of, 88–89, 151; *The Innocent Man* and murder of, 69; Tweel on family response to exonerations, 71; visual portrayal of, 80

HBO/HBO Max: *Atlanta's Missing and Murdered* on, 67, 72; *The Case against Adnan Syed* and *The Paradise Lost* trilogy on, 72; documentaries of, 40–41; prestige TV original content production on, 38; *The Staircase* scripted show on, 241–42

Hearst, William Randolph, 17

high-profile crimes coverage, 17, 74; Chancer on, 5, 18, 182; New True series from, 16, 182–83

Hillegas, Ryan, 62, 162, 194

Holland, Terri, 152

ideal victims: crime news and crime entertainment on, 78–79; Lee as, 79–80; photos of, 82; of white, middle class, attractive females, 6, 19

ideological messages, 4–6

inadequate defense: in *Serial*, 134–35; for wrongful convictions, 11, 133–35, 180

incentivized witness. *See* witness

The Innocence Files (2020), 42, 228, 234

Innocence Lost documentaries (1991, 1993, 1997), 36

innocence movement, 41, 44, 208–9; DNA evidence and, 8–9, 228; films for emotional reactions to innocence, 9, 27; wrongful conviction and, 8–12

Innocence Project, 9, 153, 208; *The Case for Innocence* documentary and, 36–37; on DNA exonerations and official misconduct, 12; *Making a Murderer* and, 59; Williamson and Fritz exoneration by, 68

Innocence Protection Act (2004), 9

The Innocent Man (2018), 3, 40, 72, 156; alternative suspects in, 70–71; on characters negative case impact, 71; deviance and guilt in, 109–10; false confession in, 11, 58, 59, 63, 69, 88–89, 137–41, 147–48, 162–63; Grisham book and, 70; Holland as jailhouse informant in, 152; incentivized witness testimony in, 135; objects of interest in, 85, 88–89; official misconduct prominent concern in, 12, 69–70, 141, 144–46, 150–52, 180; Peterson, B., official misconduct in, 150–52; Reddit views on, 177–79; truth in, 186. *See*

also Carter, Debbie; Fontenot, Karl; Fritz, Dennis; Haraway, Denice; Tweel, Clay; Ward, Tommy; Williamson, Ron

The Innocent Man (Grisham), 70

The Journalist and the Murderer (Malcolm), 187

junk science critique, of forensic science evidence, 26–27

juries, 239; confirmation bias and, 144; convictions based on forensic science evidence by, 26; crime-scene photos impact on, 77; cultural assumptions of, 105; documentarians on, 131–33; false confession as highly persuasive to, 11; New True and, 130–33; *Paradise Lost* misconduct from, 130–32; positions at deliberation beginning of, 132–33, 164; reasonable doubt and, 198; Reddit views on, 180

jury decision-making: defendant character impact on, 130; false confession as highly persuasive to, 11, 137; forensic evidence as basis of, 26; in *Making of a Murderer*, 164; pretrial publicity impact on, 130–31

Just Mercy (film), 27, 229

Kachinsky, Len, 60, 61, 72, 195

Koenig, Sarah, 1, 53–57, 72, 184–85, 205, 231, 237; on cell phone records, 89–91; experimental recreations of, 101; on Lee crime scene photos, 82; on Lee diary, 79–80; on reasonable doubt, 198–99; on Syed and sociopath label, 123, 124, 126; Syed description by, 111–12, 117–18, 180

Kratz, Ken, 181; as district attorney in *Making a Murderer*, 60, 61, 72, 148, 163–64; media attention pleasure of, 60, 62, 164, 202; Reddit views on, 201–2

Ku Klux Klan theory, of Atlanta murders by, 65, 66, 67, 149, 174
Kunstler, William, 66, 68, 148

Lancaster, Roger, 103
Lance Bottoms, Keisha, 67–68
Law and Order: SVU, 23, 25
law enforcement officials: Lenk and Colburn misconduct as, 60, *72*, 95, 99, 145–48, 163; misconduct examples of, 12, 35
Law & Order, 23, 25, 26
Lee, Hae Min, 14, 57, *72*, 198; crime-scene photos of, 82; Facebook group on, 156; family objection to *Serial* presentation of, 57; Koenig on diary of, 79–80; murder of, 53, 90, 101, 184; qualities of, 53–54, 79–80
legal dramas, 22, 25
Lenk, James, 60, *72*, 145–46, 148, 163
Leo, Richard, 129–30, 228
Lindsey, Payne, *72*, 186, 200; on alternative theories, 66–67; *Atlanta Monster* podcast of, 63–64, 66, *72*; case uncertainty of, 184–85; recording use by, 98–99; on Williams, 66, 196
Lippke, Richard, 229–30
Lofquist, William S., 219–20

Making a Murderer (2015, 2018), 40; absence of blood in, 84, 161, 162; on Avery and official misconduct, 145; Avery portrayal by, 122; celebrity attention to, 58; Dassey and Avery bias critique in, 63; deviance and guilt in, 108–9; deviance and true self in, 118; EDTA testing in, 95; evil in, 122; exoneration with DNA evidence in, 2, 59; experimental recreation of Hallbach's drive off Avery property, 99–100; Facebook followers on, 156; false confession in, 11, 58, 61, 137, 139, 162–63; Hillegas as Halbach ex-boyfriend in, 62, 162, 194; Lenk and Colburn law enforcement official misconduct in, 60, *72*, 95, 99, 145–48, 163; media coverage for, 2, 59, 61, 164; objects of interest in, 85, 161; official misconduct prominent concern in, 12, 59–60, *72*, 95, 99, 141, 144–48, 163, 180; presumption of innocence and, 201; RAV4 as Hallbach vehicle in, 59–60, 62, 85, 87–88, 99–100, 146–47, 161–62; Reddit views on, 3, 156, 157, 159–64; truth in, 186; victim family response to, 193, 194. *See also* Avery, Steven; Buting, Jerome; Colburn, Andrew; Dassey, Brendan; Demos, Moira; Halbach, Teresa; Kachinsky, Len; Kratz, Ken; Lenk, James; Ricciardi, Laura; Strang, Dean; Zellner, Kathleen
Malcolm, Janet, 126, 187–88
Martinson, Robert, 215
mass incarceration, 134, 210–15, 219, 237
Mayer, John, 70, 186
McClain, Asia, 56, 92
meaningful items. *See* objects of evidence
media, 18; *The Case against Adnan Syed* impact from, 56; crime stories and, 4–8; Halbach family on coverage by, 61–62; Kratz pleasure of attention from, 60, 62, 164, 202; on *Making a Murderer*, 2, 59, 61, 164; presumption of innocence disregard by, 20; *The Staircase* importance of, 51; on violence, 5; on WM3 satanic ritual abuse, 47, 106. *See also* social media
Mind Over Murder (2022), 3, 71
misapplication of forensic science, 11, 12, 26, 36, 133, 134, 180

Misskelley, Jessie: false confession of, 11, 45, 137; life plus forty years sentence for, 45; as *Paradise Lost* defendant, 45, *72*

monster and monster theory, 103; deviance and guilt in, 105–13, 123–28, 176–77, 227; deviance and true self in, 19, 114–20; evil and true identity in, 120–27; New True and, 127–28; poverty and race in, 104

Moore, Michael, *72*, 81

multiepisode documentaries, 42

Murder in Alliance, 235

Murder on a Sunday Morning documentary (2001), de Lestrade as director of, 34–35, 50

Murley, Jean, 16, 28, 29

National Center for Missing and Exploited Children, 21–22

National Registry of Exonerations (2012), 9–10, 12, 133, 153

Netflix, 239; *Making a Murderer* on, *72*; most well-known series of, 40–41; multiepisode documentaries of, 42; new documentary popularity on, 40; *The Staircase* on, *72*

The New Jim Crow (Alexander), 209, 211–12

news value criteria, 5, 18–20

New True, 8, 38–52, 227; ambiguity and uncertainty in, 14, 44; contemporary American culture and, 13–14; on convictions and innocence issues, 43; criminal justice system critiques by, 41; documentarians as advocates and activated audiences in, 43–44; excessive attention to detail in, 76; high-profile crimes coverage beginning for, 16, 182–83; imperfect category of, 71; juries and, 130–33; monster and monster theory in, 127–28; multiepisode documentaries in, 42; New documentary in, 40–41; prison setting and, 230–31; from production to reception in, 179–80; reality and entertainment relationship in, 4–5; on reasonable doubt, 196–203; victim family response to, 191–96; wrongful convictions and, 133–35, 152–54

New True synopses: *Atlanta Monster* and *Atlanta's Missing and Murdered*, 63–68; *The Case Against Adnan Syed*, 52–57; *The Innocent Man*, 68–71; *Making a Murderer*, 58–63; *Paradise Lost* trilogy, 44–49; *Serial*, 52–57; *The Staircase*, 49–52

Nisha call, in *Serial*, 91

objectivity, in true-crime documentaries, 33, 187–96

objects of evidence, 84; audience fixation on, 85; of blow poke in *The Staircase*, 85–87, 135; of documentation for *Serial*, 89–92; of Haraway flowered blouse in *The Innocence Man*, 88–89, 151; of RAV4 in *Making a Murderer*, 87–88

official misconduct, 11; assumption of guilt and, 142–43; in *Atlanta Monster* and *Atlanta's Missing and Murdered*, 135, 141, 144–45, 148–50; confirmation bias and, 134–36; exonerations from, 12, 142; *The Innocent Man* prominent, 12, 69–70, 141, 144–46, 150–52, 180; *Making a Murderer* prominent, 12, 59–60, *72*, 141, 144–48, 163, 180; tunnel vision and, 134, 143

An Ordinary Crime documentary (2002), 37

owl theory, in *The Staircase*, 51, 77

paperbacks, mass-market, 28–29

Paradise Lost (1996), 72; crime-scene photos in, 83; defendant solid alibis and, 45; on defense presentation and community character in, 46; deviance and true self in, 118; evil in, 122; false confession in, 11, 45, 137–38; jury misconduct in, 131–32; objects of interest in, 85; prosecution satanic-ritual theory in, 45, 106; Reddit views on, 174–76; on teenager sexual murder of three eight-year old victims, 44–45; theory of Byers, J., as suspect in, 46; victim family portrayal in, 194–95; victim visual portrayal in, 81. *See also* Baldwin, Jason; Echols, Damien; Misskelley, Jessie

The Paradise Lost trilogy (1996, 2000, 2011), 40–41, 44–49, 71, 72; audience web technology response to, 48; celebrities support of, 48; deviance and guilt in, 106–8, 176–77; deviance and true self in, 119–20; Reddit views on, 175–77; truth in, 186. *See also* Berlinger, Joe; Byers, John Mark; *Paradise Lost*; *Purgatory*; *Revelations*; Sinofsky, Bruce; West Memphis Three

pedophile ring theory, in *Atlanta Monster*, 66–67

penal harm: Clear on, 214, 229; Frost on, 229; Gould on cultural punitiveness on wrongful conviction for, 213–19; prison inhumanity and, 218–19; punitive states and, 214, 225; revenge and retribution and, 216–17

penny papers, 17, 28

perpetrators, sexual, assault family or friends, 6, 19

Peterson, Bill, 150–52

Peterson, Kathleen, 72, 74; crime-scene photos of, 82; as murdered wife in *The Staircase*, 50; visual portrayal of, 80, 84

Peterson, Michael, 72; *Alford* plea and, 51, 189, 204, 206–7; bisexuality of, 50, 51, 75, 110, 113; defense preparation and cost to, 132; deviance and true self of, 116–17; de Lestrade on truth of, 188–90; de Lestrade presentation of, 51–52, 110–11, 188; previous wife, death of, 50, 51; Reddit views on, 168–70, 201; Rudolf trial preparation for, 74; sociopath identification of, 123, 124–25; *The Staircase* on wife murder by, 49; trial demeanor of, 125

plea bargained cases, 203; criminal convictions in, 130; exoneration in use in, 10; false confessions leverage in, 11. See also *Alford* pleas

The Plea documentary (2004), 37

podcast: of *Atlanta Monster*, 41, 63–64; emergence in 2004, 39; format and topics, variety in, 40; most popular, 41; *Serial* as most downloaded of all time, 1, 41, 53. *See also specific podcast*

politicization, of crime, 210–11

politics, truth and, 239–41

Pollard, Sam, 67–68, 72

Poniewozik, James, 38

postmodernism, in *Serial* and *Atlanta Monster*, 181–86

poverty: criminal justice system impacted by, 113; dehumanizing impact of, contributing to monster theory in relation to race, 104; of WM3, 107–9, 113, 121–22

Pratt, Ray, 129

The Presentation of Self in Everyday Life (Goffman), 115

prestige TV: HBO original content production of, 38; *The Sopranos* credit for, 38

presumption of innocence, 10, 137, 196, 199–200, 202–3; Lippke on, 229–30; *Making a Murderer* and, 201; media disregard for, 20; official misconduct and, 142–43; tunnel vision and, 197; wrongful convictions and, 197–98

pretrial publicity, jury decision-making impacted by, 130–31

prison, 215; Brown on, as sites modern suffering in films, 8; cultural criminology and, 230–32; Dassey sentence of life in, 58; Fontenot sentence of life in, 69; penal harm and inhumanity of, 218–19; Syed DNA testing and release from, 57, 237; Ward sentence of life in, 69; Williams sentence of life in, 64, 65. *See also* mass incarceration

producers. *See* directors/producers

prosecutors: *Brady* violations from misconduct of, 12; event accounts of, 75–76; improper behavior or intentional wrongdoing by, 12; Kratz as district attorney in *Making a Murderer*, 60–62, 72, 148, 163–64, 181, 201–2; misconduct examples, 12; *Paradise Lost* satanic-ritual theory of, 45; Peterson, B., as district attorney in *The Innocent Man*, 150–52; presumption of innocence and power of, 10; Ross as assistant district attorney in *The Innocent Man*, 150

protections, of US constitution: in criminal justice system, 10, 226; of Fifth, Sixth, and Fourteenth Amendments, 198

pulp nonfiction magazines, of 1920s to 1960s, 28

punctum (surprising, unintended element), Barthes on, 80, 82, 139

punishment practices, 14, 104, 208–9; audience ideological messages about, 4; death penalty methods for, 218; innocence concept expansion in, 219–23; mass incarceration and popular culture, 210–13; offender denigration in, 216; penal harm and will to punish

in, 213–22; politicization of crime and, 210–11; retribution as, 23. *See also* prison

punitive states, 214, 225

Punnett, Ian, 126

Purgatory (2011), 46, 72; Byers, J., on WM3 innocence and support in, 47, 195; on DNA testing and new trial petition, 47, 205–6; on documentary role in case solving and prosecution, 49; *Paradise Lost* sequel, 45; Reddit views on, 175; victim family portrayal in, 195; WM3 *Alford* pleas in, 47, 204–6

race: in monster and monster theory, 104; *Serial* on class issues and, 53–54

Racial Innocence (Bernstein), 81

racial role: in *Atlanta Monster*, 64–65; in *Atlanta's Missing and Murdered*, 64, 68, 171–75

Rafter, Nicole, 6, 7–8, 16, 24

RAV4 vehicle, of Halbach in *Making a Murderer*, 59–60, 62, 85, 87–88, 99–100, 146–47, 161–62

reasonable doubt, New True on, 196–97, 203; juries and, 198; Rudolf on, 200–202; in *Serial*, 198–99

Reddit, 187; on *Atlanta Monster* and *Atlanta's Missing and Murdered*, 171–75, 200; on *The Case against Adnan Syed*, 165–67, 179–80; case comments in, 3, 156–58; crime-centric groups of, 48; on Echols, 176–77; guilt or innocence assessment by, 158; on *The Innocent Man*, 177–79; on juries, 180; on *Making a Murderer*, 3, 156, 157, 159–64; on *Paradise Lost*, 174–76; on *The Paradise Lost* trilogy, 175–77; on Peterson, M., 168–70, 201; on presumption of innocence, 199; on *Serial*, 56, 155, 158–59, 165–67; on *The Staircase*, 168–70, 179–80, 201; true-crime series discussion on, 3, 155, 156–58;

Reddit (*cont.*)
    on Ward, 177–79; on Williams, 171–75;
    WM3 views on, 175–77; on Zellner tests,
    161–62
Religion and Its Monsters (Beal), 103
Requiem for Frank Lee Smith documen-
    tary (2002), 37
restorative justice programs, 222
retribution, as punishment, 23
Revelations (2000), 72; Byers, J., fall from
    grace in, 46; on documentary role in
    case solving and prosecution, 49; as
    Paradise Lost sequel, 45; on process of
    passive spectator to engaged citizen,
    48–49; Reddit views on, 175; victim
    family portrayal in, 195
Ricciardi, Laura, 58, 61, 72, 119, 186; on
    Avery and official misconduct, 156;
    Avery support by, 190–91; Zellner and,
    63, 100, 147, 194
Rogers, Gary, 150
Ross, Chris, 150
Rudolf, David: Peterson, M., trial prepa-
    ration by, 74; as Peterson, M., attorney,
    49, 51, 52, 72, 74, 75, 188–89, 200–203,
    207; on reasonable doubt, 200–202;
    The Staircase use by, 51, 52
Rule, Ann, 31–33

Safer, Morley, 21
Sanders clan or Sanders brothers, in
    Atlanta Monster, 149
Sasson, Theodore, 23
Second Chance Act (2007), 238
Seltzer, Mark: on forensic-based televi-
    sion, 26; on true crime of fact that
    looks like fiction, 28; on the wound,
    48, 137; on wound culture, 8, 48, 78
Serial (2014), 1–2, 52, 57, 72, 237; AT&T
    agreement in, 91–92; cell phone
    records, pings in, 53, 54, 89–91; devi-
    ance and guilt in, 111–12; elusiveness

of truth in, 181–86; experimental
    recreation of drive to Best Buy in, 54,
    92, 101; inadequate defense in, 134–35;
    as most downloaded podcast of all
    time, 1, 41, 53; Nisha call, 91; post-
    modernism and, 181–86; on race and
    class issues, 53–54; reasonable doubt
    in, 198–99; Reddit views on, 56, 155,
    158–59, 165–67; victim family response
    to, 192, 200; Wilds's implication of
    Syed as murderer, 53. *See also* Koenig,
    Sarah; Lee, Hae Min; Syed, Adnan
serial killers, 8, 28, 33
Sex Panic and the Punitive State (Lan-
    caster), 103
sexual assault, 18; Avery conviction for,
    58; exonerations and rates of, 10; by
    family or friends, 6, 19
Sheley, Joseph F., 227
Shots in the Mirror (Rafter), 6
Sinofsky, Bruce, 48–49, 72, 107, 119, 122;
    on innocence of subjects, 186, 206;
    as *Paradise Lost* director/producer,
    45–46, 72, 186; as WM3 advocate, 47,
    186, 205
Sixth Amendment, US Constitution, 198
60 Minutes, 21
social constructionist perspective, 227–28
social deviance, 104, 113, 128
social media, audiences as active part of,
    3, 155–56. *See also* Facebook; Reddit
sociopathy, in documentaries, 104, 123–27
The Staircase (2004, 2013, 2018), 3, 40;
    blood at the scene in, 49, 50, 83–84,
    95–97, 168–70; blow poke in, 85–87,
    135; Candace as Peterson, M., sister-
    in-law in, 72, 86, 191, 207, 217; court
    proceedings impacted by, 52; deviance
    and guilt in, 110–11; experimental
    recreation of call for help in, 98;
    experimental recreation of hitting
    Styrofoam head in, 96; Facebook

followers on, 156; forensic expert, 135; Fuhs on, 187, 200; media importance to, 51; objects of interest in, 85–87; owl theory in, 51, 77; Peterson, K., visual portrayal in, 80, 84; Peterson, M., charge of murdering wife in, 49; on Peterson, K., as murdered wife in, 49–51, 84–87, 95–97, 168–69, 189; Reddit views on, 168–70, 179–80, 201; truth in, 186–90; victim family response to, 51–52, 191–92. *See also* de Lestrade, Jean Xavier; Peterson, Kathleen; Peterson, Michael; Rudolf, David

Stout, Martha, 126

Strang, Dean, *72*, 145–46, 202–3

The Stranger Beside Me (Rule), 33

streaming television, 3, 38–39

surprising, unintended element (*punctum*), Barthes on, 80, 82, 139

Syed, Adnan, 1, *72*; *Alford* plea consideration by, 56, 204–5; deviance and true self of, 116, 117–18; DNA testing and prison release of, 57, 237; McClain as alibi witness for, 56, 92; murder of ex-girlfriend by, 1, 53; Pakistani heritage and Muslim religion of, 53, 112, 114; qualities of, 54, 111–12; sociopath identification of, 123, 124, 126; Wilds testimony against, 53

television, 6, 15, 25; binge watching, 2, 38–39, 208; forensic-based shows, 26; streaming, 3, 38–39

"Theorizing Conspiracy" (Pratt), 129

The Thin Blue Line documentary (1988), 34

This American Life, NPR, 1, 53

Toobin, Jeffrey, 93

trials: attorney dominant narratives in, 75; Echols presentation during, 46; entertainment and drama in, 74; exoneration from penalties in, 10;

exoneration from waiver of rights to, 10; exonerations for cases from, 10; process of, 75; representation in popular culture, 104–5

"Trials of Postmodern" (Fiske and Glynn), 181–82

true crime: activity books, 232; binge watching and, 2, 38–39, 208; literature, 15, 16, 28–33; Murley and, 15, 28, 29; punishment practice relationship with, 4; risk and violence understanding from, 15; Seltzer on fact that looks like fiction in, 28; streaming television and, 3, 38–39; victim body obsession in, 77–78. *See also* audiences, of true crime

True Crime (Seltzer), 8

true-crime documentaries, 15, 16; Bruzzi on, 33, 187; case solving role of, 49; of *The Central Park Five*, 20, 35–36; criminal justice system critique in, 33; on defendant trials and wrongful conviction, 33–34; evil in, 121–23; forensic-based television shows and, 26; *Frontline* on criminal justice issues, 36–37; of HBO/HBO Max, 40–41; of *Murder on a Sunday Morning*, 34; objectivity in, 33, 187–96; political conspiracy thrillers as, 27; sociopathy in, 104, 123–27. *See also specific documentary*

Trump, Donald, 239–41

truth, 204–7; documentary, objectivity and problem with, 187–96; in *The Innocent Man*, 186; de Lestrade on Peterson, M., 188–90; in *Making a Murderer*, 186; in *The Paradise Lost* trilogy, 186; politics and, 239–41; presumption of innocence and, 196–203; *Serial* and *Atlanta Monster* elusiveness of, 181–86; in *The Staircase*, 186–90; Trump and, 239–41

tunnel vision, 133, 148, 153; official misconduct and, 134, 143; presumption of
innocence and, 197

Tweel, Clay, 80, 109, 186; on Carter family
members, 194; on Haraway family
exoneration response, 71; as *The Innocent Man* director, 68, 70, 72, 122, 150;
on official misconduct, 150; on Ward
dream, 138

Type II errors, crime-control model for
reductions in, 226–27

United States (US), Constitution of, 10,
198, 226

US. *See* United States

victim families: on *Atlanta Monster* and
child unsolved cases, 64–65, 174, 195–
96, 199–200; *The Innocent Man* and,
71, 194; *Making a Murderer* response
from, 193, 194; New True response
from, 191–96; *Paradise Lost* portrayal
of, 194–95; *Purgatory* and *Revelations*
portrayal of, 195; *Serial* response from,
192, 200; *The Staircase* response from,
51–52, 191–92. *See also* Candace

victims, 6, 19; of Atlanta impoverished
section of 28 Black children and 2
men, 72; Black Americans higher
rates as, 29; crime-scene photos of, 8,
74, 77–79, 82–83; New True docuseries criticized for neglect of, 57; in
Paradise Lost trilogy, 72, 81; visual
portrayal of, 80, 81, 84; will to punish
by, 221–22. *See also* Carter, Debbie;
Halbach, Teresa; Haraway, Denice;
Lee, Hae Min; Peterson, Kathleen

victims' rights movement, 216–17, 237–38

violence: crime entertainment and, 7–8,
16; media on, 5; Murley on unrealistic
whiteness and, 29; Seltzer wound
culture on mass-mediated scenes of, 8,

78; true crime and understanding of,
15; victim crime-scene photos and, 8

visual portrayal, of victims: in *Atlanta
Monster*, 81; in *Atlanta's Missing and
Murdered*, 81; of Carter, 80; of Hal-
bach, 80; of Haraway, 80; of Peterson,
K., 80, 84

Wacquant, Loïc, 211

Ward, Tommy, 72; *Brady* violation for,
70; conviction overturn for, 70, 178;
false confession of, 69, 137–39; on
Haraway flowered blouse, 88–89, 151;
life in prison sentence of, 69; murder
conviction of, 69; official misconduct
and, 150; Reddit views on, 177–79

Westervelt, Saundra, 152, 229

West Memphis Three (WM3), 46, 156; *Alford* pleas of, 47, 204–6; Berlinger and
Sinofsky as advocates of, 47, 186, 205;
Byers, J., on innocence and support
of, 47, 195; DNA testing in *Purgatory*,
47, 205–6; media on satanic ritual
abuse of, 47, 106; poverty of, 107–9, 113,
121–22; Reddit views on, 175–77. *See
also* Baldwin, Jason; Echols, Damien;
Misskelley, Jessie

What Jennifer Saw documentary (1997),
36

"What Works? Questions and Answers
about Prison Reform" (Martinson),
215

white-dominated true-crime literature,
29, 30

Wicca practice and occult exploration, by
Echols, 45, 107, 122

Wilds, Jay: Black and negative racial associations of, 54; implication of Syed
as murderer, 53, 166

Williams, Wayne, 72; as *Atlanta Monster*
murder suspect, 64, 148; background
of, 66, 114; Baldwin, James, on, 185;

Brady violation and, 149; deviance and true self of, 116; Kunstler and Cook, B., attorney representation of, 66, 68, 148; life in prison sentence for, 64, 65; Lindsey on, 66, 196; Reddit views on, 171–75; sociopath identification of, 123; trial demeanor of, 125

Williamson, Ron, 69, 72, 138, 178, 194; DNA evidence and exoneration of, 68; Innocence Project and exoneration of, 68; murder conviction of, 68; official misconduct and, 150, 152

The Wire (2002–2008), 24–25

witness: incentivized, 11, 12, 133, 135, 152; McClain as Syed alibi, 56, 92

WM3. *See* West Memphis Three

women, true-crime literature and, 30–31

the wound, Seltzer on, 48, 137

wound culture, 48; Seltzer on mass-mediated violence scenes and, 8, 78

wrongful convictions, 1, 4, 33–34, 43, 186, 209, 213; critical criminology of, 224–30; cultural criminology on, 230–35; *Dateline NBC* special report on, 22; economic inequality and racism for, 219; eyewitness misidentification for, 11, 36, 37, 133, 180; forensic science misapplication for, 11, 12, 26, 36, 133, 134, 180; Gould on cultural punitiveness of, 213–19; Grumman on death penalty and, 21; inadequate defense for, 11, 133–35, 180; incentivized witnesses for, 11, 12, 133, 135, 152; innocence movement and, 8–12; *Just Mercy* on Black men death penalty, 27, 229; Leo on, 129–30, 228; Lofquist on, 10, 219–20; National Registry of Exonerations on, 9–10, 12, 133, 153; New True and innocence issues on, 133–35, 152–54; presumption of innocence and, 197–98; social deviance categories and, 128; Westervelt and Cook, K., on, 152–53, 229. *See also* false confessions; official misconduct

Wrongful Convictions Tax Relief Act (2015), 9

Zellner, Kathleen, 93, 114; on Avery and official misconduct, 95, 99, 145–47; as Avery appellate attorney, 58, 62–63, 72, 119, 145–48, 191; belief in Avery, innocence of, 58, 99–100, 119; on Hillegas potential murder involvement, 62, 162, 194; on RAV4 evidence, 62, 99, 146–47, 162; Reddit view on tests of, 161–62; Ricciardi, Demos and, 63, 100, 147, 194

About the Author

DIANA RICKARD is Associate Professor of Criminal Justice at Borough of Manhattan Community College, CUNY. She is the author of *Sex Offenders, Stigma, and Social Control.*

Alternative Criminology

General Editor: Jeff Ferrell

Pissing on Demand: Workplace Drug Testing and the Rise of the Detox Industry
Ken D. Tunnell

Empire of Scrounge: Inside the Urban Underground of Dumpster Diving, Trash Picking, and Street Scavenging
Jeff Ferrell

Prison, Inc.: A Convict Exposes Life Inside a Private Prison
K. C. Carceral, edited by Thomas J. Bernard

The Terrorist Identity: Explaining the Terrorist Threat
Michael P. Arena and Bruce A. Arrigo

Terrorism as Crime: From Oklahoma City to Al-Qaeda and Beyond
Mark S. Hamm

Our Bodies, Our Crimes: The Policing of Women's Reproduction in America
Jeanne Flavin

Graffiti Lives: Beyond the Tag in New York's Urban Underground
Gregory J. Snyder

Crimes of Dissent: Civil Disobedience, Criminal Justice, and the Politics of Conscience
Jarret S. Lovell

The Culture of Punishment: Prison, Society, and Spectacle
Michelle Brown

Who You Claim: Performing Gang Identity in School and on the Streets
Robert Garot

5 Grams: Crack Cocaine, Rap Music, and the War on Drugs
Dimitri A. Bogazianos

Judging Addicts: Drug Courts and Coercion in the Justice System
Rebecca Tiger

Courting Kids: Inside an Experimental Youth Court
Carla J. Barrett

The Spectacular Few: Prisoner Radicalization and the Evolving Terrorist Threat
Mark S. Hamm

Comic Book Crime: Truth, Justice, and the American Way
Nickie D. Phillips and Staci Strobl

The Securitization of Society: Crime, Risk, and Social Order
Marc Schuilenburg

Covered in Ink: Tattoos, Women, and the Politics of the Body
Beverly Yuen Thompson

Narrative Criminology: Understanding Stories of Crime
Edited by Lois Presser and Sveinung Sandberg

Progressive Punishment: Job Loss, Jail Growth, and the Neoliberal Logic of Carceral Expansion
Judah Schept

Meth Wars: Police, Media, Power
Travis Linnemann

Hacked: A Radical Approach to Hacker Culture and Crime
Kevin F. Steinmetz

The Gang's All Queer: The Lives of Gay Gang Members
Vanessa R. Panfil

Skateboarding LA: Inside Professional Street Skateboarding
Gregory J. Snyder

America's Jails: The Search for Human Dignity in an Age of Mass Incarceration
Derek S. Jeffreys

The Little Old Lady Killer: The Sensationalized Crimes of Mexico's First Female Serial Killer
Susana Vargas Cervantes

Halfway House: Prisoner Reentry and the Shadow of Carceral Care
Liam Martin

Ghost Criminology: The Afterlife of Crime and Punishment
Edited by Michael Fiddler, Theo Kindynis, and Travis Linnemann

The New True Crime: How the Rise of Serialized Storytelling Is Transforming Innocence
Diana Rickard